Aaagh!

I Think I'm Psychic

(And You Can Be Too)

Natasha J. Rosewood

Queries regarding rights and permissions should be addressed to:

Natasha J. Rosewood
Box 1426
Gibsons, B.C. VON 1V0

Web site: www.natashapsychic.com

Printed by:	Friesens
Cover Artist:	Heather Waddell
Imaging Engineer:	Charles Stenton
Graphic Artist:	Tim McLaughlin
Copy Editing:	Judith Hammill
Book Design:	Natasha J. Rosewood
Photo:	Shooting Stars Photography

Note for Librarians: a cataloguing record for this book that includes Dewey Classification and US Library of Congress numbers is available from the National Library of Canada. The complete cataloguing record can be obtained from the National Library's online database at: www.nlc-bnc.ca/amicus/index-e.html

ISBN 1-4120-2821-3

Printed in Canada

*

If you want to become psychic, you can.

If you think you are psychic, you probably are.

If you are uncomfortable with being psychic, you are not alone.

When you choose to see your psychic ability as a blessing,

it becomes one!

*

Aaagh! I Think I'm Psychic
(And You Can Be Too)

What do you feel when you hear the word "psychic"? Spine-chilling goose bumps or a thrilling allure? A burning desire to discover more or the impulse to run? Fascination or fear?

We all have intuition, perhaps even a psychic ability. So why don't we use it? Fear of the unknown, fear of losing control, fear of meeting our dark side or the fear instilled in humankind during the Spanish Inquisition that still sits in our cellular memory and holds power over our otherwise unlimited minds? In this enlightening, entertaining and empowering book, Natasha Rosewood brings the word "psychic" out of the witch's closet and into the light of the New Age. "Now, more than ever in our history, the planet needs all of us to acknowledge our power by paying attention to our inner voices. But first we have to embrace and trust our intuition."

Warning: This material contains mind-illuminating content.

Aaagh! I Think I'm Psychic (And You Can Be Too) is a sometimes humorous, sometimes heartbreaking account of Natasha's reluctant psychic awakening. Her story is accompanied by metaphysical endnotes to help the reader recognize and develop his or her own inherent intuitive ability, and to offer a deeper understanding of the psychic forces that were at play when Natasha magnetized these events to her.

Prepare for a sense of déjà vu. Aaagh!

Coming soon ...

OTHER TITLES

By

NATASHA J. ROSEWOOD

Aaagh! I See Spirits
(And You Can Too)

Above The Clouds
Inspirations for Dynamic Spirituality

Into The Valley of Death
And Other Ghost Stories

 *Dedications*

Divine Thanks and Gratitude go to:

- ❖ Divine Intelligence, my spirit guides, and all the angels for showing me the way, providing the wisdom, protecting me and giving me the courage and strength to just keep going.
- ❖ My mother and all my other upside-down angels who motivated me to go deeper and find my power.
- ❖ Carol, Sally, and my other right-side-up angels.
- ❖ My family for being my teachers.
- ❖ NRB who shone his light upon me during labor and birth of this book.
- ❖ Christian, Emily, Celestina, Tyler, Laura and Spencer just for being sparks of the divine.
- ❖ CRD for giving me a glimpse of heaven.
- ❖ All my friends who are my clients and clients who are also my friends who continue to validate my work and inspire me to go further.
- ❖ And all my writing "feedbackers": Heather Waddell (Cover Artist), Dorie Tentschoff, Janet Miller, Diane Foley, Louise Lefebvre, Kathy Enns, Anne Marie Evers and Jo Hammond.
- ❖ The major talents of the Sunshine Coast who lovingly provided all the other important talents a book requires: Heather Waddell (Cover Artist), Charles Stenton and Tim McLaughlin (Imaging), Don Enns (Computer Maintenance and my sanity), Shelley West (Photographer), Judith Hammill (Ms. Angelic Picky, Picky, Copy Editor & Proofreader), Annette Humphries (Handholder @ Trafford) and Terry Lussier (Layout Technician @ Trafford).

And the Oscar ™ goes to...

- ❖ Betty Keller, Writing Mentor Extraordinaire, without whom this book would still be in the ether or sitting in my drawer.

Thank you. Thank you. Thank you.

"Angels aren't just in Heaven. They can be right in your house."
— Celestina, 8 years.

How To Get the Most Out of This Book

The Intention of the book is to enlighten, empower and, perhaps, entertain. The information, therefore, has been broken down into two parts, the story and the metaphysical endnote, the latter intended as the amplification of the energetic and spiritual motivation for the preceding story. These endnotes are meant to enlighten and empower. Some readers have found, however, that rather than read the book straight through, they preferred to read the stories first, then go back to read the stories again and absorb the teachings of the endnotes. Try it your way and see!

Your Beliefs: I have not written this book to beat you over the head with my beliefs, nor to discredit any religion, nor to try to change any tenet that you hold dear. Our beliefs, whatever they may be, serve us in some way until they are no longer valid, and then we change them. If this book offends you, therefore, know that it was not the author's intention. (Just donate the book to the local doctor's office.) However, I will not apologize for expressing my truth. If this is also your truth, you will recognize it. Validation, excitement, relief and even joy may resonate within you. What I do hope is that these writings will empower you, help to heal old hurts or even just put a smile on your face. But mostly I hope that they will inspire you to shine your light as brightly as possible.

Amen!

Disclaimers

Although this book is a work of non-fiction, all the names have been changed to respect each person's privacy. This is my story and written purely from my perspective. All the people in my book are the other cast members in my "movie," and, therefore, my teachers. I have tried to honor them as such.

On occasion in the metaphysical endnotes, you will notice that I have alternately chosen to use "he" or "she" rather than "he/she." My choice of gender does not reflect any bias towards or against either gender in any way but has been used merely as a means to enhance the flow of the writing and, thereby, make it easier for the reader to understand.

CONTENTS

CHAPTERS	METAPHYSICAL ENDNOTES

FOREWORD

by

REV. ANNE MARIE EVERS

I was very honored to be asked to write a foreword for **Aaagh! I Think I'm Psychic**. As an ordained Minister, I can only commend Natasha, a gifted, well-respected and powerful psychic, for making this much-needed information available.

In **Aaagh! I Think I'm Psychic**, she has successfully taken the needle of Divine Wisdom and with it woven the threads of her psychic development into the intriguing tapestry of her life. She brings out the truth by gently "popping" outdated ideas and misinterpretations of the psychic world, replacing them with such intelligent and demystified explanations that readers are able to clearly identify for themselves whether they are intuitive or psychic. And if those readers choose to develop their abilities, Natasha shows them, with her honest and forthright approach, how to safely and responsibly progress.

Having worked in the personal growth field for 35 years, I am impressed with the way Natasha, through her stories and metaphysical endnotes, subtly introduces the wisdom of positive thinking, affirmations and an updated understanding of psychic phenomena. While keeping readers on the edge of their seats, she teaches by example, encouraging us to live up to our fullest potential.

I know this book will instill an instant love for Natasha and her work, and while readers will experience a roller-coaster of emotions—suspense, joy, sadness, despair, courage and hope—most of all they will be left with *the urge to learn more*. I found it most refreshing and uplifting to read a book that creates a thirst for knowledge of the supernatural.

As a Reverend who teaches, through my books and workshops, the power of affirmations—the science of changing negative programming of the subconscious mind through positive re-programming—I now affirm and believe that this book, **Aaagh! I Think I'm Psychic** is, deservedly, one of the best-selling books on the planet.

Rev. Anne Marie Evers

Ordained Minister	– The World Federation of Unity Churches
District President	– International New Thought Alliance (INTA) for B.C., Canada
Creator/Reader	– The Cards of Life

Author of three books:
    Affirmations: Your Passport to Happiness
    Affirmations: Your Passport to Prosperity/Money
    Affirmations: Your Passport to Loving, Lasting Relationships

And from a psychic student...

For those people exploring their psychic/intuitive abilities, Natasha has illustrated in a gentle, safe and humorous way not only how to move through the fear of being psychic but also how to embrace one's own psychic abilities. Today, in a world of great spiritual hunger, this book provides the necessary information to move us all forward while empowering us to believe in our own inner voices. Poignant, inspiring, funny. A must read!

Thank you, Natasha.

Love and Blessings,
Charlotte Cox

*

The moment

we open our minds

to magic

is the precise moment

the magic appears

*

WHAT IS A PSYCHIC ANYWAY?

*B*eing psychic isn't easy. Ask any psychic. Blessed and cursed. Shunned and revered. Who in their right mind would choose this path? Not I. Not consciously. It was as if the psychic fairy landed on me because I was walking around with a big "psychic" sign on my head only visible from the sky. Or that's how it felt.

In the not-so-distant past, psychics were branded with many labels: witch, witchdoctor, fortune-teller, Gypsy or even less complimentary terms. Now in this age of relative enlightenment, we are able to step out without quite as much fear of being ridiculed, disrespected or burned to a crisp. Even the names we are called ring gentler: channel, spiritualist, clairvoyant, spiritual counselor, healer, light worker and of course, psychic.

But what does the word "psychic" actually mean?

While the word "psyche" comes from the Greek meaning "mind," according to *New Webster's Dictionary and Thesaurus*, the definition of "psychic" is "being able to see and feel things of a non-physical nature." But how many times have *you* thought about an old friend and that person showed up on your doorstep the next day? Or *you* met someone for the first time and felt an unexplained delight or revulsion. Does that make you psychic? To a degree, yes. We all have it. We just pass it off as accidental. "Isn't that a coincidence?" we'll say. Or, "Oh, I just had a feeling …."

Coincidence is God's way of remaining anonymous.

Although we do predict potential futures, the label "fortune-teller" is not necessarily synonymous with psychic. I prefer "spiritual healer," one who, at least, facilitates healing, a healing of the soul, the spirit,

1

the mind, the emotions and consequently sometimes, the body. With help from above, I am also a guide, one who reassures, validates, breathes life into potentials that lie dormant and sheds the light of deeper understanding. A few of my clients have called me "angel." *Me? Angel?* I don't think so. But I'm so happy I could help.

Let's assume you would like to visit a psychic. How are you going to find the right one? Be very picky. You wouldn't just go to any old brain surgeon, would you? No. Well, psychics can also mess with your head. Some of them can be downright hazardous to your health.

But how do you choose a good one? Unfortunately, there is no master's degree for psychic practitioners, not that I'm aware of at least, although I would like to introduce some measure of distinction into the psychic arena. Until there is a certificate on the practitioner's wall, we are forced to rely on the age-old referral system, recommendations from family and friends. Once you have found a reputable psychic, feel free to ask questions like "How will you impart bad news if you see it?" and "What are your beliefs?"

Being a psychic, a good one at least, involves a lot more than sensing things before they happen. And yes, there are variations on the theme. Speaking only from my experience on both sides of the table, I have encountered the good, the not-so-bad and the "ugly" psychics.

The ugly psychics are those who will have no compunction in telling you really bad news and put the capper on it by declaring that your fate is decided before birth and there's nothing you can do to change it. While you sit there devastated, they will add insult to injury by pointing out, "Well, it's good you know about it now so you can be prepared." Wrong.

A client of mine came to me, terrified. An ugly psychic had told her when she was 17 that she would not live a day past her 40th birthday. I worked very hard with the 45-year-old woman to assuage her fear of psychics by explaining the mechanics of reading energy, and not just *why*, but *how* her psychic had misread her. Susan is now one of my most avid psychic development students. The more fragile of us could have made that prediction a self-fulfilling prophecy, like a 21-year-old girl in England who committed suicide after a psychic told her she couldn't see anything good for the rest of her life. Now that is a really ugly psychic.

The not-so-bad psychics are those whose perceptions are limited by their own traumatic histories and depressed psyches. They have not worked through their own painful pasts, spiritually or psychologically. Consequently, their interpretation of your energy may be limited, depressed or disempowering. While their predictions might be quite accurate, there may be no spiritual wisdom within them, leaving you feeling unsettled, inadequate, downright doomed or sucked dry. Yes, psychics can suck *your* energy too.

Good psychics, on the other hand, will perceive you as an honored spark of the divine. They trust that you possess the intelligence and the good sense to find your highest path, given the variables you have to deal with such as soul Agreement, challenges, talents, personality and karma. Even though you may not know on a conscious level at the time which direction to choose, a good psychic will encourage you to follow your own intuition, making you aware that what he/she is "seeing" for you is just one potential. Like a weather forecaster, many psychics base their predictions on the energy they see/feel/hear/smell from the past up to the present and then prognosticate the future from that information. But there may be other potentials that we miss, just like the weather, and therefore the outcome and the timing can also differ.

A good psychic will also be compassionate in imparting bad news and give you a) an understanding of why it's happening, b) an indication of whether and how you can change it or c) an idea of what is to be learned from the experience. In the larger scheme of the Universe, every experience is neither good nor bad, it is how we perceive it. An experience is just that—an experience—though some can hurt like hell at the time!

A good psychic will give you the gift of encouragement, enlightenment, empowerment. You will leave the reading feeling as if you just received a big warm hug from your spirit guides, angels or your deceased Aunt Ethel.

Remember, no psychic is 100% correct 100% of the time. According to statistics, even really good psychics average a 75% accuracy rate. That should mean that even on a good day, we are 25% inaccurate. Some of my clients though have validated 100% of my readings while others could only vouch for between 50 and 75%. If your outcome meshes with what a psychic has foreseen, great. If not, it means he/she misread the energy, or you, having been forewarned, chose to divert to another path. Or...it hasn't happened yet.

Only you, the client, will know what does or does not come true.

Curse or blessing, I do not own this psychic ability. I am merely the messenger. This channel that I am owns me. And my soul. Apparently my soul chose it (just *what* was I thinking?) before I came to this physical, densely mattered, emotional and egotistical plane.

Why are people so fascinated by psychics? Well—and this is just my theory—it's because underneath their skepticism or their enthusiasm, they suspect (quite rightly) that they also have the gift. They might be scared of it. Or they want it. Let's face it, the whole topic is intriguing. But what most inquirers want to find out is *how* and *when* did I *know* I was psychic?

Every psychic will tell you a different story. Theirs. I'll tell you mine.

Warning: Subject matter may contain mind-illuminating content.

Metaphysical Endnote 1

Where Does a Psychic Ability Come From?

Why does one child in a family possess the ability "to see" while the others don't? Is it inherited? Sometimes. Or it can look that way. If you had an old Russian grandmother who read tea leaves, she probably passed down to you her understanding of the symbolic pictures in the teacup. She would, thereby, have opened a door into the spirit and psychic world for you, her offspring.

Perhaps all of us would retain such inherent psychic abilities if we had parents who, when we told them as children that we had a lovely chat with our deceased grandfather the previous night, would respond with "Really, dear? And what did he have to say?" instead of "Don't be so ridiculous!" or "You have an overactive imagination but don't worry, you'll grow out of it." The sad part is, we usually do. We then buy into the adult-world concept that what we see is all there is. What a tragedy! We are then cut off from all the magic that our minds and the Universe have to offer.

Of course, the parent probably suspects deep down that the child is telling the truth but *their* parents responded the same way to *their* otherworldly sightings and that's all they know.

Does a psychic ability evolve out of a survival instinct? For many, a psychic ability is not a consciously cultivated luxury. Often honed instincts are necessary for a child's very survival. My theory is that most professional psychics you will encounter have, as children, experienced serious trauma, or at the very least, survived precarious upbringings.

Childhood, for most of us, is no picnic, especially if the environment is not secure. This is where many of us will sharpen our abilities to sense danger—incoming mood swings, violence or the impending wrath of a parent/sibling/authority figure. This heightened sensitivity to our environment protects us and lets us know whether to run and hide, be silent or, to save our skins, just plain lie.

The Mind has its own inbuilt safety mechanism. As Richard Bach writes in *Illusions*, "There is no problem so big that it cannot be run away from," for a while at least. And if something happens to us that is too overwhelming for the mind to absorb, the psyche will split off from itself to prevent insanity. Hence multiple personalities. We all have them to a degree—early morning persona, private persona, happy persona, pms persona. Repressed memories, habitual astral traveling and psychic abilities are also symptoms of a split. During trauma, if children, especially, find that what they are experiencing is particularly overwhelming, their spirits can vacate their bodies and fly away for a while. Trauma catapults the mind into that in-between world, that place where we can disconnect from our own conscious mind and body but stay connected to, and safe within, another reality. Some might call this astral traveling, psychologists might understand it as disassociation, but I call it a survival instinct and the beginning of a gifted psychic ability.

Or is your psychic path predestined? Yes, it can be. Being a healer or an artist might be the Agreement we made before we came here. We are all born with gifts and challenges, the gifts helping us to overcome the challenges or the gifts arising *out of* the challenges. (More about this later.) So while the budding psychic might have been abused as a child (the challenge), it also provided an opportunity to overcome and to learn to heal the Self and others (the gift). Many of us at this time in world history have chosen to be healers and light workers, contributing to this planet's accelerated evolution. So we have been put "through the mill" so that we could learn compassion, humility, understanding and the opportunity to further develop this gift. And it *is* a gift. Honest.

Can a psychic ability be developed? Absolutely! Whatever the degree of your present ability, by unleashing your mind you can experience an enhanced psychic ability *and* a spiritual reawakening. If you so desire, it can be the same thing. If you have the desire to learn, you can do anything. (I could sing too if I took up singing lessons—lots of them!) All that is required is an openness, a willingness to explore the outer reaches of your limitless mind, a desire to study and, like any other talent, practice, practice, practice.

CHILDHOOD – IT'S A SET-UP

"So," they ask in a hand-on-hip tone of voice, "when did you know you were psychic?"

The question is posed with naked child-like enthusiasm or hungry fascination. Or sometimes with blatant skepticism. But whether from loyal clients or from the morbidly curious, the question always comes as if I might have wakened one morning and, suddenly finding a lump in the middle of my forehead, screamed, "Aaagh! I think I'm psychic!" But of course, it didn't happen quite like that. Not for me anyway.

"Well," I announce glibly, "if my mother hadn't been psycho, I wouldn't be psychic."

That's the quick answer. The discovery of my gift was a journey, a long, up and down, in and out, complex trip filled with ruts in the road, mountain highs and, to keep me sane (yes, it's official), a lot of laughter.

Unlike some of my esteemed colleagues, I don't have memories of seeing spirits as a child. If I had, my mother would have soon made sure that I didn't. I do remember that she sneered if I made any of what I thought were perceptive observations. "Oh, don't be so ridiculous," she would say. I saw the boogey man, yes. I was paralyzed with terror in the dark because I was sure I was being watched, yes. I had an invisible friend, yes. But all those things are pretty normal, aren't they? Just say yes...please.

At the very moment I was born in the hospital on that April afternoon, my grandmother, who was pumping water from the well in our back garden, glanced up and "saw" my mother standing in the kitchen. Mystified and frightened, convinced that something had gone terribly wrong, she rushed into the house where my father was making himself a cup of tea.

"Where's Sylvia?" my grandmother demanded, her eyes searching the shadowy kitchen.

"In the hospital having the baby," my father responded, momentarily wondering about my grandmother's mental stability.

"But I just saw her here!" Grandie insisted.

This visual transference of energy might have been a sign of my grandmother's and mother's ability to communicate telepathically. But perhaps it was also a sign of what was to come for the baby born that day.

Some might say that I grew up in paradise. Given the birth name Kate, I was number four in a line of five children—two older brothers, Mark and Alex, an older sister, Janet, and then four years later another brother, Luke. After my father returned from the Second World War with all his silent and horrific memories, my parents rented an old water-mill house in the Oxfordshire countryside. "The Mill" was a rambling gray-bricked property two miles from the closest shop, post office and school, so most of the time we only had each other for playmates. A "deep river," as we called it, flowed under the silent mill wheel-house, a babbling brook ran along the side of the property, an orchard grew in the front, and at the back of the house, the fields went on forever. I was unaware of anything but living in this nature haven and the love I had for my family. The fact that we were poor as church mice, that we wore faded hand-me-downs and that I nearly died at six months due to inadequate nutrition didn't seem to tarnish my mother's nostalgia or mine for our days at The Mill. Indeed, the older she got, the happier she believed she had been there until in both our memories The Mill became a mythical heaven.

The first recollection I have of my life was when I was three years old. At that time we often played outside on the country road in front of The Mill, the only traffic being a rare car, a few bicycles and the feverish, thundering horses and bloodthirsty hounds of the weekly foxhunt.

One day while playing on the road, I looked up into a cloudless sky and, seeing nothing but blue, I suddenly *knew* that there was much, much more to this world than what was here on earth. There was something much greater "up there." What I did not know at that time was that I would spend my whole life demystifying the secrets of the Universe, searching, studying and finally integrating what was "up there" with the Universe that was inside me.

I was also three when I became aware of the ability to vacate my body. My mother had put me to bed for an afternoon nap while my older brothers played with their friends on the road. For whatever reason, whether I was afraid to be alone in that spooky upstairs room or whether something else had frightened me, I suddenly found myself, or my spirit at least, outside in the bright afternoon sunshine floating above my brothers and their two friends as they played a ball game. They were completely oblivious to my spiritual presence as I hovered twenty feet above them until it was time for me to return to my little body and wake up.

The Mill, where all five of us experienced the formative years of our lives, was a place in time where my mother was loving, where she was happy. She often fussed over us just before we left for our two-mile daily trek to school, giving Janet, Alex and me the perennial warning, "Now don't talk to the Gypsies."

One day, on the long walk home, my sister suddenly put her hand out to stop me in my tracks. A vivid blue Gypsy wagon blocked our way, standing silent and still in the middle of the long, flat road. My sister wanted to take another route in a wide loop up through the fields back to our home. But my five-year-old legs were already wobbling like jelly from the two-mile hike. And I was too fascinated. As we attempted to tiptoe past the wagon, an old thickset woman with a neat crop of coarse, black hair and dark, dirt-tinged skin, called out, making us jump. Her vivid blue dress matched the paint of her canopy and she sat like a man with her knees unceremoniously planted wide apart on a wooden bench at the front. Her brown, hypnotic eyes barreled through my childish defences straight into my soul and held my intrigued stare.

She smiled wryly, revealing yellowed and missing teeth. Then she pointed at me. "You've got the sight, you 'ave, dearie."

It wouldn't be until years later, when I finally owned up to my clairvoyant abilities, that I understood what she meant.

My parents were not religious. Apart from instilling the usual moral mores into us, like not telling lies (to them anyway) and always showing respect (for them anyway), they did not tout any specific set of beliefs. So at the age of seven, after we had moved into suburbia, I'm not sure what inspired me to take myself off to church. What I do remember is sitting on a large shiny pew amongst an adult congregation, a lone child with just my curiosity for company. The vicar, waving his white-cassocked arms around, proceeded to lambaste these adults with, "You're nothing but miserable sinners." They just sat there and seemed to accept his version of them. "Jesus Christ died so that you could be born," he accused some poor woman in the second row. I shifted on the unforgiving wood. How did *he* know if I was a miserable sinner? *Uh, excuse me,* I thought, *I think you are mistaken. God is a loving, forgiving God. I think you have it all wrong, Mr. Vicar.*

The Church, I decided, wasn't going to give me the answers I was seeking.

Only two weeks later, as I lay in my bed at night, something wakened me from a deep sleep. I had to blink to make sure I was truly awake because in front of me, near the top of the room where the wall meets the ceiling, I saw the very golden profiled head of an angel. No body, no wings, just the head turned sideways as if giving me a silent message. It wasn't so much what I saw but the feeling it left me with, one of peace, of being watched over, of being protected and loved. I was right. God was a loving God.

Then ghosts entered my life. As well as being teased and tormented by my older siblings, I would listen to the ghoulish ghost stories my family told as a form of entertainment. And as my older sister served up this steady diet of supernatural tales in the dark under the bedcovers with a torch contorting her pretty features into something malevolent, I was not aware it would fuel my fascination for all things non-physical.

As a teenager, the only vaguely psychic involvement I recall, apart from dabbling unwisely in unruly séances and being fascinated by what made people tick, was cursing my own excruciating sensitivity and suffering everyone else's feelings. My emotional edges were blurry as if I didn't know where mine stopped and those of other people began, as if I had climbed inside their skins. This blurring might have been due to my own fascination with what it would be like to be someone else, to actually *be* him or her, to think their thoughts, then perhaps to be able to revert to my own body and personality but still remember what I had felt. But I didn't realize I was actually *doing* it. Sometimes, when in groups of people, I would experience sudden paranoia. Before I had entered a room, I could be filled with the joy of life. The next, after I had been in a social setting, I could retreat to my room in a devastating depression. I didn't know why. Was I absorbing others' miserable energy? Or were the dramatic mood swings just typical for a hormone-infested, neurotically insecure woman-child?

In those days, our house was always packed with friends and neighbors, lots of them. While my father retreated to the sanctity of his garden, my mother loved the laughter and warmth that filled our kitchen. I can remember on one of those occasions making a casual comment to her about one of these visitors. "I can see Sheila living in Zimbabwe, becoming a gynecologist, having triplets…."

"Don't be so silly!" she snorted, oh-so-encouragingly. But later, when my prediction came true, it did not occur to me that I might be psychic. Like most teenagers, I just *knew* I was right.

But some things I saw I rejected because I didn't want to be right. Like the nightmare I had one night. It was so disturbing and felt so real that I leapt out of bed, panicking. Had all my family really been murdered except for Luke, my younger and closest sibling? Once I had checked all the rooms and was assured that my beloved family was all safe and sound, I went back to bed. But I didn't forget the dream, maybe because at some level I knew that it was a symbolic foreshadowing in the movie of my life.

It is written in *The Book of Runes* that "We are in the process of becoming who we already are." So as a psychic child, it was a blessing that I could not see my own future.

Metaphysical Endnote 2

But We Shall Overcome

The next time you watch a dramatic movie, take note of the structure. The protagonist always has, right from the beginning, a problem to overcome—a bad guy/woman or a negative situation or a character flaw. The whole purpose of the movie *is* for the hero/heroine to overcome that problem, normally with a great deal of struggle, before emerging at the end of the movie victorious.

In case you hadn't noticed, this is also the purpose of your life: to overcome. Socrates talked about it. Plato and Aristotle wrote about it. Art doesn't just *imitate* life, art *is* life and life *is* an art form. If all goes according to your plan, you will be able to celebrate the gift of your soul's evolution by having overcome your challenges as you disappear into the sunset at the end of your life.

Your script, otherwise known as the contract, Agreement, destiny, fate, kismet or *schicksal,* is *not* written in stone. When you are born, your script's outline is firmly implanted in your subconscious mind. However, as soon as you are born, you become *consciously* oblivious to your story line. And as you progress through the scenes of your life, you decide on the rewrites and adaptations. That is your creative free will in action. The underlying theme of your script, however, remains the same. The Universe will not force us to grow at a given pace. The only problem with *not* growing, however, is that the same old obstacles keep rearing their ugly heads. Ever noticed that? And whichever lessons you *don't* face in this life, you have to come back and face, do another take of the whole movie. *Yawn!*

Your Agreement, for example, might have been to come to the planet as a healer. Your guides probably warned you before you came that this would mean going through some major painful events in order to learn/remember what you need to know in order to help others—compassion, humility, forgiveness, spiritual awareness. *No problem*, your spirit said in a moment of wild abandon, probably having forgotten just how tough things can be in the physical plane.

In the early years of your life, especially if you are born into poverty, abuse or violence, it becomes immediately apparent that just surviving this chaos surrounding you is paramount. Unconsciously you sharpen your wits, hone your instincts, learn very quickly to tune into your environment, probably often seeing your angels, invisible friends, and deceased relatives who are there to comfort, guide and protect you. You also learn that, if life gets too unbearable, your spirit can just fly away for a while.

The message you may get from your family environment in the early years is that "Spirits don't exist except in your imagination," so you start to distrust your Self, your instincts and even your own eyesight. You might possibly be abandoned emotionally or physically by your family, rejected or otherwise made to feel different and separate from the world. But you still survive. If you happen to express what you want to be when you grow up—actress, astronaut, trapeze artist—your parent, teacher or sibling might respond with a "Just-who-do-you-think-you-are?" or "*You*-can't-do-that!" So you bury your natural talents in the basement of your being.

As you grow up and observe the world, your psyche will probably become compartmentalized. In one compartment you are seeing what is presented to you in the outside world where you are bombarded with the message that "Seeing is believing." But inside, your intuition tells you something else. There is a conflict between these two. That's why psychics often exist in a duality. At first, you probably opt to believe the outside world because it's safer, you want to be accepted as "normal," and you need to be loved. These other things you are feeling, your instincts, just seem to get you into trouble and you are told, or it is implied, that you are crazy, weird, different or strange. It is not safe, you discover, to listen to your own truth.

When you finally get over the set-up of your childhood (for some this may take 40 to 60 years) and understand that all of what happened to you was merely your training ground and not some curse, you realize that you were right all along. All those instincts you experienced inside were/are your truth. And you were/are always right about what you felt/feel. Eventually—and sometimes you might need help to do this—when you have excavated your authentic Self, the child within you will finally trust and honor the fact that you *do* know, you *are* right. The outside world was just a set-up to test you, to get you in touch with how powerful you truly are.

Restriction, you see, can be a great teacher.

And your feelings are not weird, strange or even crazy. They are the truth. You will realize that it is the outside world and the many people in it who are so afraid of that truth that they hide behind a protective and superficial layer of what they call reality. *Their* behavior you now recognize is coming from fear and could be deemed strange, weird or crazy while *you* can now pronounce yourself officially sane. Amen.

BOMBED AGAIN

*I*t wouldn't be the only time in my life that I returned from a holiday to have my post-vacation euphoria shrapnelled with bad news. The powers that be did not even allow me to pause briefly and check back into reality but sent me headlong into a nightmare. Or that's how it felt.

It was a sunny Thursday evening when my landlady left me the message. *Call your mother at your grandmother's.* Now what could that mean? I was 17, tanned and relaxed after arriving a few days earlier from my first holiday on the Costa Brava. On Montpelier Street, just ten yards from my flat in Hove, the familiarity of the English red telephone box gave me a vague reassurance as I inserted a shilling into the slot. While I waited for someone to pick up the phone, I noticed, scrawled across the plastic that protected the list of area codes, the words, "My mother made me a homosexual." Underneath in a smaller, neater print, was written, "If I gave her the wool, would she make me one, too?"

The tense edge in my mother's voice soon took the smile from my face.

"I need to see you," she said.

My stomach clenched as my senses were bombarded by her wired agitation. "What is it?"

"I'm staying at Grandie's," she responded, ignoring my question. "When can you come?"

My secretarial-cum-personal assistant job at BMW was very hectic. Sometimes it demanded my Saturday as well as Monday to Friday.

"Saturday afternoon probably."

"Can you be here before twelve?" Though it was posed as a question, that familiar commanding tone was in her voice.

"I'll try," I said meekly, the lining of my stomach beginning to loosen and shift from its walls.

On the hour-long train ride from Brighton to East Croydon that Saturday morning, as the Sussex countryside whisked by to the rhythmic swaying of the train, I didn't allow my mind to explore any possibilities of what the news could be, probably because on some level I already knew.

I always loved the sense of anticipation between stepping off the red double-decker bus and the thirty-yard walk down Havelock Road to my grandparents' house, a happy childhood memory. Their old, gray-bricked two-storey house with long bay windows and a glass summerhouse that had barely survived a bomb during World War II had been home to all of us. With all my parents' frequent moves, this house had been and still was the one constant home in our lives.

When my mother flung open the wooden front door, her drastically changed appearance still didn't prepare me for what was to come. All the roundness had melted off her now angular frame, the cheekbones prominent as she sucked on a cigarette. *When had she started smoking again*? Her short black wavy hair was light with gray and even though she wore a pretty blue sleeveless summer dress which showed off her now slender figure, there was something fractured about her whole being. In a new and strange wildness in her eyes, I saw a flicker of satisfaction at my undisguised shock.

"Where's Grandie?" I asked as I entered the shadowy hallway, the oh-so-familiar sweet, nutty smell offering me some small comfort.

"Sleeping," my mother snapped.

Oops! I should have waited to enquire after Grandie. My mother had always resented my closeness to my grandmother.

"Come into the kitchen." She bustled ahead of me, her energy frenetic, almost itchy. If it were possible, she probably would have crawled out of her own skin.

"Luke!" I beamed as I saw my younger brother sitting at the kitchen table. His shoulders beneath the navy sweater, white shirt, and gray school tie were slouched. *Whatever the news is, at least I won't be going through it alone,* I thought.

In the last year since I had left home, he had grown into a bespotted fourteen-year-old, with lank blond hair hanging down around his sullen face. He stared at me with a look of...what was it...pity, shame, guilt? As if I was a lamb about to be slaughtered.

"What's going on?" I muttered, feeling weak now.

Mother and Luke exchanged grimaces. "Luke, make some tea, will you?"

With just a grunt, my brother wearily pulled his tall, slim frame to full height as if he suddenly weighed triple his size.

"Sit down," my mother commanded, pointing to the far end of the table as she positioned herself facing me, at the opposite end.

Noon sunlight poured into the kitchen from the summerhouse windows and all the counters were uncharacteristically bare of Grandie's usual knick-knacks. A sign of my mother's occupation, I decided. No clutter. This kitchen, where I had shelled peas with my grandmother, where my whole family had laughed around this old oblong table while we enjoyed roast beef dinners, with Grandie's enormous fluffy Yorkshire puddings, followed later by sumptuous Sunday teas, was now empty of warmth, almost sterile. The air was hushed as if still waiting and listening for a second bomb to drop.

Maybe it was the blue and white checked tablecloth that gave the optical illusion of my mother being miles away from me instead of just a few feet. Her eyes were cast down. She was preparing her speech. Luke stood at the counter, facing a blank wall, his stiffened back to us while he busied himself with needlessly stirring the tea in the teapot.

"Your father and I," she announced regally, "are getting a divorce."

All the tension in her face seemed to let loose then and her features crumpled as she broke down and cried. The word *divorce* was rattling around in my mind while my mother shook her head and wept as if trying to shake off the concept, like this wasn't really happening.

Above her sobs, I heard sniffling. It took me a while to realize it was my brother. Poor Luke. Of course, he had already heard this. How long had he known?

This couldn't be. My parents never fought, did they? I had only been gone from home a year. Could things have changed that much?

"Why?" I breathed.

"Your father," she snarled, raising her head and staring straight at me as if I was responsible for his actions, "has been having an affair for two years...*two years.*"

Tears brimmed over and rolled down my cheeks. I saw a trace of a smirk on my mother's face. My God, she was enjoying this! Was it my pain she reveled in or was it merely the attention she was finally getting that was making her gloat?

My father. An affair! Part of me wanted to laugh. But he was a conservative businessman who came home every night, who never swore or drank. He hardly fit the picture of a philanderer. And an affair implied sex. I didn't even want to think about that.

"An affair?" I repeated inanely.

"Yes," my mother hissed with so much venom that I shuddered. "Barbara Stevens, his s–s–s–secretary, that cheap s–s–s–slut."

With shaking hands, Luke set a cup of tea before me, then sat down between my mother and me. With eyes fixed on the tablecloth pattern, his square-tipped fingers, nails bitten down, just kept turning the cup in his saucer. I wanted to reach out to him but I was all curled up inside myself. My mother, I noticed for the first time, was nursing a gin and tonic. *She had graduated from sherry then.*

As I sipped on my tea, her angry, bitter sobs reverberated in the silence of the kitchen. Her hysterical cries were punctuated with snarls of "That bitch!"

I didn't know which was more frightening, the fact that my parents were getting divorced after 25 years of marriage or the depth of my mother's pain and unhinged rage.

Finally, when her weeping had subsided, I asked tentatively, "How did you find out?"

"O–h–h–h." She waved a hand in the air as if it was obvious. "I suspected for a long time. I even asked him, time and time again. But he kept saying, 'Oh, no, darling.'" She mimicked him in an ugly sneer. "'What are you talking about, darling?' U–g–h! He lied and he *lied...*" Her voice was rising with each "lied" and I was scared. I expected Grandie to make an appearance and save us from this horror show but her bedroom door, which I could see through the slit in the doorframe, remained closed. "...and he *lied* and he *lied.*" She spat out the last word as if that was the most low-down, abhorrently disgusting thing one human being could do to another. I glanced over at Luke just as his eyes found mine. His terrified, devastated expression mirrored my own disturbed thoughts. *Was she going insane?*

"How could he *lie* like that?" she demanded of some invisible person sitting by her side. She didn't get an answer. I didn't have one either. I felt stupid sitting there, a helpless witness to my mother cutting herself loose from her tenuous sanity and allowing herself to sink into a dark pit of mad despair. *Come back!* I screamed inside. *Come back!* But I knew it was too late.

I tried to imagine what it had been like for her, keeping this awful betrayal to herself for two years. The damage to her mind and her body was evident. Now she couldn't stem the well of tears that she had been crying inside all that time.

"Do the others know?" As if someone had died in the family, I considered it might be my duty to continue passing on the bad news to my siblings.

"Huh!" Impatiently, she wiped her nose as Luke passed her a box of tissues. "Your sister thinks I should stay." Her wild eyes flashed anger at even more betrayal.

Oh, God, trust Janet to stick up for my father. The relationship between my mother and sister had always been like two gladiators in a ring, dancing around each other, swords drawn, tentatively stabbing at each other.

"What about Alex and Mark?" My oldest brother would be easy to locate in Canada but Alex, who lived only a few miles away somewhere in London, was an elusive challenge.

My mother just nodded, head bowed, cheeks red with tears and gin and tonics. *What had their reaction been?* I wanted to ask. Shock, mild surprise or a slightly raised eyebrow as if they had foreseen the inevitability of this day? *Two years.* That would have meant I was still at home when he was having the affair. Why hadn't I seen it? Maybe my mother was right: I was selfish, always lost inside my own little world. Had I been the only one asleep at the wheel?

A hush settled again on the kitchen as each of us succumbed to our own grief.

My memories of this kitchen will never be the same, I thought. But then nothing would ever be the same. Not now.

Grandie must have assumed from the silence that the worst was over. Without a sound, she appeared in the doorway of the kitchen, leaning on the door handle for support and clutching to her chest her lace-edged handkerchief rolled into a tight little ball as if it would give her strength. It was the first time I had ever seen my grandmother look so scared. And little did she or I know that this was just the beginning.

Metaphysical Endnote 3

It's All about Balance

In this current level of vibration, most of us are still learning through pain. Pain is resistance to *what is*. But we don't have to go through pain.

The Universe gives us plenty of signs, warnings and messages—sometimes from psychics—about our paths and how to avoid pain. But so many of us blunder on alone, oblivious to all the help and support that is there. Even our spirit guides are yawning as they stand idle wanting to help but unable to interfere until asked for guidance.

Avoiding pain and choosing to learn through joy is about listening to intuition, following the centerline. If we ignore this guidance, we get off track (which I have been known to do and paid the price!). And if we continue to stray even further from that center, and the pendulum swings too far, we become excessively out of balance. Finally, if we are still not listening, the Universe finds it necessary to metaphorically, and sometimes literally, pull the rug from under our feet, or even hit us over the head with the proverbial two-by-four. These reminders can manifest in the form of a car accident, illness, loss of relationship, breakdown of a marriage, robbery or other loss. If we just listen, if we are more sensitive to the energy, if we pay attention to the signs, if we trust that inner voice, we won't have to go down that destructive path only to have to crawl all the way back up again. But the soul always seeks balance, and one way or the other, sooner or later, kindly or brutally, we do come back to the center.

BRAM-HELL

*T*he long distance call came during breakfast. Down a crackling telephone line, the distraught headmaster of Pangbourne, Luke's boarding school, told my mother that Luke had defected again. This time my brother was caught in his pajamas scrambling across the roof of the old school. Hardly The Great Escape.

It was just three days before Mark and Sarah's wedding. The young couple, my parents, Grandie and I were all enjoying pre-festivity relaxation at the lake where Sarah's parents had their cottage just outside Kingston, Ontario. My mother and father had reconciled again for the wedding but the harmony between them was like my mother's sanity, precarious.

And in her presence I never breathed properly. I had to be vigilant, constantly aware of the early glint of hatred, the twitch in her cheek, the hard set of her jaw line, the frenetic body movements, all signs of an impending explosion. And now here it was.

"*You* deal with him." Anguished, my mother thrust the phone at me. "He'll talk to you!" She, the outsider of the mutually protective bond between Luke and me. I, the accused. Somehow it was all my fault again. She ran outside then, punching her fists into the air, shouting her rage, renting the peaceful fabric of the lake scenery with her gut-wrenching sobs. Sarah looked up from her coffee cup, stunned. *Welcome to the family, Sarah. So what do you think of us so far?*

Somehow my mother instantly turned Luke's defection into being all about her failures. If I had dared to speak, I could have told her that this was Luke's revenge on his father for not paying for him to come to Canada and Mark's wedding. But I kept quiet. The last thing she wanted right now was my opinion and the last thing I wanted was to be shredded.

If I could have paid for my younger brother to join us, I would have gladly, but I had only just scrambled enough together for myself. My heart was torn in two as, at the other end of the line, so far away, 15-year-old Luke sounded like the frightened three-year-old I used to comfort. But I had no means of solace now except to listen to his hurt, anger and frustration.

"I hate it here," he sobbed. "I hate it here."

"I know, Luke," I said. "I know." But I didn't really.

Ten days later, we were back home. Or that's what we called the flat in Bramhall. Luke had been conveniently filed away into yet another boarding school out of harm's way. Or so my parents claimed.

God knows what had possessed my father to move my mother and him from our family home, a large, light four-bedroomed house—albeit full of good, not-so-good and latterly nasty memories—to this tiny, square box of a two-bedroom flat. Yes, it was on a serenely peaceful residential street, but the dense tall evergreens that overshadowed the windows only accentuated the sense of incarceration. As far as I could tell, his thinking was that if they were going to reconcile, my mother needed a fresh start. New memories. And the flat would only be for mid-week, he told her, when he was working. And not so much housework, not that she did any. Then they could enjoy weekends at the cottage in Wales. Or that's what he said. Didn't he know that my mother abhorred the cottage even more than the flat? Probably something to do with Barbara Stevens, "that dammed bitch" who had enjoyed illicit weekends there with my father, sitting on their furniture, eating off their china, sleeping in their bed. Maybe it was my father's sanity I should have been more concerned about. Did he just make arbitrary decisions about "what was best for Sylvia"? Or did he consult with her and she gave him her martyr response, "Whatever you want, Charles. Don't worry about me." *Aaagh!* But she would make him pay for it later. Oh, yes.

My parents had grudgingly agreed that I could stay with them while I scraped together enough money for my next trip, hitchhiking around Europe with Erica and Hilary. To live at home for a month seemed like a good idea at the time or at least the most practical. But when I think back now, it would have been less painful to sleep under a bridge on a bed of nails and eat worms than to witness what I did. I was toying with emotional masochism and don't know why I did it. Maybe I believed it was my only option or that I could somehow save my parents from each other. For a while anyway.

"You're not going, it's too dangerous," my mother intoned when I talked of my impending adventure. I knew that her parental concern was a cloak for her hatred of me and my freedom. But I wasn't going to let either her paranoid fears or her jealousy stop me. *Misery loves company*, I thought and her protestations only strengthened my resolve to escape this flat, the gray pettiness of the North and her schizophrenic outbursts. Not that I didn't have some of my own fears. She was right, of course. We could be raped and murdered. But I didn't want to think about that. I focused on the adventure, seeing all those different countries, the history, the languages and happy, normal people.

A week later, Erica, my only pipeline to the real world and sanity, rang. "We're leaving on the 25th of July, two weeks earlier than we planned," she announced. *How would I get enough money together in time?* "Can you still come?" she asked.

"Yes," I told her quickly. I would have to work in dark and dingy Dickensian offices, typing and filing, treated as the alien outsider but I would somehow make enough money for the trip.

"Are yer courtin'?" the black-haired secretary asked. She was probably only 45-ish but like many northern women, old before their time, she already walked with rounded stooped shoulders.

"No," I responded as I sorted the yellow NCR forms into alphabetical order. How I hated the red-bricked, dark and musty-smelling offices of Stockport. And the monotony of filing. *All for a good cause though*, I told myself.

"Oh, dear," she groaned, as if suddenly understanding that I had been condemned to some awful death. "'Ow old are yer?" There was a tragic tone to her voice.

None of your business, I wanted to say. "Nineteen."

"O–o–o–h–e–r." She stepped back from me. In her eyes, I was condemned to the eternally barren hell of spinsterhood. My head was on the chopping block now. I could say goodbye to any hope of happiness.

"Don't yer want to get married then?" A last ditch attempt to save my life.

I groaned inwardly. If one wasn't pregnant and married by 18 (normally in that order), there was "no 'ope fer yer." *Get me out of here!*

"Yes, but not yet." *I'm only 19 for God's sake! What's the big deal about marriage anyway? People live together for 30 years, share their whole lives, bring children into the world, endure all the hardships and then turn around and tear each other to shreds. What exactly is the point?*

The woman returned to her desk. I was a hopeless cause. I didn't care. I hated the North. I hated this job. And my mother was getting crazier and crazier.

Finally there was talk of Mother's going to see a psychiatrist. Thank God. Now maybe there was hope. I would have suggested it my-self a long time ago, but I knew the response I would get. *Who the hell do you think* you *are, you little bitch?* she would have shouted. *You think you know everything, don't you?* And I would have shrugged helplessly. There was no defence against my mother's attacks.

I remember coming home that Tuesday full of hope. As I reached the front door, I tried to shake off the gray dreariness of the wet misty fog that had enveloped the whole day. But when I entered the flat, the grayness had leeched in through the walls. There were no lights on even though it was dark inside the flat.

"Hello?" I called out. "Anybody home?"

I heard a whimper from the living room. Uh-oh. My stomach lurched. One day I anticipated coming home to find my mother sprawled on the kitchen floor, finally having stuck her head in the oven and gassed herself to death as she often threatened to do. Well, today at least, she was alive.

It took me an eternity to move along the darkened, straight, short hallway towards the living room. What would I find? Already I wanted to cry.

There was my mother, sitting in the somber shadows in the middle of the three-seater settee, nursing a full glass of sherry, staring hard at the blanket of dark green branches just outside our window. She was weeping, quietly, eerily, as if the tears themselves were cutting into her cheeks with her pain.

I sank down onto the chair facing her, needing the strength for what was to come. "What happened?" I finally asked.

A barely perceptible shiver, like a mild electric shock, passed through her body.

"Did you see the psychiatrist?"

"Oh–h–h–h." She waved a hand in the air as if to push the reminder of him away. Or me and my questions.

I waited. I didn't like the look of terrible hurt in her eyes. Already I wanted to kill the psychiatrist. What had he done to her? She had had to drive all the way up to Liverpool, a distance of at least a hundred miles round trip on this horrible dreary day, and for what?

"Do you want a cup of tea?"

She barely shook her head in response, still refusing to speak but clutching her glass of sherry as if it was the only solid thing in her world. *How many had she had?*

I got up, put down my jacket on the chair and moved to the kitchen. I needed something hot, liquid, comforting. I returned to the living room and resumed my position on the edge of my chair, legs crossed. Waiting. Tears of hurt and rage still poured down her cheeks, spilling out like a geyser from some deep bottomless pit of despair, as if everything good that she had ever known had all just been stripped away. I had never seen this much grief. What should I do? Stay away? Let her be? Or just sit here until she was ready to talk?

Her whole body was stiff, frozen to the middle of that settee, holding herself intact, afraid that if she moved she might fall apart. I would have offered to make her something to eat but I knew that it was futile. Her diet, since our return from Canada, consisted of large bars of Cadbury's Fruit and Nut chocolate and copious glasses of sherry. And she was already so skinny. I wasn't sure that she was even eating the chocolate. She stuffed the purple-wrapped bars down behind her and the settee cushion. Every now and then, I would hear a rustling of foil and a snap as she broke off another piece. It was a protective habit from when we were all at home, hiding her treats from our gluttonous eyes.

"What did he say?" I ventured. *Maybe I should just shut up.* At first she didn't move and then she suddenly swiveled her head around at me, wild eyes fixed on mine, flashing hatred, insanity, grief.

"What did he s–a–y?" she snarled, like a wild cat, spittle flying from her mouth. "I'll tell you what he said." But then the rage that I braced myself against disintegrated into grief again and she sobbed. I wanted to move over to her, take her hand, comfort her. But my mother didn't invite comfort. I wished I could at least turn on a light instead of sitting here in the dark shadows. Instead I sat melded to my chair.

Oh, God, Oh, God, Oh, God. Where was everybody? My family? My father? He would be home from work soon but would that make it better or worse? Sometimes the sight of him only seemed to ignite the fires of hatred within her.

"He told me," she hissed, "that I should…oh …," she shook her head in disgust, "pull… pull myself together." The last three words trailed off into another fit of sobbing.

If only it were that easy.

She turned her head quickly towards the window as if repelling some revolting slime. Even in the descending darkness, I could see swollen eyes, her cheeks wet and red from rage and sherry. Yes, I definitely wanted to kill this psychiatrist. Too bad he lived all the hell way up in Liverpool.

"That was it?"

"Oh, no."

Uh-oh.

"He said," more tears flowed down her florid cheeks, sarcastic indignation in her voice, "he said I should be thankful." She spat the last word out. "Thankful."

"What for?" Even I couldn't follow this line of thinking.

"Oh," she half-snorted, an ugly sneer contorting her features, "that I had a good figure for my age."

I had always suspected that psychiatrists had to be a little batty to work with insane people but I wondered if this man was on the wrong side of the bars.

Suddenly I needed life in this suffocating box of a flat. I was drowning in her misery. Light, people, sound.

"Do you mind if I switch on a light?" I asked tentatively even though I was afraid to see her grief in full technicolor.

She waved a hand. Nothing mattered any more.

There was a click at the front door. My father was home. What would it be tonight? Screaming, yelling, slapping of faces with indifference to my presence or whispered conciliatory discussions, overly concerned that they talk out of my prying earshot. As if every one of my happy childhood memories hadn't already been dismembered, my mother not bothering to keep the dirty laundry of family secrets hidden any more. I would never be able to trust again, not my own judgment or myself because I would never know what was real. Nothing was as it seemed. I didn't blame my parents for lying to us about their less-than-perfect pasts; they had done it to protect us. I blamed myself for being stupid, for not seeing.

That night, as I concocted a dinner from leftover vegetables and tinned goods, I watched, through the kitchen door, my father's back as he sat on the settee, leaning over her, making commiserating noises while she sobbed and ranted. I don't think he understood her pain. I could only guess at it. And that's why I felt so helpless.

For the next three days, my mother stayed in that position on the settee, as if nailed to those cushions, a bottle of sherry at her feet, her heart and my heart breaking. *If she could*, I thought, *she would cry herself to death.*

Metaphysical Endnote 4

The Six Levels of Consciousness

Sigmund Freud wasn't a psychic, not officially at least. And that's why he would disagree with me. He would argue that there are only three levels of consciousness: the ego, the id, and the super ego. But after years of tuning into the whole mind, my experience tells me that there are indeed six layers, which though largely separate, can and do communicate with one another.

Imagine these levels of consciousness as horizontal layers in a pyramid, starting at the base and working upwards. (See diagram on page 31.)

1) *The Soul*: The soul, situated at the base of the pyramid, is the foundation and largest of the layers. It is your essence, yours for all eternity. When we reincarnate, I believe that part of our soul stays at "home" in the world of spirit while a large part is also embedded, with the spirit, in the physical body. This might account for our deep fear of abandonment or always searching for wholeness, as we subconsciously know that a part of us is somewhere else.

2) *The Spirit*: Second from the bottom is the spirit, which is an aspect of the soul expressing in this lifetime and constitutes our personality, our gifts and challenges. Whatever the spirit learns, it takes back to the soul, adding to the soul's overall evolution.

3) *The Subconscious*: The third layer is the vast subconscious. It is a limitless databank which holds *everything* that has ever happened to you, been thought or said in this or any other lifetime. (Scary!) The subconscious can recall in acute detail conversations, events and feelings from any time period or dimension when you a) trigger those memories b) go under hypnosis c) dream or d) access the subconscious through the alpha state. Like a computer hard drive, the subconscious accepts whatever belief systems are programmed into it and, therefore, it is this level that drives our lives. Agreements, contracts, karma, fate or destiny are all implanted into the subconscious and it steers us automatically in the direction that our souls and our spirits agreed upon. How do you know what beliefs you are holding in your subconscious? Just look at your life, your relationships,

your health, and your level of abundance. Your results reflect your beliefs.

4) *The Unconscious or Alpha State:* Above the subconscious is the alpha state. At this level, you can access your subconscious where you can be hypnotized and change belief systems. The alpha is a relaxed state where you can do effective creative visualization, meditate, receive visions and premonitions and daydream. It is the state we experience just before dropping off to sleep and when watching TV. The alpha is also the state I put myself into when doing readings. It is from this level that I "scan" all the levels of consciousness in your mind.

5) *The Ego Conscious Mind*: At the top of the pyramid is the conscious mind where the ego lives, the separate "I." It is our daytime waking state. I call this the "pea-brain" part of the mind as it is so small and limited compared to the other levels. The conscious is the only level of mind that experiences separation from other consciousness. And so it is also the only level to experience fear. The purpose of the ego is to act as a small filter through which we perceive and receive the data from our world. This filtering process is designed to prevent the ego from going into overload, splitting off from itself or descending into the chaos of insanity. Of course, when pushed the ego can be overwhelmed. Ego is also the level of mind that judges our experiences, decides on our beliefs and files them away into the subconscious. Much of this we do through the process of dreaming. And yes, we all dream.

6) *The Higher Self*: The sixth and final level does not sit in the pyramid but extends up and out from the top of the pyramid, stretching into infinity. This is the higher self, the access to your spirit guides and your higher power. It is limitless. Your guides represent aspects of who you are in the process of becoming. Metaphysically, access to the higher self is represented by your crown chakra which is the energy vortex located on the top of your head.

From my alpha state, I tune into all these levels when I read the mind. The difference in vibration and density tells me which level I am reading. The more attuned we are to ourselves, the more the various levels of consciousness vibrate in harmony with one another. However, sometimes our ego mind wants something other than what our subconscious is driving us toward, creating conflict within our Selves. Conflicts are most common between the subconscious—where our programming lives—and the ego, our waking state—where fear lives.

So despite my constant words of encouragement to my mother that she could move on, do anything with her many talents, find happiness again, her image of low self-esteem was so deeply entrenched in her subconscious—which is why she attracted this situation in the first place—that my support fell on deaf ears. What I didn't realize at the time was that she needed to change her subconscious, not just her conscious state. But *can* you change the beliefs in your subconscious mind?

Absolutely.

The Six Levels of Consciousness

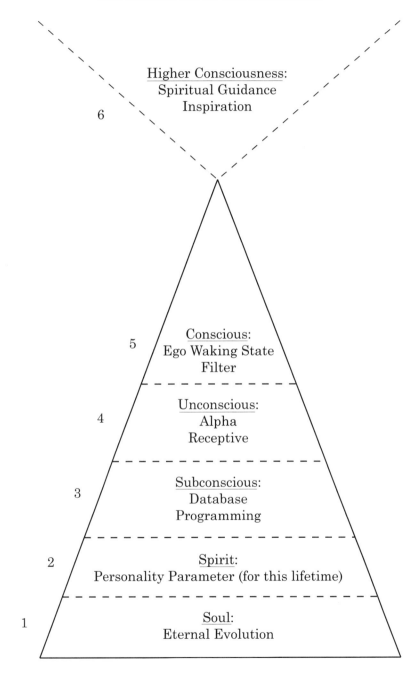

5

ANGEL OR DRUG DEALER?

*I*t was August 1971, the year of my great adventure. Erica and Hilary, my two 19-year-old traveling companions, and I were sitting on our bunks in a Corfu Youth Hostel debating whether we should use our dwindling funds to travel on to Athens or stay put for a week on this still unspoiled Greek island. We opted to stay, enjoy more local Greek salads, learn their dignified plate-smashing dances and relax on white sandy beaches. Then we would hitchhike home through Italy, Switzerland and France to England.

Now nine days later, under a cloudless blue sky, we were crossing the border from Italy into Switzerland. After the relentless honking of horns, persistent leering shouts from the Italian men and the general raucousness of the country, the hushed silence of Switzerland was for me a welcome relief.

"I love the Italians but I could never live in Italy," I told Erica and Hilary as we stood on the side of the road heading for Zürich, our thumbs in their usual hopeful, vertical position. In stark contrast to the chaos and messiness of Italy, all around us were lush green hillsides and pristinely clean, neat wide roads. I was also glad to be out of Italy as the cheap bread that was our perpetual diet was salty and spongy and left me feeling hungrier than before I had eaten. Not that the Italians didn't make great bread. They did. We just couldn't afford it.

Before we had left on this adventure across Europe, the three of us had agreed that there would be no lending. We would all take the same amount of money. But when I had returned in July from my brother's wedding in Canada, the girls informed me that they had brought forward the date of our departure. While Erica and Hilary had each left with 45 pounds, the most I could scrabble together through temporary secretarial jobs and other acts of desperation was a mere 40 pounds. Oh, well, I thought. I'd manage somehow.

My stomach was rumbling now. I would have to get used to that. My funds were almost out. I would only have enough for one more meal, but then it was going to take two days to get through Switzerland and France to Dieppe where we would catch the ferry to Newhaven and home. I *hate* being hungry, must be the Taurus in me. We like our food. But at least I had my ferry ticket. *I will survive*, I told myself. *I won't like it, but I will survive.*

A turquoise blue Volvo was slowing down. Excitedly, we ran towards it. I was the one with the smattering of French and German so the girls had appointed me as professional front seat passenger.

"*Wohin fahren Sie?*" I asked the middle-aged businessman in polite German.

"*Zürich. Und Sie?*"

"*Das ist gut,*" I responded, sounding like a tacky tourist.

"*Moment mal,*" he gestured for us to wait before climbing in.

Stiff-shouldered, he stepped out of his car, came around the back, opened the boot and indicated that we should unload our huge grubby backpacks into the vacant space.

Before he had pulled back out into the traffic, he announced, "If you don't mind, I would like to practice my English." His pronunciation was amazingly clear of the usual formal accent. "I do a lot of business in Japan and we always speak English," he explained.

After hitchhiking in Europe for four weeks, we were in the habit of assessing our drivers. Contrary to my mother's dastardly prediction that we would all be raped and murdered, the kindnesses that we had been shown—people driving for hours out of their way, taking us home and making us lunches, buying us dinners, even giving up their beds for us—had more than reinforced my faith in humanity. Dressed in the mandatory charcoal suit, this man with short graying hair and intelligent brown eyes set in a squarish face appeared to be a typically Swiss, conservative businessman in his mid-forties. *Married, quiet, refined, sophisticated, worldly*, I surmised.

"Where have you been traveling?" he asked as the green hills whisked by us.

"We started in Dieppe and then hitchhiked down through Strasburg, Luxembourg, Italy and then over to Greece."

"That's very brave of you," he said, his "v" sounding faintly like an "f."

I shrugged. Wasn't the whole world hitchhiking these days? The hostels were bursting with multinational hoards, all catching rides to somewhere, many of them around the world. Their stories made our adventure sound like a stroll in the park.

"Have you had any bad experiences?" he inquired, eyes on the road ahead.

Just hunger, I wanted to say but he might take that as an unsubtle hint. "No, actually people have been exceedingly kind, even when we didn't speak each other's language."

We drove in silence for a while as if he was contemplating his next sentence.

"I am meeting my wife in Zürich for lunch. Would you and your companions like to join us?"

My stomach thanked him immediately but I showed polite restraint. "That would be wonderful but I need to consult with my friends." With eyes glistening at the thought of real food, even if it was a bratwurst, I cranked my head around the headrest and told the two girls we had been invited to lunch. I was afraid Erica might turn the invitation down, thinking we were not dressed appropriately. She was unpredictable. But they both nodded vigorously, salivating as I was at the prospect of anything other than salty bread.

"Yes, we would love to," I told the man. "By the way, my name is Kate and my friends are Erica and Hilary."

"I am Walter Weiss and my wife is called Regina."

Erica might have been justified in saying we weren't fit to be seen with this smartly attired man. As we entered the Mövenpick Restaurant on the Bahnhofstrasse in Zürich, all eyes turned on us. Office workers in uniform-like suits of gray or navy were dressed in dignified contrast to us, three ragamuffins in faded jeans, t-shirts barely covering suntanned arms, our sun-blonde hair scraped back into scruffy pigtails. Mr. Weiss didn't seem to mind the gaping stares but strode through the lively restaurant as if he arrived every day with three urchins he had just picked up off the *autobahn.*

His wife, Regina Weiss, when we found her sitting at a table next to the window, was equally non-plussed. A pretty lady with piercingly tragic blue eyes, she recovered quickly when her husband explained in his quiet manner that he had just encountered us on the outskirts of Zürich. When he told her that we were traveling around Europe, her eyes sparkled momentarily. Then she checked her emotions as if it was unseemly to show delight. "You must tell me all about it," she said, sucking needily on a cigarette.

A waiter instantly appeared with the largest menus I had seen since being in Canada. *What do we pick?* I thought, embarrassed. *Bratwurst or steak?*

"Pick anything you would like," Mr. Weiss offered, reading my mind.

After a steady diet of bread and cheese and vitamin C tablets for a month, we had lain in our bunks for the last five nights describing to each other in minute detail the first meal we would eat on our return home. I fantasized about a nice big steak with a beautiful green salad, Hilary wanted a humongous bowl of sweetened red raspberries loaded with Devonshire cream and Erica, the skinniest one of us all, wanted a plate piled high with fish and chips.

"Why don't you order for us?" Erica piped up, addressing Mr. Weiss.

Thank you, Erica.

"If you like," he responded.

Immediately, three glasses of coke arrived, and Regina watched, a slight smile on her lips, as our English manners temporarily forgotten, we guzzled the contents of the glasses. Mr. Weiss waved a hand and immediately three more cokes appeared.

"It is such a shame," Mrs. Weiss said, "but we are leaving tomorrow to go on our holiday in Tessin." I understood Tessin to be the Italian-speaking region of Switzerland, full of rolling hills and vineyards. "Otherwise we would *love* to have you come and stay with us." Something caught in her voice as if she really didn't want to go on holiday now, something desperate.

"That would have been charming, nicht?" Her husband, I noticed, was watching his wife very carefully as if he was afraid she would... what?...disintegrate into little pieces, give away a secret? Her petite elegance and the way she held her cigarette between long slim fingers with perfectly manicured nails contradicted the aura she was emanating. There was something else.... What *was* it? Loneliness? Fear? Fragility?

Plates with green melon and delicate slices of pink Parma ham were suddenly placed before us. *Oh, heaven. Real food.* "But you must stay and explore Zürich," Mr. Weiss added looking for agreement from his wife. "It is such a beautiful city."

Mrs. Weiss nodded as she took another sip of her gin and tonic. "Oh, yes, very beautiful."

I peered out of the restaurant window down the long straight street. A blue and white tram hummed quietly past, and an array of shops promised expensive chic. Nothing in our price bracket.

"Maybe we could stay with you next year," Erica said, blue eyes twinkling. We had already played with the idea of a sequel adventure.

"Oh," Regina gasped, "that would be so wonderful."

In between the blissful taste of sweet-on-savory, I wondered about Regina Weiss. She was on her second gin and tonic, she wasn't eating much, just picking at the food, and her eyes bothered me. Had she been crying? And why were they so desperate for us to stay with them? Maybe they had lost a child and we were a brief consolation prize. There seemed to be an easy intimacy between the couple but knowing how my own parents could put on a show, I thought it could have been for our benefit. There was definitely something hidden, something terribly sad.

The main course arrived on a silver trolley from which the waiter deftly carved wafer-thin slices of Chateaubriand. He placed the rare meat on large white platters, topped them with Sauce Béarnaise and filled up the empty white space with a mountain of crisp French fries and green salad. Once we were all served, silence descended upon the table as the three of us drifted into gastronomic heaven.

"We've been dreaming of a meal like this," Hilary told them between mouthfuls.

Mrs. Weiss lit another cigarette. "So how long are you going to stay in Zürich?" she asked brightly. Was her mood lightening with our company or was it the effect of the g & t's?

I shrugged. "Not too long." I didn't want to disappoint her, tell her we couldn't afford to stay in their wonderful hometown, even in the hostel. This meal would make the journey home a lot more bearable though.

She leaned across the table towards her husband and said something in German which I couldn't catch. Mr. Weiss nodded and got up from the table.

"Excuse me, I have to make a phone call."

"We had a strange experience the very first night in Reims," Erica was telling Mrs. Weiss. "The lights were on, sleeping bags on the beds, clothes everywhere but no one was home. Like the Mary Celeste."

Mrs. Weiss didn't know about the Mary Celeste, a cargo ship found sailing in the Atlantic in the late 1800s mysteriously empty of passengers and crew.

"Anyway, we ended up staying with a young French couple who rescued us from sleeping in the local jail."

Mrs. Weiss's eyes glistened with something, as if on the edge of great joy or terrible sadness or both. She was drinking us in like a woman dying of thirst, except that she'd had enough to drink.

Her husband sat down again. "I am very sorry but after dessert I have to go to a meeting, so I will take you back to the car and you can get your bags."

Was Herr Weiss psychic? Three bowls piled high with raspberries and dollops of fresh whipped cream arrived. Hilary and I exchanged looks. This meal was spookily reminiscent of the menu all three of us had envisioned.

When lunch was over, the businessman suddenly stood up, our signal to leave. Somewhat hurriedly, we scribbled addresses on scraps of paper and in return we were each given Mr. Weiss's business card.

With warm goodbyes, we left Mrs. Weiss alone again at the table, a fresh gin and tonic for company. The brightness that had been briefly rekindled in her eyes was already dimming again. Then her husband led us back to the underground where he had parked the car. En route, he pointed to the bridge and the other side of the Zürich See.

"The hostel is over there," he said.

With exceedingly full stomachs, we struggled with our backpacks while Mr. Weiss rummaged in his glove compartment. We stood and waited. He emerged with something small in his hand. In the shadowy darkness of the underground, it was difficult to see what it was.

"Here is approximately twenty-one pounds in various currencies." I recognized then that he was clutching a roll of banknotes. "I really want you to stay and see Zürich. I am just sad that you can't be our guests."

All three mouths were agape. "No," was the first word that came out of all of us but then Hilary spoke. "It's very kind, but no thank you."

"But I want you to see Zürich," he persisted, thrusting the roll towards Hilary.

"You've been kind enough, the lunch…," Hilary responded while Erica and I just nodded. "No, we can't take any money from you."

"I insist," Mr. Weiss responded. And then he threw the roll into the air and it landed expertly between Hilary's breasts, where the slit in her t-shirt opened onto her ample chest.

Initially stunned, she finally reached in and pulled out the roll. By this time, he was halfway across the parking garage. We all stared at one another and then after him. Eventually, when our eyeballs had settled back into our heads, we ran to catch up with the retreating figure.

Who was he? I wondered. *An angel?* People on our journey, especially women, had been kind. But in my short and cynical experience of men, I found that they normally wanted something in return. But he didn't seem to want anything. We called after him as he hurried along the street away from us. "Thank you," we shouted into a light breeze that carried our voices away, "Thank you."

Mr. Weiss didn't even turn but waved a hand as if suddenly tired of us. Or was he concealing some other emotion? Stunned, we stood rooted to the spot in the afternoon sunshine, watching him disappear into the mêlée of Friday afternoon shoppers.

"Amazing!" Erica exclaimed.

"Exactly," I added, unable to put into words how uplifted I felt and not just by the food.

"What shall we do?" Hilary asked, staring at the thick roll of notes held together in a rubber band still in her hand.

"Let's go and get the money changed first," Erica, ever the practical one, suggested. "Find out exactly how much we have before we make any plans."

"*Sechsundzwanzig pfund,*" the man behind the bars of the Bureau du Change informed us as he pushed the notes under the grate. Twenty-six pounds! We were rich!

"This will give us another two weeks traveling," Erica calculated.

"Where shall we go?" Hilary asked, still stunned by this miracle.

"We could go back to Athens?" Erica suggested.

"Or Yugoslavia?" I offered.

"How about the south of France?" Hilary proposed. "We could have a week on the beach, then head straight home."

"Yes!" Erica and I chimed in unison, the idea of beaches and sand beckoning yet again.

The next day, after a good night's sleep and a hearty breakfast of *ruhrei und speck* (scrambled eggs and ham), we stood on the steps of the hostel overlooking the bridge and the skyline of the city with its onion tower. Mr. Weiss was right. Even in the rain, Zürich was like a beautiful, dignified older lady. As I stood there, a voice inside told me, *You will come back here to live and learn German.*

"What do you think?" Erica asked.

"Let's keep moving on," Hilary muttered.

Yes, sorry Mr. and Mrs. Weiss, but it won't be any fun sightseeing in this rain. As we turned in the direction of the *autobahn*, I felt a twang of guilt as though we were betraying our saviors. But it was time to head south.

Erica was right. The extra money extended our freedom by exactly a fortnight. Unfortunately, the postcard that I had sent my mother advising her of our extended trip arrived in England two days after we did. For two whole weeks, she had envisioned our nasty demise. I paid the emotional price for that extra freedom.

The voice that told me I would return to Zürich was also eerily right. As fate would have it, through my father's business connections I was offered the position of *au pair* and landed at Zürich airport just one month later. I had left through the back door, but now, at the airport with "my family," the Simmels, to greet me, I was returning to make a dignified entrance into that fair city, through the front door.

Six weeks later, after I had settled in and quickly acquired a rudimentary knowledge of basic German, I clutched Mr. Weiss's white business card in one hand and the Simmel's red space-age phone in the other. I was both shy and excited. Wouldn't he be gratified to know that at least one of us had fallen in love with Zürich, enough to return for a year? How would he react?

I dialed, then waited. Instead of a ringing, an obnoxious monotone droned in my ear. Hmmm?

I checked the number on his business card and dialed again. Same tone. Maybe they had moved.

Oh, well, call him at the office in Winterthur, an area ten miles north of Zürich. The same drone tone.

The phone book! But no Weiss let alone W or R. This is strange. Maybe the operator could help.

"*Tut mir leid,*" the operator apologized in her guttural Swiss, "*Es gibt kein Walter Weiss.*" No Mr. Weiss.

But he had looked like a solid, respectable businessman with a wife and no children. Even if he had moved, wouldn't he have left a forwarding telephone number, an address, something?

Finally I sought out the assistance of my employer. Frau Simmel's sister worked for the government and she could find anything out about anybody. Though Switzerland was far from a communist regime, it was still law to register a move from one canton to another. They knew where their citizens resided, for the most part. But even the government had no record of a Walter or Regina Weiss.

Did he even exist? Maybe he was an angel who had arrived in our hour of need, or mine anyway. He *was* an international businessman as evidenced by his impeccable English and the roll of bank notes in various currencies. But what kind of business? Industrial espionage? Arms? Drug dealing?

Angel or drug dealer? Drug dealer or angel? Hmm?

Maybe all I needed to know is that he was an angel to me.

Metaphysical Endnote 5

You Are Being Watched...Over

You may be wondering why I shared the previous story with you. Several reasons. This event demonstrated how energy can work on many levels.

Did we manifest the meal, the man and the moolah?

When we want something very badly, many of us use our minds unconsciously, achieving the results we want without even knowing what we are doing. So wouldn't it be beneficial to you to understand *how* you manifested what you wanted, so that in the future you can employ these tools at will, apply them when and as you need them? (More details in Chapter 32, Leap of Faith.)

While lying in our lumpy hostel beds at night, we had been visualizing our desires in great detail. The image of that food became so clear, we were salivating. This intensity of desire is often required to bring us what we want. Although this process feels magical, manifestation works according to the universal laws of physics. So is this why we were treated to this wonderful meal even before we got home? Maybe.

Or was it fate that put this man in our path? Was there a written soul Agreement before we came to this life that Mr. and Mrs. Weiss would show up just when we really needed them? Maybe.

Or was it karma? Erica, Hilary and I were withdrawing from our karmic bank account when we really needed to. If so, it was nice to know we had some karmic credit.

But it could also have been our complementary energies that attracted us to each other. We needed to be fed and watered and they needed...? Maybe we didn't need to know their needs, we just needed to be there.

There is also the possibility that I had unknowingly employed a technique which I often suggest to my clients. Ask the Universe for what you want, envision it, know that it is yours and then let it go. Ask yourself what is the worst thing that can happen if what you desire doesn't show up. Then face that possibility. In my case this was two days without food—not pleasant for a Taurus! Truly accepting the worst outcome eliminates the fear factor which, if allowed to fester, will only negate the manifestation. If you can't handle the worst scenario, change your plan. And if you can accept the worst as the possible outcome, then hope for the best and move forward.

It is the acceptance of what is and the subsequent letting go of fear that I believe allows the magic to happen, because you are not imposing any negative restraints on creation. My grandmother used to marvel at how I "could fall into mud but always come up smelling roses." I may have had angels working overtime, or I just implicitly believed that somehow it would always work out. It had to. And so it did.

In Zürich, I felt the Universe rewarded us for our faith, not just with the meal that we had all dreamed of, but the added bonus of two more weeks of adventure. Often when we do something for ourselves, especially if it involves overcoming a fear, the Universe will let us know we did the right thing by awarding an extra prize. Giving to the self is not an act of selfishness unless of course it's actually physically harming others.

My conclusion about this "miracle" was that a higher power was at work. We all have spirit guides, guardian angels, fairies or hobgoblins watching over us. They don't materialize or flutter down in front of us, their golden wings wafting magnificently, nor do we hear celestial music when they are about to do their work. (Well, okay. It *can* happen!) Mostly these higher entities make it look like a coincidence or luck. You think of someone, they show up. You need a lawnmower, it just so happens your neighbor wants to give away his old one. Coincidence is God's way of remaining anonymous. And the angels regularly work through us mere mortals, using us as the channels or mouthpieces for that higher knowing. It's not necessarily just those of us who appear angelic or even clean. I once received a significant message from a bedraggled street person outside a liquor store. I knew from the way he peered deep into my soul that the wise words coming out of his mouth weren't coming *from* him but *through* him. Out of the mouths of babes have also come pearls of wisdom that I knew were intended as guidance.

On that occasion in Zürich, the angels chose this married couple, who in some way mirrored my parents, to take care of us, feed us and, with a little money in our pockets, send us on our way. So it was not for me to judge whether Mr. Weiss was really a legitimate international businessman or something less savory. As far as I was concerned, our angels were watching over us. And who knows? In some small way, maybe my friends and I brought a little light into their lives, too!

TAKING FLIGHT

I am sure that each of us, in our quieter moments, glances back down the highway of our life and wonders about the off-ramps that we took. I often question the signposts of fate, fear or just plain fickleness that motivated me to veer into the fast lane, stay comfortable in the middle or take a rapid exit. But I never even thought about the sign that steered me onto my psychic highway until I was asked numerous times, "How did you become a psychic?"

Since I had joined an airline six months previously in May of 1974, my life had already changed drastically—for the better. Detesting my lot working as a temp for a London secretarial agency for two years, I had been encouraged by both friends and relative strangers to pursue a new career as an air stewardess. How had people who barely knew me recognized that the life of a Gypsy was my perfect niche?

I loved my new lifestyle flying short-haul routes all over Europe. I loved the lack of routine. I loved the people—crew and passengers. I loved being able to use my knowledge of French, German and Italian. I even loved everything about planes including the dirty diesel smell of the tugs that brought in a just-landed aircraft.

Love had also found me. It was because of Tom, my new gentle and funny boyfriend, that I decided to move from London to Crawley. I now shared a large comfortable neo-Georgian house with my two friends and flat-mates, Sheila and Debbie, both "stewies" flying for the same airline. I was living within dating distance of Tom now and twenty minutes from the airport. Instead of being miserable and lost, I was finally happy and excited about life again.

Ironically, I had always believed that at the age of 22 I would die.

43

But my life was just taking off. *Must be a memory of a past life*, I decided.

Of course, all was not perfect. My parents had finally, after five years of vacillating between loving reconciliations and trying to kill each other, got divorced.

The seeds of the future are often hidden in the present, and anyone who was awake could have perceived them drifting apart long before the final battle came. My mother, as I glibly diagnosed, had gone crazy. She was still scrawnily thin, still substituting nutrition for gin and tonics, and appropriately, giant bars of Cadbury Fruit and Nut chocolate. She now spent her days screaming accusations of betrayal at anybody and everybody who would listen, mostly me because I was there, either in person or on the phone, and she cried and cried and cried. Feeling helpless and totally inept, I tried to rescue my mother from her misery with inane suggestions like, "You're free now. Just think of the possibilities!" But she wanted or needed to wallow in the injustice of it all.

Still unpredictably switching between her former bright, chatty self and her more recent hysterically vengeful, scorned personality, my mother was now a scary stranger to me. My grandmother, as much as I adored her, didn't help. She constantly validated my mother's belief that she was a victim. "It's all Charles' fault," they both moaned. "All men are bastards." "They all cheat and lie." "They only want one thing." And on it went.

I didn't know where my father was and I really didn't care at that time. My memories were always of him enraged, shouting at me, at all of us, especially at Mark, my eldest brother.

He was lost in his own world, his brooding, detached, escapist silences his only defense against the chaotic family in which he, through *his* choices or fate, had found himself.

Whether it was my grandmother's influence or my own questioning of who or what was culpable for all our pain, I chose to blame my father for the emotional bomb that had dropped on our family, sending us all devastated, scattering in opposite directions and shattering my mother into a thousand tiny little pieces, like Humpty Dumpty, never to be put back together again.

My four siblings not only made themselves scarce as if our mother had contracted Ebola but also "didn't want to talk about it" as if the disintegration of our family wasn't really happening. I realized that this nutty clan of mine wasn't my only motivation for studying psychology and metaphysics. My pursuit of knowledge was also a necessary defense against my own suspected encroaching insanity.

I was like a four-year-old with my unceasing why? why? whys? What made people tick? Okay, what made my mother tick? Why did bad things happen to good people? Like my mother. Why was my family so cruel? Especially my mother. Why had this happened to my parents? What had caused my mother's insanity? Was it the pain of my father's betrayal or had that triggered something deeper? Was it punishment or fate? I wanted to know if a person's upbringing dictated their future life or, as my grandmother would have it, was my mother merely a victim of circumstance? So even I knew that my motivation for burying myself in books on numerology, pop psychology or any other available illuminating information I could get my hands on was my own search for answers.

Although the world *appeared* to function out of chaos and people talked as if life was something that happened *to* them, I sensed another truth. Behind the apparent randomness of events, good or bad, there was a rhythm, a pulse, a plan, or at least a capitalist plot. But it was a secret and like a code had to be deciphered. If I just kept digging, I thought, the mystery of this silent powerful mechanism that ruled our lives would eventually be solved. I would not only be able to make order out of the chaos in my life but I would also understand other peoples' motivations. Like the Lone Ranger off to rescue Tonto, I decided I would unravel the mystery of the Universe.

But there was no one to teach me. Except everyone, life and books. I threw myself into self-help writings and metaphysics like *Your Erroneous Zones* (or was it Erogenous?) by Wayne Dyer, the I Ching, and the back pages of women's magazines where Dear Somebody solved everybody's problems.

Then a magical thing happened. A little, tattered, purple paperback landed in my hands. The book was called *The Complete Book of Palmistry* by Joyce Wilson. It changed my life.

I couldn't know the huge impact that this little book filled with fine print and numerous diagrams would have upon me. And to this day, I couldn't tell you why that book hooked me like a gambler to a casino except that it "spoke" to me. Palmistry, after all, is a hugely elaborate science. The information took time to absorb. I would periodically grab people's hands, while avoiding getting arrested, study the lines, then have to revisit the text and the diagrams. As the author kept making references to astrology, I found a copy of *Sun Signs* by Linda Goodman.

And though I bought into the basic premise of astrology—that each planet in our Universe emits its own vibrations and we mere mortals are subject to their influences—I wasn't attracted to learning all its complexities. Maybe astrology just wasn't personal enough. And I had made my choice—palmistry.

As a flight attendant in the roaring seventies, I was definitely a people person. Not only did I, for some insane reason, love the challenge of dealing with often insufferably rude passengers and interesting travelers, I also immensely enjoyed my fun, adventurous colleagues. Consequently Tom and I just *had to* attend a lot of parties. It went with the territory.

It was at these free-spirited gatherings—yes, a lot of the spirits were free though customs never did find out—I began my apprenticeship as a palmist. While airline staff talked endlessly in airline lingo about their eventful flights, whacko passengers, idiosyncratic captains and scary incidents, boring anyone who did not work around airplanes, I would indulge in my palm-reading ability on woolly-minded and willing victims.

The correlation between the shape of people's hands and their personalities fascinated me. As I peered into the person's outstretched palms, I proceeded to point out prominent personality characteristics and future events. "I don't know what I'm doing so don't live by it," was my regular preamble.

But some of the faces of my "victims" would turn pale or their pupils would become enlarged, and they exclaimed, "How did you know that?" Their reaction was often incredulity, almost accusatory, as if I was a spy with MI-5 or had been interrogating their close friends and family.

I just shrugged, amazed but pleased that I had hit upon some hidden truth. "I dunno. It just comes," I slurred, unscientifically, partially proud of myself, partially a little unnerved. How *did* I know? Was it luck? Coincidence? I had no idea. The feelings and the information *just came* to me.

As my readings were limited in content at that time, it did not occur to me that I might be psychic. For me, my palm reading was a very hit-and-miss affair, probably missing much more than hitting. As most people believed then, and many still do, I thought that in order to be clairvoyant one had to possess special powers. *Psychic* definitely wasn't a word I used to describe myself. But even in those early days, I remember a certain integrity that went with the territory, an unspoken command not to say anything that I did not see or that was not the truth. Sometimes, I would simply respond to the person asking the question with "I don't know."

The lines on the hand were to me indicators of the personality type and the person's future potential. The major lines were all so varied in length, shape, form and strength, with such a myriad of nuanced interpretations, that I believed it would take a million years to become a proficient palmist. (I wasn't far wrong!) But I also knew that if I studied palmistry long and profoundly enough, it would take me to a deeper truth, that of the Universe and its workings.

It would be another thirteen years before I would understand the process and could, without an ounce of doubt, say, "By George, I think I've got it. I *am* psychic." But at that time, my question was, *Do I need to be psychic to see or could I just know someone's innermost mind and their future from reading the lines on their hands?* I wanted to understand it all, especially *how* a psychic could see.

Fate must have heard my question because it wasn't long before I would have my first experience with a real psychic.

Metaphysical Endnote 6

Why Palmistry?

Your hands reflect your personality, your challenges and your gifts in life. They convey the story of your soul, your spirit for this lifetime, your beliefs, your hidden potentials, your hopes and your dreams. And they let me know, as your reader, what stage you have reached in your evolution.

Like any other medium used for divining—Tarot cards, the I Ching, Rune Stones, goat entrails or coat buttons—palmistry is a tool. The reason I am attracted to the lines and the shape of the hands is that they are intensely personal, and the story they tell is totally specific to the person to whose arms, mind and soul they are attached.

Just as the six billion faces on the planet all have the same structural elements—two eyes, a nose and a mouth—there are six billion permutations and combinations of those elements. No two faces are alike, except identical twins, of course. Quelle creativity! Well, your hands are even more unique. Same elements but no set alike. Even the right is different from the left. That's what makes palms so fascinating.

While astrology and numerology can provide tremendous insights into the psyche for me, the reading is not as personal as in palmistry because other people can be born on the same day, at the same time and even given the same name. But your hands are unlike those of any other individual and will reveal your past lives, childhood, present and future potential.

The Chinese hand-reading art is to read the thumb and the area around the base of the thumb only, because the thumb represents the will. It is said that there are thousands of nerve endings in this area from which the trained reader will be able to tell a person's story. The Gypsy way is to read the headline as the marriage line and the marriage line as the lifeline and the lifeline as the headline. Confused yet? Wait until you start to read books on palmistry. As if palmistry in and of itself is not complex enough, some books will give you diametrically opposed interpretations! When in doubt, I defer to my intuition.

But take heart. What I have found in my many, many years as a practicing palmist and perennial student of metaphysics is that it all comes out the same in the end. There is only one truth, with many different viewpoints of that same truth. Palmistry is not an exact science either. When I read a palm, I use the lines as a guide, a confirmation of the energy I am already feeling.

Studying the lines is a focal point for my client and for me. Focusing on the lines occupies the client's conscious ego mind, allowing them to go into a relaxed alpha state and giving me easier access to their subconscious, that being the level of the mind on which I am concentrating.

But it really does not matter what tool or medium psychics use to tune in. What is important is how well they know their chosen medium and how confident they are in their psychic abilities. Sometimes the only way to advance a psychic ability is to practice on real live people. But a word of warning: a little knowledge can be a dangerous thing. So before you start grabbing people's hands or offering to read cards and claiming to be a psychic, let them know you are an apprentice. That way, at least, your victim can choose to discount the information and you will do no harm.

MRS. TINSLEY

*I*t was late summer. The other two stewies and I were sitting at the front of an empty BAC 1-11 which was due to take off for Majorca within half an hour. Having finished our pre-flight duties, we had a little time to relax before the passengers descended on us for boarding and our work would begin.

"I just went to see ziss amazeeng psycheec," Joseline, who was perched on an armrest, announced in her thick French accent. "Everyone is talkeeng about 'err."

"Where?" I asked.

"Brighton. 'Er name ees Mrs. Tinsley."

"What does she read?" the other stewardess inquired absently. "Tea leaves, palms, Tarot?"

"She just reads ordinaree playeeng cards. But she told me my seesterr would 'ave a baby girl and zat I would be leaveeng on 'olidays very soon." She shrugged the way the French do. "My sister 'ad zee babee and yes, I am leaveeng in two weeks."

"That's amazing," we both cooed.

I was intrigued. "Can I get her number from you?"

And that was just the beginning of my addiction to a long and eclectic string of psychics.

Two weeks later, my friend Lucy agreed to drive the thirty-minute trip to Brighton. The August sky was a soft blue with fluffy white clouds that reminded me of cotton wool puffs. A slight breeze neutralized the potential mugginess of the summer's day. And we were all excited about our imminent readings. Lucy was newly engaged to Neil, I was about to move into my first purchased home with Maggie and Lucy as my new lodgers, though Lucy would be there just a short time until she got married, and Maggie was just coasting in her job with British Airtours with nothing particularly exciting on the horizon, except traveling all over the world.

Mrs. Tinsley lived in south-coast suburbia. Her semi-detached house with black framework and latticed windows was fronted by a small square of grass and a thin border of wilting flowers. Like so many English suburban areas, the only feature that set her house apart from her neighbors' was the shade of blue on her front entrance.

A tall, slim, dark-haired, bespectacled man opened the door. Whether because he emanated an eerie intensity or because he leaned too far forward, peering invasively at all three of us, we instinctively shrank back from him.

"We're here to see Mrs. Tinsley," I said timorously.

Without responding, he turned his back, and with a careless flick of his hand beckoned us to follow him into a front room where a buxom white-haired older lady in a flowered dress was sitting at a small square table. As she signaled for us to sit down, she sighed long-sufferingly as if she was already weary of the questions we had yet to ask. She shooed the man out of the room with the same impatience. "Stop gawkin' an' go an' make the tea, will yer?" she snapped. To our relief, like an obedient dog he left.

Mrs. Tinsley pointed to Maggie. "You...sit over there," she commanded, inclining her head toward the opposite side of the table where there was a vacant chair. Lucy and I took up the two spectator chairs behind Lucy.

While Lucy and I watched fascinated, Mrs. Tinsley plunked a deck of playing cards down in front of our friend. "Shuffle them and then split the cards into three piles," Maggie was told. "An' do it again," the psychic ordered, and Maggie repeated the exercise.

When Maggie handed the pile back to Mrs. Tinsley, the psychic flipped them over expertly in rows of five across and four down. She made expressive grunts as she noticed which cards appeared. Then, like a tap turned on, she began to gush information. "I see a move. You like the dark-haired men, don't you, dear?" Maggie frowned at me. *Who was she talking about?* "Oh, there's going to be an upset around the job, but don't worry, it'll be all right in the end," she continued.

I noticed that much of the information was generic. "Dark-haired man" could be ten per cent of the population. "An upset on the job" could be pesky passengers, at least one of whom we encountered on every flight. Maybe she heard my thoughts because then she announced, "A man with the initial 'P' is going to be very significant. Is your father experiencing health problems? 'E's got to watch 'is bladder. I see problems there." Now *that* was specific. I sat up.

While I studied the psychic at work, Lucy, afraid that she might miss a single prediction or morsel of wisdom, frantically scribbled on Maggie's behalf what Mrs. Tinsley was saying. *How could this psychic get all this information from playing cards?* I wondered.

Suddenly, as if the tap had been turned off, Mrs. Tinsley stopped, gathered the cards together back into one pile and abruptly told Maggie, "You're done." She nodded at Lucy. "Next." A little stunned, Maggie moved out of the hot seat and Lucy took her place, handing me the notepad and pen.

"I see a wedding..." she started. "June." That's when Lucy and Neil had planned to get married! Maybe she was good after all. "You're also moving to a bungalow. I see a lot of trees where you are ..." Mrs. Tinsley seemed to warm to Lucy. Maggie and I gasped frequently as she mentioned people, places and events that we recognized as already having happened in Lucy's life or that were planned. *Was it possible that psychics are more tuned in to some people than others?* Then there were more details we did not recognize, occurrences that were way out in the future. The time went quickly and suddenly it was my turn. As I sat down, I held my breath.

"There's been an upset with a dark-haired man and you had a hard time gettin' over 'im but he wasn't really for you." *Yes! Keith.*

"But don't worry, you're getting married this October." *Maybe Tom was going to ask me to marry him,* I thought. She flicked a second layer of cards over the first layer, sucking in her breath as she did so. *What? What?* I wanted to ask but stayed silent. "There's an offer of a new job. You're going to be involved with a big building and some people are really happy for you but some are jealous. Watch out for a dark-haired lady." Maggie and I exchanged glances and smiled. I knew it wasn't her. "Hmm?" Mrs. Tinsley continued. "The initial 'M' will cause you some heartache." *Uh-oh.*

Then she peered straight into my eyes. "Be careful when you're driving, dear. I see something round goin' flyin' and you're too young and pretty to die." *Oh, God!* I envisioned a wheel flying off my car and me crashing into a ditch.

As if Mrs. Tinsley had rung her servant's bell, her husband (or was he the butler?) entered the room perfectly timed for the end of the readings and formally presented us with a tray of tea and a plate of custard creams. As he set the floral tray down on the card table, I noticed that where his dense black hair joined his scalp, there was a thick unnatural seam. I shuddered. The cheap wig, for some reason, made him appear even creepier.

"Drink yer tea and I'll read the leaves, dearies," she instructed. The three of us sipped on our tea, ruminating on all of our individual futures. I would be driving up to London that night, I remembered. I would have to make sure the wheels of my car were on tight.

The hot liquid felt good, soothing my shock at her prediction. I was the first to hand her the dainty teacup. She swirled the dregs around and peered intently into it as if trying to read a newspaper without glasses.

"Oh!" she exclaimed. The excited inflection in her voice soothed my fears. "A man with the initials 'J,' 'T' or 'L' means something." I scanned my mental black book of acquaintances, family and friends and came up with several potential candidates but nobody in particular. "And you're going on a large ship, dear, like a cruise. You'll 'ave the time of your life." *Oh, good. Is this before or after I die in the car crash?*

When all three cups had been read and she was collecting our money, antsy for us to be gone now, I asked her, "Do you think that our fate is written in stone or do you think we have the ability to alter it?"

In response, she peered straight into my eyes. "Your life is decided the day you're born and there ain't nothing you can do to change it."

Hmmm? That didn't bode well for me and my car then.

Half an hour later, Maggie was slathering her French bread with gooey Brie. "She was bang on with you, Lucy," she said.

In a state of bemused amazement, we had driven straight from Mrs. Tinsley's house to a cozy pub where we could assess our readings and were now scoffing down a ploughman's lunch accompanied by a potent homemade blackberry wine.

"Yes." Lucy just grinned complacently. Everything was settled for her. Despite having boyfriends, both Maggie and I were still in that no-man's land of singledom and anything-could-happen futures. I took out the notes that Maggie had recorded for me and re-read them.

Going overseas. Fulfillment of both wishes. Receive a letter in the post from a lady. I love animals. Upset about a light-colored animal dead. Watch health in 78th year. I don't like children, two children not bothered about. Have I had an affair with a professional man? Watch out because he's a bit of a so-and-so. Dark man smasher abroad. Fate alters. Lady gives birth to a girl, urgent call starts big changes in your life, traveling before next Tuesday. Happiness over a wedding ring. Lady dies suddenly. Watch something on car.

Well, she was wrong about me not liking children. I loved the little blighters. As far as the rest was concerned, *We'll see,* I thought.

When my flatmate, Eric, arrived home that night from his office job, I told him about the psychic's warning and asked him to check my wheels. Despite his cynical teasing, without stopping to change out of his business suit, he went outside in the early summer evening. From the living room, I heard the "prang" sound as he proceeded to remove the hubcaps on my little green mini. I went to stand in the front door-way and watched as he tightened the wing nuts on the wheels and banged the hubcaps back into place. I breathed a sigh of relief as he reported that the wheels were all "secure."

An hour later, I had the country road almost to myself as I drove to-wards Knightsbridge in South London. While I marveled at the golden glow that bathed the winding hedgerows and surrounding green fields in the summer evening, I was still pondering my reading and wonder-ing how much of it would actually come true when I heard a "ping" followed by a loud tinny noise. My rear-view mirror reflected the sight of a metal hubcap rolling back down the road, heading towards the ditch. I surmised it had become detached from *my* car. Mrs. Tinsley's words, "something round goin' flyin'," echoed in my brain.

Maybe it was the shock of her prediction coming true so quickly but it didn't occur to me to stop and retrieve the round metal disc. I continued driving, clinging tightly to the steering wheel while the implications of what had just happened sank into my mind. Was the prediction now fulfilled and therefore over, nothing more to worry about? But if I hadn't asked Eric to check the wheels, the loosened hubcap might not have become detached. And, if Mrs. Tinsley hadn't warned me, I would not even have asked Eric to touch the wheels. So did I save myself from a wheel going flying and make the prediction come true or would it have happened anyway? Was the cart before the horse or the horse before the cart? Or worse, was the disaster still in my future?

On that beautiful summer's evening, where all seemed otherwise right with my world, I chose to believe that what Mrs. Tinsley had seen was just an errant hubcap that might have come loose anyway. Now it had "gone flyin'," I could relax, look forward to getting married in Octo-ber, going on a cruise and having the time of my life.

Metaphysical Endnote 7

Interpreting the Energy

In the old days at Delphi, the readings were not just between client and psychic seer. There was a third person. Their task was to interpret what the psychic saw for the "querent"—the person asking the questions. This interpreter was adept at understanding psychic energy, its symbols and the myriad of ways energy can be construed. These days, as psychics, we are the readers *and* the interpreters of energy. In my process, I adhere to three rules.

The First Rule: *Be gentle and do no harm!*

As every experience is for our ultimate growth, there is no good or bad news. But very few of us would declare when going through hard times, "Oh, goodie, another painful learning experience."

When something negative presents itself in the reading such as an impending illness, as the reader, I have several choices.

❖ Blurt it out. "Oh, look, you're going to get cancer!" Trust me, I have been to this kind of psychic and you need to avoid them like the plague. While the psychic information might be correct, he/she could also be misinterpreting. The potential might exist for cancer but it may not manifest. But what this psychic has done with his/her forecast is implant the seed of an idea in the client's consciousness. If you water and feed that belief with fear, it could become a reality.

❖ Avoid the topic altogether. Avoiding the beginnings of something negative is also a disservice to your querent and not practicing integrity. Denial, apathy and resistance can get us into as much trouble as diving headlong into the abyss without wings.

❖ First check with my client to see if he is already aware of this problem. I might ask, "How's your health?" He might respond, "I've got cancer." Or "Something's not right." Or "Great!" Then I present his potential future in a way that empowers him to change it and at the same time deepens his spiritual understanding of why this illness is manifesting. If we believe that the mind/spirit absolutely has power over the body, then it does. So I remind him that he can choose to heal or not to heal. Going through the illness might be part of his pre-life Agreement. And even that can be forgiven.

❖ Ask for guidance. When distasteful news doesn't match my

perception of the person I'm reading, I sometimes push it aside. But if it is the truth, it will continue to nudge me. In fact, the truth almost nags at me until I put it into words. Then I ask for guidance. *How should I phrase this? In what context should I put the information, literally or symbolically?* Miraculously the words then just come tumbling out of my mouth, and I hear the news being communicated in a very wise and loving way, almost as if I am listening to another entity speaking through me which, of course, I am. I often experience a surge of relief as the client seems to understand the information without fear.

And whatever the news, always, always, remind the client that psychics can be wrong at least 25% of the time. Our future is a result of the choices we make from the thoughts we think which come from the beliefs that we harbor in our subconscious. If we want to change our outcome, we need to change our beliefs. Our thoughts and then our actions will automatically readjust.

The Second Rule: *Don't expect to be right, at the time of the reading.* My advice to both budding psychics and clients is to give yourself latitude when interpreting. The energy is never wrong but your translation of it might be. You also need to remember that you are seeing the energy through your limited perception. You will find that the longer you read, the more you will understand that there are many different ways to interpret energy. As in translating dreams, it is about peeling away the layers. I am often able to be extremely specific, giving the minutest and strangest of details. But when I don't feel that absolute knowing, I let the querent know this, and I give as many interpretations of the energy as possible. Clients can then superimpose their reality on my information. They will anyway.

The client receiving the information might often dispute the predictions. Some may even want to argue, especially when most of the reading is about future events and people of which they are not yet cognizant. Beware the denial factor! À la Monty Python, *I didn't come here for an argument.* I can see over the wall and they can't. So I gently remind them that they won't do anything that they don't want to do. And if I see it, I have to say it. That's my job.

In the preamble to my readings, I also advise the client that what I am in fact doing is reading the six levels of consciousness of their energy: soul, spirit, subconscious, unconscious, conscious and higher consciousness. On those levels of Mind, I see what they are in the process of manifesting with their beliefs and thoughts. However, what I see is only one potential. People change their minds, go off in another direction or, because of fear, delay the predicted outcome. "Take it all with a grain of salt," I warn them. "If what I say supports you, great. If it doesn't have any bearing on your life, throw it over your left shoulder." Thankfully some clients, when cautioned of a potentially negative situation, will take heed, change their thinking and their course and avoid that disaster.

And while I like to be as specific and give as many details to the querent as possible, sometimes it behooves the psychic to be more vague. As an example, instead of saying, "Your mother is coming to see you," I might give a broader interpretation by saying, "An older female who feels like family and shows maternal-type energy is coming to visit." Or instead of saying, "I see you going to New York," I change it to, "I see a busy city, like New York." Or "There may be a strong connection with that city." The querent will often contort your information to make it fit their perception of their future. When the actual prediction manifests in a different reality, then they understand what you *really* meant. And they will know the truth. When a prediction comes true, it feels like déjà vu or a previously dreamt sequence.

Instead of promising marriage for an upcoming romance, I use words like "significant relationship." And predicting the outcome of a relationship is, I feel, robbing my client of that discovery. Unless that relationship is extremely unhealthy, of course. Then I tell them.

I find words and phrases that give me as the psychic or you as the querent, some leeway in interpretation. Giving this leeway does not incur too much liability for the psychic, and the querent then is not tempted to fixate on details. When I do have that absolute knowing, however, I certainly do give my clients the particulars.

The Third Rule: *Always give the client a gift.* When the reading is done, I like to summarize the essence of all the information that has come through in one gift. What is the single message for the client at this time? And that message is always a gift of empowerment, enlightenment or healing. Whatever is happening, in some way, is for their highest good. Order *does* come out of chaos, and sooner or later we all *do* evolve to a higher vibration and joy.

JUST AN ORDINARY BLOKE?

$\mathcal{B}$y the time I had been flying for eighteen months and studying palmistry for just twelve, my intuition was honed enough to save my own life but sadly not another's.

It is nine o'clock at night. The Captain and First Officer are leaning like bookends sandwiching two female cabin crew and myself between them at the bar of the Manchester Airport Hotel. John Davis, a popular BAC 1-11 Captain is a health nut with a crew cut topping his tall lean frame. The First Officer, Paul Reid, in his mid-fifties, is even leaner, taller and grayer. New to our company, Paul, rumor has it, is fairly embittered. After having reached the higher echelons of Fleet Captain with his former airline until it teetered into bankruptcy, he is now forced to fly with our charter outfit as a mere co-pilot.

The three females, including me, all have our backs to the room, which is long and somberly lit.

"Hey, did you know that Kate reads palms?" John suddenly pipes up.

The girls coo interest.

"Well," I shrug modestly, "I'm not very good...."

Paul stretches out his thin, spindly hand in front of my face. "Read it."

I give him one of my disdainful glares normally reserved for rude passengers.

"Please," he adds.

"Looks like you're going to live a long time," I mumble, surprised. The man is so ashen, he could die tomorrow. "You could experience some troubles in your marriage. If you are discussing divorce already, it is up to you how you manage it as to what the result is. It could get very nasty. Very nasty, indeed. Or not. It depends on you. Don't let your anger get the better of you."

Paul groans, retracts his hand suddenly and resumes sipping on his beer.

"How do ya do that?" John slurs. "See things in people's hands jush from the lines?"

"I don't really see anything. It's more feel," I respond, not sure myself exactly how the information comes.

"Talking about intuition," Kathy hisses out of the side of her mouth, "that man sitting behind us hasn't taken his eyes off us all night."

"I know," I nod. "I sensed him ogling us when we first came in."

Jane shivers as she says, "Psycho-man's giving me the creeps."

I do a surreptitious turn. A tall, big man in his early thirties, smartly but casually dressed, returns my casual glance with a soulless icy stare. The word *killer* comes to mind. I shudder.

Our cheery conversation suddenly dries up. "I'm tired," I say, "but I think we should all leave together." In silent agreement, we stroll out of the bar, along the carpeted foyer and into an empty lift.

The elevator doors open onto the third floor. We walk in silence. Jane's and Kathy's rooms are first. They say goodnight and disappear. John's room is at the end of the corridor just before it turns right. He unlocks his door and stumbles into the shadows. Now it is just Paul and I. His room is next on the left and then mine is the last on the other side of a pair of heavy swing doors. Paul is behind me. Just as I am about to say goodnight, he pipes up, "Why don't you come and have a nightcap with me?"

I turn to say, "No thank you," but then I freeze. Looming behind Paul is psycho-man from the bar!

"That would be lovely," I respond, grabbing Paul's arm and pushing him towards his door.

Once inside, Paul hands me a brandy and pats a spot on the bedspread beside him. Shaking, I take the glass and sink down gratefully onto the bed. He instantly slings a possessive arm around my shoulder.

Oh, God. "No, Paul," I say exasperated, "I can't stay. That man, that man from the bar...."

"What about him?"

"He must have followed us up here. And where was he going? My room is the last door in this corridor."

"Oh, don't worry about him," Paul takes the brandy from my trembling hand and pushes me down on the bed.

"No!" I yelp and struggle into a standing position. *What to do?*

"Paul, you *have* to come with me to my room."

"Okay." His eyes light up.

"Check the hallway first," I hiss over his shoulder as he opens his door. It is the silent stealth of psycho-man that disturbs me.

I unlock the door to my room and Paul barges in. "Thank you," I say as I attempt to close him out. But he is forcing his way in. *Not two psychos in one night!* The determined flinty cruelty I see in his eyes makes me nervous.

"Paul," I say, shamelessly coy. "You are a very attractive man but I'm really tired tonight. Maybe another time...?"

His eyes soften and he backs away.

"Goodnight, Paul," I say firmly and shove the door in his pouting face.

God. His poor wife.

I glance nervously around my room. It's empty but I still feel psycho-man close...and waiting. I look up and see the loose panels of the heating ducts. I envision one of the panels sliding back.... I dial Jane's number.

"Hi. It's Kate."

"Are you okay?"

"You know that man in the bar? He followed us up here."

"No. We were the only ones...."

"He suddenly appeared by my door...."

"Oh, my God. Get down here!"

"It's me," I pant breathlessly a few minutes later, feeling vulnerable in that empty hallway before a wide-eyed Jane peers out from the sanctity of her room.

Gratefully, I snuggle into the spare bed and realize that a movie Jane is watching is about an invalid girl stranded alone in an isolated cottage knowing that a knife-wielding psychopath is coming to get her. Neither of us sleep.

The next morning, as Jane and I are tucking into bacon and eggs in the hotel restaurant, Kathy appears.

"I had nightmares all night that psycho-man was climbing in my window, even though we were on the third floor," she grumbles.

Before we leave the hotel, we enquire at the front desk about the eerie stranger. The hotel employee shrugs. "Just seemed like an ordinary bloke ter me, luv."

So did the First Officer.

Ten years later, one of my ex-flying buddies asked me, "Did you hear what happened to Paul Reid?"

That night in Manchester instantly sprang to mind.

"No."

"He's in jail."

"What!"

"He murdered his wife."

"Oh, no." The palm reading. *Our character determines our fate.*

"Yes, he put her in concrete, apparently. Chartered a small plane and dumped her in one of the bottomless lakes in the Lake District. Some trainee scuba divers discovered her perched on a large protruding rock."

"The story goes that she was suing for divorce and when she went for half of everything, he didn't want to share."

Metaphysical Endnote 8

The "Why Me?" Syndrome

Like energy attracts like energy and/or complementary energy. Whatever thoughts you are putting out into the Universe, consciously and unconsciously, like a boomerang come right back at you. The easiest way to rate your core beliefs is to assess the results you are getting in your life right now. Take an honest look at the quality and the quantity of energy you are emitting into your world. If you are not satisfied with your results in your home, your relationships, your finances, your health, then re-evaluate the beliefs that keep you stuck in that negative condition. Elements of fear or guilt may be holding you back.

"It's not that easy," you say. Well, it is and it isn't. The trick is to see life as simultaneously mind-numbingly simple and infinitely complex. The complexities are merely the limitless manifestations of fundamental laws of energy. You only need to know a few universal laws to be able to reduce those complexities to their simplest essence. Once you understand these laws, you can do the programming instead of being programmed.

❖ Like attracts like or complementary energy.

❖ Thoughts are magnetic impulses. Whatever you focus on will be drawn to you.

❖ Whatever you hold as true, the Universe will make you right.

❖ Fear vibrates on the lower frequencies and is a heavier, darker, denser energy.

❖ Love vibrates at the higher levels, is lighter and cleaner and has power over fear.

❖ Whatever you fear or love can have power over you, if you allow it, in the mental/emotional if not in the physical realm.

❖ Bad things happen to good people because on some level they believe they deserve the negative. Or they seek the lessons that the bad teaches, otherwise known as the gift, though it may not seem like a gift at the time.

❖ To erase a certain behavior, in yourself or others, change your thinking around it. Or remove yourself, physically and emotionally, from its influence.

So why did Paul Reid's wife attract a nasty demise at the hands of her embittered husband? I do not know what transpired between husband and wife. Just the outcome. We can often determine the initial intention by the end result. According to the law of vibration, she attracted him first as her husband. The relationship might have been karmic. That would be my first guess. And at some level, she must have continued to participate because she needed to learn from her mirrored experience with him and his low vibration. It does take two to play the game. If one walks away, the destructive game stops. If we stay, it means we are still willing to participate on that same vibration because we haven't learned to honor who we are!

Maybe she was just as fearful as Paul and wanted to fight it through to the end ("like" energy). Or she could have been a very sweet person with such low self-esteem or some huge guilt that she felt she deserved what he doled out (complementary energy). Whatever her beliefs, the results were sadly the same.

And, of course, there is a higher justice. Was it his guilt that attracted those scuba divers to her concrete-embedded corpse? Or her spirit that avenged her death by perching herself on a rock where she could be found and he could be punished? In death, as in life, we can throw boomerangs!

BREAKDOWN/BREAKTHROUGH

*I*t wasn't just the purchase of my first home that sent me into a downward spiral. Like the cause of most plane crashes, it's never just one thing.

The flight should have been a quick LGW–MXP–LGW, (London/Gatwick–Milan–London/Gatwick) but as on so many of those chaotic summer days, major delays caused by air traffic snarl-ups created rush hours in the sky. Changing weather conditions, especially fog, only exacerbated the situation. (Why do they always build airports in fog-prone bowls anyway?)

This particular flight extended from a seven-hour duty into a twenty-three-hour marathon. Instead of returning to Gatwick, we ended up diverting into Bristol where our captain, without consulting the cabin crew, oh-so-kindly volunteered us for another two sectors, this time to Zürich and back to Gatwick. Chauvinism was alive and well in those days! But the fog still lay thick on the ground at Gatwick, and so we diverted again into Bristol. With delays at each turn-around, and after a twenty-hour duty, we ended up having to taxi from Bristol back to our airport base.

When I finally arrived home, I remember falling into bed and not waking for two days. When I did, my whole body, right down to my bones, was excruciatingly *sore*. And something was different about me, inside me, as if something was coming to an end, a kind of death. I knew I was in trouble.

How did this happen? I try to remember. It was sudden, as if one minute I was walking along under a blue sky in a sunny, open field and then, with no warning, the earth collapsed under my feet. I fell into a black hole. I remembered to grab the sides and I clutched at a clump of grass on the edge of that hole. I am hanging by one arm, praying that this clump of grass will not break away and leave me to fall into the abyss. I must not let go. I must not let go. My strength is waning and I am tired and I want to go to sleep but I mustn't let go or I will disappear into oblivion, into darkness, lost in outer space and I will never be able to get back.

I look up and see the light in the field where I had been walking. Faces appear around the rim of the hole, peering over the edge, looking down on me, some curious, some frowning, some scared. Some want to reach out and they lean forward, offering their hands to pull me back. But somehow, I don't have the strength to even raise my arm to meet theirs. It is not that simple. So I stay in my dark pit, holding onto the light by a thin blade of grass, looking up at their silent, helpless faces.

Sometimes there are no faces, and sometimes I feel my hold slipping. Then I am terrified. I don't know how to get out.

To venture into the unknown without any road map is too terrifying. I have no reference point because I have never been here before. I am in the dark, lost in outer space. I feel close to insanity. Anything could happen. All possibilities flash through my mind, too fast for me to grasp or know them. Only a feeling of fear remains, great fear. Some terrible, terrible thing is going to happen to me if I am not vigilant. I must stay vigilant. I must have something to hang on to, a reference point. Always. Then I know I am safe, forever. The ultimate fear is not death. Death would bring sleep, peace, a place where no one can hurt me again. Death is a thing I am not afraid of. What I do fear is being lost, floating in the Universe. Darkness. Insanity.

The phone rings and I burst into tears. I know it is Crewing.

"Miss Rosewood?"

"Yes?"

"We'd like you to do a Frankfurt, Zurich double tomorrow reporting at 06:00."

"I can't," I barely whisper.

"Why not?"

"I'm sick."

"What's wrong?"

"I–I don't know."

"When will you be fit?"

"I–I don't know." I want to cry. "I'll let you know."

"Well, when? Tomorrow? Five days from now? When?"

"I don't know." I feel pathetic and I hate the harsh voice on the end of the line.

"I'll call again in two days."

I crawl back to bed and cry, but I don't know why. Then I sleep.

Part of me wants to let go but I am terrified that I am slipping away into oblivion where I will be alone forever. Never again will I be able to reach anyone. Most of the time, I hold on, even with just one hand. It takes so much strength that I just don't have.

My bones are aching with the tiredness. It's all too much. I think— thought—of myself as tough, a strong person. I could always do it alone, but now I am not so sure. There is a doubt there, a small but nagging one. I will never have complete faith in myself any more. I will never be the same again. A piece is missing. There will always be that fissure, that weakness in my strength.

If I am not vigilant, I could fall through that crack. So I am constantly aware of that weakness in my mind, and I watch for it. I treat it with care. I will have to go more slowly now my confidence is shattered. I won't push or overload myself like I used to. I was adventurous but now I will be cautious. Where I was fearless and free, I will now fear that hole.

I'm sad that I have lost the freedom that courage gives. I thought I was impervious to hurdles. It seems I just kept leaping over them or going around them as each one hit, denying any weakness, pushing down any feelings of sadness or grief. I always had to stay strong. Who taught me that there is no room for weakness? Grandie, my mother, my siblings. I realize I was brought up to be tough like a boy. Not allowed to cry. No matter what happens, keep going, don't stop, not allowed to grieve, no time for weakness, it's disgusting, it's self-pity. To be human is not allowed.

Or did I maintain my façade because there was just nowhere to go, no one to understand? If I show my feelings, I am shamed, as if I revealed my nakedness to them, and they turn away, disgusted.

That's why I need to be alone, to sleep. Please let me rest, I am so tired. I can't do it anymore. Not like you want me to do it. I can't pretend. I know I have to stay in the race. And I know that if I don't stay in the race, I will be left behind. I will be left alone.

Why is there always this sense of urgency?

I hate the phone. It jangles and jangles on my frazzled brain as if I have no protection for my eardrums, and I weep.

It's Crewing again. "When are you going to be fit, Miss Rosewood?" This is not just a demand but also an accusation. What does he think? I am taking a holiday?

"I don't know." I am trying to be honest.

"It's been eight days. We'll need a doctor's note."

"I can't...," I say, but he's not interested and he hangs up.

Nobody understands. They are looking at me strangely, confused by what they see. I am not what they thought I was. I am not what they want me to be. I am not behaving the way they expect me to behave. I am letting them down. I should be performing for them, making them laugh, being happy, coping.

And so it is more painful. There is no comfort, no safe place to go and just be in my pain. The pressure is there to be something more than I am. I am not enough, not good enough.

It's been two weeks now. Crewing calls every three days, but I just let the phone ring and I cry, afraid that they will come and bash my door down and make me go back to flying. But I can't, I just can't.

The voices in my head tell me to get better now, right now. They tell me to smile and laugh and be normal, but my body rebels. It does not want to move. The need to sleep is overwhelming. The blackness engulfs me and I have to sleep.

The pain is all over me, in and around my body now. I am one piece of excruciating pain, as if all my nerve endings are uncovered and raw. Any touch, any movement hurts. When someone speaks, meaningless words jangle in my ears just as if someone had hit me with a hammer on my bloody, exposed nerves.

I see my face in the mirror. I am gaunt, gray. My eyes are dead. I pray to God, please, please, let me die. I don't ever want to wake up to this pain again. To life. What is it but hurt and struggle? The joy that they speak of is just a trick. Maybe for others there is love, and for them I am happy. But not for me. They don't understand me; I am an alien on this planet. I am tired of trying to explain myself and failing and being misunderstood. I am alone and isolated. But I am scared to be alone. Has no one else been in this black hole?

Some days, it feels as if I will never, ever be better again. I will always feel this terrible weariness, as if my body is a dead weight and I must succumb finally to this force trying to suck me down into its vortex. Other days, I feel light and I even have the hope that if I can just hang on, I will get my strength back and get out of this hole.

I ache all over my body. I ache to feel some warm, strong arms around me. I know Tom knows I am sick, and he stays away. That hurts. I ache for him to hold me and tell me everything will be okay. But he doesn't. There is only absence, a void. His presence feels stronger because of his absence. People don't like it when you are depressed. Nobody wants you when you're down and out.

They look at me in disgust and turn away, leaving me with the shame of my weakness. No sympathy. You must be happy or else we don't want you, they think. I know this by now but still it hurts. Who can I tell how I'm feeling? There is no comfort, so I go to bed and sleep and beg God to just let me slip-slide away into death, into peace. I am the walking dead. I want to be the sleeping dead.

Some days, because the voice in my head tells me I should, I get up and sit in the chair in the living room. I obey. At least I can pretend that I am getting better even if I'm not. I feel guilty that I am sick for so long. It hurts to move so I sit very still in the velour dressing gown that has become my only wardrobe.

Maggie, my flat mate, bounces in, vibrant, fully of energy. *I have forgotten what it feels like to have that kind of energy and I envy her. So I feel even weaker.*

She's in love. She argues with her new boyfriend, Peter, a friend of Tom's. They are flirting. But the noise of their voices, though they are not speaking loudly, hurts my ears. I can feel the energy underneath their voices, the aggression, the defensiveness behind their game. I look at them and wonder, "Why bother?" Why bother to do anything? It is all meaningless. I hear them talk but I can't distinguish the words they are saying.

To me it is just a cacophony that jangles in my ears and causes me pain. I want total silence. I need total silence.

Maggie says, "Why don't you go for a walk? You'll feel much better, you know."

John, Tom's best friend, drops in. We sit at opposite ends of the oak dining room table. It is badly scratched from years of use, but it is my one and only family inheritance, apart from this insanity. He talks of nothing. I make polite noises, trying to distinguish the words. It is an effort even to sit on that dining room chair that offers no support and even more to make intelligible responses. I see his concern. He wants to help me, I know. I keep hoping he will say something about Tom, some little bit of news for me to hang onto.

But he says, "Why don't you try going out for a walk, get some fresh air?"

I am the character in Edvard Munch's painting, on the bridge. I am screaming but no one can hear. John doesn't understand and I can't explain. I don't understand myself. I am scared because I don't know what is happening to me.

I want to get out of this vacuum but I don't know how. When I am not in my pit, it's as if I am in a thick glass bottle. People can see me and I can see them. They talk to me but the words are muffled. I watch their lips but still it doesn't mean anything. I look within myself for strength, even a little push to open the door to my vacuum. I try to push myself to speak, to do something, but there is nothing left. I have been running on reserve for years, and now even that is empty.

Maria comes over and just sits on the couch. She can see that I don't have the energy to talk. My brain has disconnected itself from my lips. But I am comforted. She is the first person who knows I am in mourning. I don't know what I mourn for. We watch TV. I don't listen to what is being said. Nothing goes in. I am just glad that I am not alone and that I don't have to perform. She makes me tea and doesn't want anything from me. She doesn't mention the word "walk." She doesn't peer at me frowning, only with understanding. I relax a little.

Then Amanda calls. Amanda knows pain. She knows what it is like to be like an orphan.

"Are you okay?"

"No."

"Are you eating, Kate?"

"No." I know that my skin is starting to cling to my small frame. "I don't have the energy to make food. Lucy and Maggie don't cook for me. They think I'm lazy." I whimper as I tell her how they keep telling me I just need to go for a brisk walk and then everything will be fine.

Amanda grunts condemnation at the other end of the phone. But I don't blame my flat mates. They are afraid. But it hurts that they, the two friends who share my home, cannot reach me in my darkness.

"I'm coming over," Amanda announces. She does and she brings me dinner.

I think of Mother. Her craziness haunts my every waking and sleeping moment. Am I going crazy like her? Is this how she feels? Is this hereditary? Of course, insanity is hereditary. Am I out of control just like her? In her dark, evil moments, is she this scared?

But wait a minute, I am not lashing out at others, screaming obscenities and hurting people as she does. I am not threatening suicide. I am just thinking it. I won't tell anyone of my schemes. I will just do it and then no one can talk me out of it. It will be a done deed. I spend much of my day thinking about how I can kill myself. The flat is only three storeys from the ground. If I throw myself off, I will only break a leg. How can I get enough sleeping pills to put myself to sleep forever? But I don't even have the energy to get dressed, let alone leave the house. I think of who would miss me, who I would hurt by leaving. I decide I couldn't hurt my little brother like that. He's been through enough.

I realize then that my mother will never commit suicide; she wants to live because she has so much vengeance and vindictiveness in her. Her rage feeds her, keeps her alive. Revenge is her purpose.

I need no longer worry about my mother killing herself. I know who she is now. And I am different.

After I finally dragged myself to my doctor's office, Amanda called. "What did he say?"

I groaned. "He asked me if I had a cold and then proceeded to tell me about his weekend fishing trip in Scotland." I shook my head, remembering how I had cried all the way home. Not even a doctor could figure out my problem.

"Those GPs!" Amanda snorted. "I'll take you to see Doc Lemon, the airline doctor. He'll know."

He did. As soon as Doc Lemon (who was also a Boeing 727 captain) laid his twinkling brown eyes on me, he assessed me accurately. "Kate, you look bloody awful."

Right, so far.

He sat on the far side of a huge antique desk, and I slumped down in the chair opposite him.

"Are you depressed?" he asked.

"Yes."

"Do you cry a lot?"

"Yes!" I started crying with the relief of having someone understand.

"Do you feel exhausted, you just want to sleep?"

Yes! Yes! Yes!

"We'll have to examine you, but it looks to me like you have a bad case of nervous exhaustion."

Nervous exhaustion? The words echoed in my head. Yes, that described what I was feeling perfectly. Just exhausted. Emotionally and physically on my knees.

"So you don't think it's a nervous breakdown?" I asked between sniffles.

Now it was the doctor's turn to scoff. "No, Kate." He smiled kindly. "This airline has been working some of you to death, about eight of you to be precise. You know, you're not the only one."

I'm not the only one? Then I'm not crazy? If only I'd known that. I wouldn't have been so scared.

"I'm going to write you off for a month," he said as he reached for his pad.

A month! No more harassing calls from Crewing. I could rest in peace knowing that I wasn't crazy, just tired. It made so much sense.

If I'd had the energy at that moment, I would have leapt across that huge desk and plunked a kiss on the man's cheek. Instead, for the first time in what seemed like an eternity, I exhaled.

Metaphysical Endnote 9

The Power of Truth

When I lived in England, British society as a whole had a penchant for believing that if you only smiled, all your troubles would be wiped away. As a people, the British are famous for refusing to openly face pain, misery or depression. There is (or was) an obsessive cheeriness, no matter how devastating the circumstances, and that in itself was enough to drive one to insanity.

Revealing one's true feelings was perceived to be a weakness, but the constant denial of emotions probably accounts for the English inclination for black humor (of which I am guilty), eccentricity (that too) and heinously bizarre crimes (not those). But many of us, and not just the British, make a profession of running away from pain or covering it up in the belief that if we avoid it long enough, we will forget, or the original cause of our pain will magically dissipate.

I have often wondered if my psychic ability—this talent for seeing into people's souls— didn't derive from my lifelong habit of seeking the truth, looking underneath for what was *really* going on, wanting to understand, needing to feel safe in my own environment.

The one question I always ask as a psychic is "What is the truth?" because the truth *is* always there, somewhere deep down. Many querents visit psychics merely for confirmation of what they already feel to be true. We can also come to our truth just by stilling our minds and listening.

If I had listened to my truth, I would not have allowed myself to be pushed by the airline or by my mother over the edge into exhaustion. Evidently the Universe could see that it wasn't going to claim my attention any other way. I had to go to the bottom of the barrel before I could crawl back out again. (This is not recommended as a methodology for attaining wisdom!) I saw the truth only after I had gone where my mother had gone before. Only when I was on her vibration, or close to it, could I see the truth that set me free—she was not going to kill herself. Her rage fuelled her zest for revenge and that rage fed her will to live.

And if I had listened to my body when it just didn't want to do one more flight, or paid attention to my depressed moods, I would have known that something was way out of balance. But as I was pushed and pushed, I in turn pushed my physical and emotional body beyond its limits into overload.

I also realized I was *not* a victim. I alone had allowed that invasion of my boundaries. On some level I had believed I didn't have any other choice. Something in me had attracted that experience into my life, whether it was my thoughts, belief system, karma or just a necessary step in my growth. As Richard Bach wrote in *Illusions*, "There is no such thing as a problem without a gift for you in its hands. You seek problems because you need their gifts."

My gift out of this experience was to recognize the truths that a) my mother could not hold the threat of her suicide over me any longer and b) I had limits. I had to learn to protect myself, to say no. It was them or me. In order for me to survive, I had to choose me. It was a brutal way to learn about boundaries.

The gift of truth didn't stop there. Years later, when I became a professional psychic, I realized how prevalent burnout is in our society and how important it was that I had experienced that pain so I could understand it. In my current practice, I see many a burned-out client in tears and can totally understand how they feel because I have been there. Once they understand that they have fallen into the abyss because they lack boundaries and they have been remiss in honoring the Self, then they understand that they also have the power to regain their equilibrium. But only if they give themselves permission. I remind them that when they emerge on the other side of their dark time, they will look back on it not as a breakdown but as a breakthrough. I also remind them that they are not crazy. As Doc Lemon did for me, I give them permission to heal. "Do nothing. Just sleep," I say. "Let the pendulum swing back. Back to center."

For that is where we find our balance and our truth.

THE OLD CHAPEL

If I stay here, with no one to take care of me, I may die. I must be get-ting better because a small part of me wants to live.

Should I call my mother? A woman who switches, sometimes mid-sentence, from a charming, even doting matriarch to a hissing she-devil? I am so, so fragile, mentally and physically. One vicious out-burst from her and she could push me over the edge into the abyss. It wouldn't take much at all. While part of me still wants to die, I don't want to die at the hands of my mother. I don't want to give her that satisfaction.

One minute she wants to care for me as if I were still her little three-year-old, and the next she wants to bring me to my knees, stick-ing in the proverbial knife, always in the places it hurts most. Being my mother, she knows where those places are. I never can defend my-self against this Samurai and the swift savagery of her venom-coated sword, sticking words into me, leaving me winded and wounded.

Only once had I hit back. When I was sixteen, I was sitting on the couch in our living room, talking to a friend. For some reason I still can't fathom, my mother flew into the room, came right over to me, her eyes flashing rage, and with her small, roughened, brick-like hand whammed me across the cheek. Something snapped inside me then. Furious at having endured years of mockery, snide remarks, wallop-ing slaps across the face and other humiliations in front of my friends, adults and boyfriends, I finally retaliated. I leapt up from the couch and slapped *her* hard across her cheek. Through clenched teeth, I hissed at her the way she always did to me, "Don't you *ever* dare hit me again."

She didn't...for a while.

But that hadn't stopped the verbal abuse.

I made the phone call to my mother on the Friday evening. I told her I was sick and that I couldn't take care of myself. My voice must have betrayed the extent of my frailty. God, what if I was doing the wrong thing? I didn't even know why I was putting myself at such risk. She could just as easily kill me as cure me. Being around her had always been like walking through a land-mine field, one step in the wrong direction and I could be blown to bits.

"I'll come and get you right away." Her hyper energy made me groan inwardly. I knew this was going to be too much.

"No. It's okay," I said with as much strength as I could muster, fearing an indignant explosion at even mild resistance to her will. "Tomorrow morning will be fine. I'm tired now and I'm going to bed." It was only seven at night but I was exhausted. She agreed without a fight. A miracle.

Mother arrived at ten sharp the next morning. While I sat on the bed like a sack of potatoes, she scurried around my bedroom and packed my bag. I had no fight left in me whatsoever and she could have blown me over just by breathing on me. But she seemed to realize how drained I was and just poured me into the car and away we drove into the Buckinghamshire countryside. Though she chatted on the journey, I couldn't keep my eyes open and slept.

Her new home was a converted chapel, a tiny cottage that basically consisted of a kitchen, long narrow living and dining room and one bedroom with twin beds. On arrival, she put me into one of the beds and let me sleep. I didn't wake up until eleven the next morning when she brought me scrambled egg on toast in bed. It tasted wonderful.

I marveled at how, when one of her children was down, my mother returned to the sane and nurturing caretaker she once was. I was grateful for this reprieve and grateful that she could be a mother to me now. But still I mustered enough energy to protect myself if necessary.

After a few more days of sleeping, being fed and beginning to relax a little around her, I got up and put on clothes for the first time in weeks. I sat in the living room, curled up in her comfy armchair and read. In the evenings, we watched television. My mother seemed to be sleeping a lot herself, I noticed. "My doctor told me I might be anemic," she explained, shrugging in response to my concern. "Nothing to worry about."

The next evening, the golden end to a sunny summer's day, we went for a stroll down the country lane, the hedgerows abundant with wildflowers, and talked. When she was "normal" like this, I always enjoyed my mother's lively, stimulating company. This was the person her friends and outsiders saw. But I never could have explained her other satanic persona. One had to witness the dramatic change from the articulate, easy-going charm to instant evil. When I had been in the depths of my own blackness, I had wondered if she still attracted that evil spirit that saw a welcome sign on her depressed psyche and decided to take up residence whenever it needed a physical vehicle for its expression.

I remembered the time in the Bramhall flat. We had been in the kitchen enjoying a light-hearted chat when I saw something, like a wind, rush down and enter my mother's body. Instantly, the warmth in her eyes changed to hatred and she started spewing obscenities at me. I had sat there transfixed, terrified, almost fascinated.

If I had known what triggered these outbursts, I would have felt a lot safer. But I didn't, so for my own survival, I honed my senses for impending attacks, always watching and acutely aware of her moods.

By the end of the week at the Old Chapel, I had enough strength to go with her for a swim at the local pool. Yes, I was definitely getting better. Maybe it was being mothered that did it or being away from people who didn't understand and who were pressuring me to get better. It was also a relief to be away from my home and the harassing calls from Crewing.

While my mother prepared lunch in the kitchen on the Saturday morning, I was cutting out a dress pattern on the living room floor. There was a knock at the front door followed by the murmur of voices. Something about the conversation made me curious. So I followed my curiosity to the door.

There stood a Gypsy. My mother had so often warned us not to talk to these people when Alex, Janet and I dawdled from the Mill on our two-mile hike to primary school every day. This Gypsy was a lady of about fifty, the dark leathery skin of her face illuminated by piercing, light-filled brown eyes. She was clutching a large round wicker basket with several sorry-looking bunches of small purple flowers which she had probably just picked from the side of the road.

When I arrived at the door, she gasped as she stared at me.

"Oh, you would 'ave made a good teacher or nurse, you would. You've got a lot o' patience," she said, peering straight into my soul and giving me a yellow-toothed grin. "I'd love to read your palm, I would."

Always a sucker for a psychic, I asked my mother, "Can we?" I was never sure of my mother's reactions to anything anymore. But she agreed, curious herself. The Gypsy followed me into the living room and plunked herself on the sofa while I quickly cleared my sewing out of the way then kneeled in front of the Gypsy. My mother sat at the other end of the couch, the observer.

"You're grieving over a lost love, dear," she announced, tracing the lines in my palm with her dark-skinned fingers, "but you're not to look back."

Grieving? I hadn't thought of my break-up with Tom like that but she was right. She paused, scrutinizing something in the middle of my hand. "In a few months' time, you're going to go across the water and meet a dark-haired man. You think he is 'the one' but he isn't."

God! Would I ever have a love in my life?

"But don't worry, dear," she continued, picking up on my thought, "'cause you are going to meet someone in the next eighteen months and you're going to be extremely happy and peaceful with him."

The Gypsy looked up then, squinting. "His name begins with 'J,' 'T' or 'L.' And you're going to have a baby daughter who will be very special to your mother." The Gypsy and I glanced over at her. My mother's face lit up briefly. "Your 'usband will be more like a son to your mother than a son-in-law." She stopped and beamed up into my face. "You're going to be so 'appy. *So* 'appy." Her mysterious eyes sparkled with some radiant image I couldn't see.

Happiness to me was just a word then. It had no meaning. But when I saw the light in her eyes, something in me connected with an old, familiar feeling. Just for a second I felt a glimmer of hope, like a butterfly alighting on a flower and then taking off again.

Now it was my mother's turn. She ordered me to leave the room, using a tone of voice that implied I couldn't be entrusted with any secrets. I complied. It didn't matter to me except that it was insulting. If anyone was the betrayer of confidences, it was my mother.

Fifteen minutes later, after we had covered her palm with pound notes, the Gypsy left. While my mother finished preparing lunch in the kitchen, with her back to me, she recounted selected excerpts of her reading. "She told me that I would not end my days in the Chapel or alone but with a man who likes me just for who I am."

Thank God. How often had I fervently prayed for a loving mate for my mother, someone to bring her some happiness.

"We'll see," she shrugged dismissively. But I could see, even with her back to me, that her energy was lighter.

A few days later, she drove me back to Horley. I was feeling so much stronger and so happy to be out of the black hole that I decided Crewing could call and I would proudly announce to them that I was fit to fly. I also hoped that the companionship I had enjoyed with my mother in the past week was a sign of a new beginning for her, for us.

But I was wrong on both counts.

Metaphysical Endnote 10

How Does the Psychic Read?

According to neuro-linguistic programming (NLP), which maps the effect of language on the brain, we all communicate and receive information in three ways, each of us having an emphasis more on one than the others. These are visually (that is, we see all communication in pictures), audially (we respond to sound), and/or kinesthetically (we translate information into physical feelings).

Psychics also receive their transmissions in three principal ways:

a) Clairvoyance – seeing visual images: premonitions, conscious daydreams, and visions.

b) Clairaudience – hearing extrasensory sound.

c) Clairsentience or kinesthesia – receiving information through extrasensory perception and feelings.

Though we experience mostly a mixture of all three, we generally have a stronger leaning towards one.

There are, however, many other ways of receiving psychic information: fits of sneezing, nightmares, the whisper in the ear, conscious flashes, and rashes on the knees. And you don't have to be hallucinating to hear voices. Honest!

What's your style?

Exactly how *does* a psychic read another's energy? I can only speak from my own experience. The following is what I apply during a reading.

Imagine for a moment that a psychic is like a television set picking up on waves, or vibrations. While those waves appear in the form of pictures and sound on your television screen, for the psychic, your energy waves show up as pictures, sound and feelings in the psychic's mind, but in a much more disjointed fashion.

So when you come to me for a reading, after allowing my mind to sink into the alpha state, I tune into the wave you are emitting and translate that energy into sound, pictures and/or feelings. The alpha state, if you remember from page 31, connects the conscious and your immense database, the subconscious, and is a neutral, receptive level. In the alpha state, I can scan your other six levels of consciousness from the soul all the way up to the higher self.

Before I begin reading, I always ask that my guides and your guides be present so that all that is to be known is made apparent. Remember, I am just the messenger, a channel for the information.

Once I "tune in" to your clear channel or vibration, I virtually ride your vibrational waves for a few minutes to sense the energy there. After settling in to your vibration, I can see, feel and hear what has been in your past (including some past lives), what is in the present, and what you are *potentially* creating in your future with your thoughts and your belief systems.

Like a TV, sometimes the reception is DVD clear and at other times fuzzy. What many clients don't appreciate, especially the more cynical, is that a good reading is a two-way communication between psychic and client. Often clients worry that if they are tired or stressed their energy won't come through. But it is not the physical energy that makes the difference. It is the willingness of the client to be open. Therefore, the more open, trusting and conscious the client, the easier it is for the psychic to see. I find the creative, the spiritually inclined and other psychics a joy to read. The images come through in full, detailed technicolor. But when clients are not as open, for whatever reason, then it is like groping my way through a foggy tunnel with just shadows for clues. Once I am able to identify something or someone in that tunnel, however, often the querent suddenly opens up. The fog clears, the images also become much clearer and we are in the flow! It's called trust.

So the next time you visit your psychic, be conscious of your own willingness and state of mind before judging your reader to be good or bad.

For a psychic, it's also not enough just to receive energy. Knowing the difference between literal or symbolic pictures is important. For example, if I see a client crashing into a brick wall, it may mean that he is literally going to crash into a brick wall. However, the symbolic message might mean that he is going to encounter a huge obstacle in his path and needs to rethink his strategy because the path he is on will only lead to a dead end. Therefore, to understand the full message, we also need to be aware of the numerous interpretations of energy so we can learn from its teachings. That is why studying the complex world of dream symbology is a good basis for interpreting psychic energy.

I believe that the urge to see a psychic is actually your spirit guide giving you a metaphysical nudge because he/she has a message for you. So unless you are going through a tremendous crisis where the circumstances might be changing regularly, I recommend that you seek out a psychic for a reading only "when the spirit moves you," or minimally every six months to a year. If you are a psychic-aholic—and they are out there!—and addicted to readings, then you may want to ask yourself if you have some trust issues and would perhaps benefit more from counseling.

As always, I encourage you not necessarily to rely on the psychic's interpretation but to listen to your own inner voice and what your higher self is trying to communicate to you. Your guides will show you signs. You can also remember and learn to decipher your own dreams, to meditate or to just wake up and listen!

After all, this psychic information is coming from the source, right inside *you*.

11

OH, IT'S JUST THE WIND

When I first bought 24 White Hart Court in the spring of 1977, this three-bedroom maisonette wasn't physically what I had envisioned for my first home. But something pulled me in. I remember, as I first stepped into the hallway, a cocoon of peace wrapped itself around me.

This is it, something whispered in my ear. I interrupted the real estate agent then as he waxed poetic about the spaciousness and the wrought iron balcony and told him he could plaster a sold sticker on his sign. Two months later, with my two flight attendant girlfriends Lucy and Maggie in tow, I moved in.

Then things in the house started to go wrong. "Toilet's broken," Maggie announced before we were even unpacked.

"Sink is plugged," Lucy called out ten days later on her way out the door to the airport.

"Fire won't go on," I told the electrician.

Was this what having a home was all about? Fixing a perpetual list of malfunctioning devices? Oy, vey!

Then the breathing started.

The one positive thing I had inherited from my parents' divorce was a huge, comfortable bed which sat in the middle of the oceanic space of the master bedroom, six feet away from the adjoining wall to Maggie's bedroom. As I lay there one night, just drifting into sleep, I became aware of a breathing sound. I opened my eyes and listened. I heard it again. Long, slow, deep breaths. It reminded me of an older man in a peaceful sleep. Where was it coming from? The wall? No. *Inside the wall, near the floor!*

Maggie was in Mauritius. And the walls were so solid I could not even hear my next-door neighbors speak, let alone breathe. I lay back down and listened again. Maybe it was the rhythmic swooshing of cars on the fairly busy road not fifty yards from the house. Somehow, by some miracle of refracted sound, the noise of the cars was bouncing oh-so-rhythmically off my bedroom wall. Yes, that was it. The traffic.

But the next week, when I gave up my bedroom to my friend, Maria, she came down the next morning, strode into the kitchen and informed me that someone or something was breathing in my room.

"Oh, it's just the traffic," I reassured her.

She wasn't buying it. "But Kate, aren't *you* the one that believes in all the heebie-jeebie stuff?" Maria probed, amazed at my skepticism.

I shrugged. A girl could be in denial, couldn't she?

"No, Kate," she continued unrelenting, "*that* is the sound of breathing and it's coming from *inside* the wall."

The breathing continued every single night for another six months until in November, as suddenly as it had started, it stopped.

"Is it true?"

My brother Mark's voice was disturbed, the Canadianized drawl even lazier-sounding, his attempt at disguising his angst. He never called from Canada just to chat. My stomach lurched.

"Is what true?"

"Mother."

Oh, God. What had she done *now*?

"I just got this hysterical call from her saying she's only got six months to live. She says she has leukemia."

Leukemia?

"But I was just with her a few weeks ago. She's fine...." And then I remembered her white-faced tiredness. "Anemia," she had told me. "Nothing to worry about."

"I...I don't know."

After my return from the Old Chapel, within two weeks back to flying, sadly my mother had instantly reverted to her venomous, enraged self. I could only guess that she resented my recovery, slow as it was. She thought I didn't need her any more. Misery loves company and I wasn't on my knees now.

Only a week ago, she had rung me to threaten suicide again. But when I, weary of her manipulations, had responded with, "Well, if that's what you feel you need to do, you better go ahead and do it," there was a stunned silence at the other end of the line.

Now that the suicide threats weren't working, was this just another ploy to get attention from us? Or was it for real this time? I realized that I spent much of my waking state tuning into my mother's energy, trying to anticipate what she would do next. Her ability to crash into my world with her dreaded phone calls (if only there had been answering machines or call display in those days!) was eerie. Even at a distance, she often knew when I was having fun, and with her biting words would revel in destroying that momentary happiness. She also knew when I was down and would delight in pushing me even further into the abyss, as if even from sixty miles away, she was intimately acquainted with my every thought and feeling. There was no hiding, no safe place from her. As if she was psychic....

And her voice always gave her intentions away. The sometimes insidious intonations or the violent energy would blast its way down the phone line leaving me feeling punched in the stomach or worse, spinning in frustration. Whether it was the unpredictability of her moods or the unknown quantity of her violence, I was continually afraid that there would be a knock at my door late one night. I saw myself walking through the hallway and opening the door. My mother would be standing there, that cold, glazed, stony look on her face and a gun dangling from her right hand. She would raise her arm and just shoot me.

"I don't know, Mark," I said, feeling the familiar blackness descend over me yet again. "I'll try and find out and let you know."

Yet when I attempted to get the actual diagnosis from the hospital where she was apparently being treated, I was frostily informed, "It's none of your business." I guess being her daughter didn't count or had she told this doctor what a callous bunch her offspring were, especially her younger daughter? So the manipulative dance continued.

In the meantime, other things were pulling at my mind.

They say that it isn't until one observes something that it becomes a reality. The ghostly presence had been an eerie nebulousness lurking at the back of my mind, still undefined like an amoeba. But it wasn't until my flat-mate Lucy had moved out and Ted, a luverly northern lad with a strong Mancunian accent, moved in that it began to take on a shape. Then it moved front and center.

Because I had been preoccupied with buying the house, living in fear of my mother killing herself and/or me, grieving for my lost relationship, and flying at a brutal pace, I hadn't paid much attention to our invisible flat-mate. But now the presence was demanding more attention.

"Do you think this place is 'aunted?" Ted tentatively asked one night, as we were relaxing in front of a now-functioning electric fire.

"Haunted?" I sat up in my chair. "Why do you think that?"

"Well, chuck, things like doors opening and closing by themselves, my shoes disappearing, then finding 'em days later in' t airing cupboard. Other strange little things."

I hadn't told Ted about the breathing. I really liked him as a flat-mate and didn't want to scare him away. The image of Maggie semi-joking about a ghost came to mind. *Oh, it's just the wind,* I had told her to explain away the frequent and inexplicable opening and slamming of doors. I brushed Ted off with the same reasoning.

"If it's just wind, 'ow do yer explain this then? One day, I were 'ere by meself and were dying for a cigar. So I went up to my bedroom to get me Hamlets. I *knew* I'd left them on't dresser but they weren't there. So I pulled that room apart, looked under bed, in the drawers, in't cupboard. Everywhere. Couldn't find 'em. I was so mad I went off down to't corner shop and bought meself another packet."

"So?" I interjected, pretending to be bored with his story.

"When I got back, blow me down if cigars weren't right there."

"Where?"

Ted scratched his head, obviously still baffled to this day. "They were sitting balanced precariously on top of the 'andle of dresser. But the lip of the dresser comes out farther than th' 'andles so they couldn't 'ave fallen *onto* them. I tried for bloody hours to balance that packet of cigars but just couldn't do it. It's a physical impossibility. I don't think that ghost likes men."

"Maybe the ghost *really* likes you and wants you to stop smoking cigars," I suggested, smiling. But I squirmed in my chair. Had all those things that had gone wrong the first six months been because of a mischievous ghost, or worse, ghosts, causing havoc or because of Murphy's mechanical law where all things break down at the same time?

What if I had bought a haunted house?

Just three months later, my theory that all the strange occurrences could be blamed on the wind was, once and for all, blown out the window.

It was a Tuesday night in July. I was on the phone with my boyfriend, James. The conversation was, at first, romantic, flirtatious, but then for some reason rapidly deteriorated into a defensively heated argument. Full of righteous indignation, I blurted, "I think this conversation and this relationship are over!" I hung up.

Distraught, I rushed over to my girlfriend's house for wine and sympathy. Though Maria listened patiently to my emotional ramblings, I imbibed more wine than sympathy, and she insisted that to prevent any further disasters I crash in her spare room. I returned home mid-morning the next day to an empty and silent house. With an aching heart and head, I busied myself with cleaning, always good therapy for a hangover and heartache.

When Ted finally arrived home after work, we shared a pot of tea in the kitchen. As I placed the steaming mug before him, he gave me an odd sidelong glance.

"What?" I frowned at his quizzical expression.

"I 'eard yer come 'ome last night, chuck," he said, grinning, "yer dirty stop-out."

I studied his face with its huge round glasses which, when he was serious, made me want to laugh. Was he joking?

"You did?"

"Aye. I went to bed 'bout eleven but you woke me up when you came in and slammed front door. Then I 'eard you staggering up stairs. I called out, 'What time do yer call this then?' But I got no answer. She must be *really* drunk, I thought. Then you just went in't bedroom and banged door shut."

"Ted?"

"Aye."

"I don't know how to tell you this...but I didn't come home last night."

Through his oversized spectacles, his eyes struggled with momentary incomprehension. "Yer kiddin'?"

"No. I did have a few consolatory glasses of wine," I admitted, "so I stayed at Maria's."

"Bluddy 'ell," he exclaimed, collapsing onto the kitchen stool, as his legs refused to support him. "But...." Ted started to rub his temple as if he had suddenly contracted a huge headache. "Maybe *you're* the ghost," he said finally.

As part of my healing, Maria had decided we should go to Barbados for a holiday in October. I didn't put up a fight. There, the hot Caribbean sun, filtering through the wafting leaves of a coconut palm, melted the iciness in my bones while the gentle breezes soothed my aching muscles. I began to heal physically. But it was the romance that I encountered on the last day of my holiday that transformed me emotionally. The new hope for love, and for life, that Alejandro stirred in me in Barbados inspired me to make a decision on my return to England.

I already knew that if I didn't switch to a long haul airline, the short haul carrier would kill me with its unforgiving schedule. So by spring of the following year, I began my long haul flying career. The airline flew to destinations mainly in the United States, but also in Europe, North Africa, Canada and sometimes even Barbados. Long haul, I soon discovered, not only offered a much more civilized lifestyle but also allowed me to stay in contact with Alejandro. During this time, I also came to realize the man that was my father was not the man my mother had painted him to be. And so on my three-day-off stints, I enjoyed driving into the Buckinghamshire countryside to visit him and his new wife.

"Just tell them to go away," Marnie said. She was just one of the four cabin crew who were sitting around the table, covered in the prerequisite blue-and-white-checked cloth, in a funky Greenwich Village bistro. Our twenty-hour layovers in New York were normally spent shopping and sampling an array of multi-cultural cuisines. The conversation had turned to ghosts, my ghosts. Apparently she had also lived in a haunted house where a poltergeist made its presence known. "Ghosts are like people. If you don't want them around, tell them to leave."

Was it that easy?

Marnie, seeing my dubious expression, added, "Just tell them they have to go. It works."

"But apart from cups flying off counter tops, heavy breathing, moaning and cackling laughter, it's a very peaceful house." I couldn't believe it. I was defending the ghosts!

"Up to you," she said, getting up from the table. "Maybe the ghosts are more to do with you than the house."

"What do you mean?"

"There's an attachment."

Marnie left me mystified that day, but soon I would understand.

Later that summer, after returning home from yet another LA trip with all its transatlantic time changes, I couldn't sleep. Maggie was in Hong Kong, Ted at his girlfriend's, so I was alone in the house. Instead of tossing and turning in my large bed, constantly checking my clock only to be told in ghostly luminous green numerals it was still three-something-a.m., I decided to get up and do something. The multitude of photos that I had taken over the last few months needed putting into albums. That's what I would do.

As I walked downstairs, I remembered that sometimes at night the eerie baby-like howling of a cat could be heard in the back lane, but to-night the air was loud in its silence. I spread the photos across the oval pine table in the dining alcove. The kitchen light shining through the open glass hatch shed an extra golden glow over the pictures.

Soon I was lost in the memories, tanned smiling faces beaming out from under palm trees on white beaches, and marveling at all the new people I had met. I was just laughing at a picture of my favorite first officer on Malibu Beach pulling a goofy expression when I froze.

Out of the left corner of my eye, through the hatch, I watched as the kitchen door noiselessly swung wide as if someone had pushed it. And was hiding. I half expected Maggie or Ted to step out grinning mischievously. But no one appeared.

I held my breath and waited. Something I felt rather than saw, something invisible like a disturbance in the air, wafted across the length of the kitchen and ended up where the small fridge stood. Then I heard it. As if coming from the fridge, a long, anguished moan, that of an old woman haunted by her own remorse, filled the kitchen. The photos stayed where they were, scattered across the table in a collage of memories. I was gone, upstairs in bed, under the covers, waiting. For what?

Was it an over-inspired imagination or was there really the spirit of a tall, dark-haired young man entering my bedroom, stealing over to my bed, leaning over me and peering so closely into my face that I felt his cold aura on my cheek? With eyes scrunched closed, and as still as a statue, I lay there paralyzed until, exhausted from the effort, I mercifully drifted into oblivion and sleep.

So when my mother called at eight o'clock the next morning, eluding my questions about her leukemia by spewing more recriminations at me and slanderous comments about my beloved siblings, it hit me. It was *she* who was haunting me. And maybe Ted was right. Perhaps because I wasn't able to express the frustration, helplessness and misery that she inflicted, I was unconsciously funneling it all into poltergeist activity.

Was that possible?

Metaphysical Endnote 11

So You've Got a Ghost?

Have you ever witnessed a caged animal in a zoo going around and around in circles? That's what a ghost does. However, poltergeist activity doesn't necessarily occur because you have the spirit of an unhappy dead person in your house. Suppressed traumas in perfectly live, otherwise healthy people have been known to create such activities as water running down walls, children dragged from their beds (*The Bell Witch*) and furniture moving from one side of the room to the other.

A ghost's behavior is not unlike that of a real live person, an unhappy person. Okay, he doesn't have a body, although he thinks he does. And there is a big difference between a ghost who haunts and a spirit who is merely visiting or guiding. While spirit energy is light, translucent, ethereal and mostly invisible to the human eye, a ghost will emanate a thick, heavy vibration, sometimes manifesting in quasi-physical form and even giving off a rotten smell. A ghost is a spirit who is trying to heal an unresolved trauma. And that means he is not likely to be a happy camper.

At the time of his death, some major issue that was integral to his peace of mind was not resolved. Therefore his spirit did not go forward through the transformation into the spirit world and "home." He is stuck in a no-man's land, an in-between world, and clings to the earth plane, repeating and repeating some pattern in the hope that the past will change. But even though he can haunt for centuries, a ghost will not stay forever. At some point, even he will tire of his own dead-end consciousness ('scuse the pun) and decide to move on. Many of us have been ghosts, and some of us might still have a chunk of our souls stuck somewhere else in time.

If a person was murdered, for instance, his issue could be that he is struggling with the way he died or who killed him. Maybe the issue is some unresolved guilt about a relationship, his own suicide or a trauma that he witnessed and is unable to process, usually because of guilt. Sad, helpless and believing that he is alone, he is now stuck in that trauma. He will express his grief, anger and frustration through various physical manifestations such as moaning and groaning, angry or subtle movements of furniture, slamming doors, running, heavy breathing, moving and hiding items, playing with electrical devices, especially lights, or even more disturbing demonstrations of grief. Like many of us who act out from time to time as a cry for help, this unhappy soul might be trying to get someone's attention.

A ghost is also a consciousness, a way of thinking. At the time of his physical death, the deceased is supposed to ascend to the light and the spirit world usually accompanied by his spirit guides and previously deceased loved ones. His low-vibratory emotions, however, will often cause the distressed spirit to reject the light, believing he has to stay behind because of guilt or anger. As James Allen writes in *As a Man Thinketh,* "According to our beliefs be it unto us."

A ghost is usually trying to work out his own trauma and doesn't necessarily want to be bothered with you. However, some ghosts are there *because* of you, because they sense you are able to help them or your life experiences are a mirror of their own pain. Like attracts like. In the same way that some people are not able to move forward past an emotionally charged event in life, ghosts often need outside help in their dimension. This help could be facilitated by a medium or the local vicar but unless the hauntings are violent in nature, you can probably exorcise the ghost yourself. You may have to do this several times, however, before the exorcism is effective. You may also want some moral support, just for your own comfort.

If you would like your ghost/s to leave, you can do the following:

- ❖ Let them know they are in spirit form now, or dead as we know it. (Even in death, we can be in denial.)
- ❖ Make a ritual of their passing. Light candles. Burn some dried sage. Go around your house with the smoldering sage and in each room, sweep out the space, especially the corners. As you go, say a prayer, ask the angels to remove the unhappy entities and to take them towards the light.
- ❖ State firmly that this is your home now. They are not welcome and there is nothing for them in this house. There is a better place for them and they have to go. Encourage them to move toward the light and go in peace.
- ❖ Imagine your home *filled* with great love and a brilliant white light. Affirm that all who enter and live in the house experience only peace, love and serenity, the highest and the best vibration.

And if that doesn't work...call Ghostbusters!

"What do you think it means?" Amanda's blue eyes were worried. Her fine auburn hair framed a deceptively angelic face.

"I don't know," I responded helplessly. It was May 1978. With a rare Saturday off together, rare for "hosties" anyway, we were sitting in Amanda's seen-better-days Morris 1100 while an early Sussex morning sun warmed us through the windshield. The huge bare concrete wall at the back of Marks & Spencers loomed directly in front and the car park behind us was steadily filling with Saturday morning shoppers.

"At first I thought it was just a coincidence that it was always 11:11 on the clock when I woke up. I even considered that it was some outside noise that was waking me, you know? But then it became more than fluky when my hotel rooms were always 111 or 1111. Every time I got something in the post, 11–11 was somehow on it."

"When's your birthday?" Maybe there was some connection to numerology.

"August 14, 1954."

"Hmm." I calculated quickly in my head. "That makes you a 5 life path. Freedom and change. I don't see any correlation between 5 and 11 but then I don't know that much about numerology yet." The vast expanse of gray wall before us reflected how I felt. Blank. "Some kind of warning...."

"Well, yes. But what?" Amanda was uncharacteristically unnerved. "You're the only one I've told...who would understand."

Even with my superficial knowledge of numerology, I was aware that 11 was a master number. Though Amanda's life path was a five, perhaps the energy of the 11 was somehow influencing her destiny at the present time. But what did I know about 11? Only that those who have it as a life path often incorporate all the characteristics of all the people with the 1–9 numbers and then some. I also knew that 11s are often highly intelligent, good at everything, super-sensitized. As far as I could tell, Amanda's life path was not connected to 11, but like palmistry and astrology, numerology is complex and a little knowledge can be a dangerous thing.

"How long...?"

"It started about nine months ago."

"Let me think about it," I offered. "In the meantime, we've got more important things to do."

Amanda suddenly brightened. "Shop!"

Over the next year, Amanda's life was anything but predictable. Weary of the slog of short haul flying, she defected to Iran Air.

"But you should see the chic uniform and *gorgeous* suitcases," she argued when I pointed out that the Shah of Iran was being deposed and the country's political status was a little precarious. "Oh, it'll be *fine*," she countered, waving a hand at me as if swatting off an annoying fly.

For an exceedingly bright and witty female, Amanda's lack of emotional stability often worried me. Right from the beginning of our friendship, I had felt it was my job to watch over her. I had given her a lift to the airport on her first flight, suggested she take over the rental of the house I was about to vacate in Sussex and regrettably introduced her to my pilot friend and neighbor, James Charlwood. She instantly fell in love with him.

"**British stewardesses are being held hostage**," blurted the voice on Radio Four. Amanda had only been in Tehran two days when Iran sank into anarchic chaos. For ten long days, there was no news. On the eleventh night just after eleven, I received the call.

"Come and get me!" Amanda pleaded, her thin voice sounding unhinged. "I'm at Heathrow!"

Sitting safe in her dimly lit living room, James and I listened into the early hours of the morning to how she and others had barely escaped a mob of marauding Iranians, had then hidden at the palace of the Shah's nephew and had eventually, with the assistance of an anonymous Iranian "angel," fled the country. A few days later, she announced she was returning to Iran "for a uniform fitting."

"But the airline is defunct," I pointed out, wondering seriously about my friend's sanity. "The whole country is defunct, Amanda."

"But they called me...maybe the airline has been reinstated," she suggested hopefully.

"Your funeral," I retorted, reluctantly acknowledging that my friend really did have a death wish.

After just two days, she returned to the UK unscathed and officially jobless.

Then James was temporarily transferred to Aberdeen the following January. Amanda was convinced that if she could claim his home, she would eventually be able to claim him and so she moved into his house. "One day, he'll see the light," she intoned.

God, I hope so.

Not unemployed for long, Amanda scooped her dream job based at Heathrow, flying on a Lear jet hostessing VIPs all over the world. I was surprised when a month later a black MGB GT rolled up in front of my home with Amanda at the wheel, her fine red hair tousled in the wind.

"When did you get that?" I asked. She just grinned, but once we were settled into our favorite spot in our local country pub with a hearty ploughman's lunch and a glass of blackberry wine before us, Amanda explained.

"Let's just say it was a gift from a passenger."

"He gave you a *car?*"

"Not exactly."

"Then what?"

"A thousand pounds."

"What for?"

"Well...," she grinned sheepishly, "as a thank you for a lovely evening."

"Amanda!"

"Well? A thousand pounds to an Arab is like a bouquet of flowers."

"Better a bouquet," I muttered.

Maybe the airline disapproved of Amanda's offering such personal service because two weeks later she was fired.

Undeterred, Amanda charmed her way into a British charter airline that must have decided they could benefit from her varied flying experiences. That summer, apart from the odd histrionic phone call late at night when yet again James had not lived up to Amanda's romantic expectations, contact with my friend was minimal.

We did have one lovely day out shopping together that summer though. But on our return, just as we were stepping into her home clutching our green Marks & Spencer's bags, I was suddenly bombarded with a sense of dread. As I glanced at my friend, a vision of her energy suddenly fading flashed into my mind. Like a photo negative, I saw her outline but her substance was evaporating. I knew then that she would soon die. As if in explanation, the words *she's not strong enough for this world* popped into my head.

"My God, Amanda, what happened?" It was May 1980. On the other end of the line her voice quavered with subdued hysteria.

"Belly landing. Undercarriage just would *not* come down."

"Was everyone okay?"

"Shaken but not stirred," she muttered.

"Seriously?"

"When we landed on the foam and skidded along the runway, it made an *awful* noise." I imagined the sound of tons of metal scraping on concrete. "The friction caused flames to lick at the windows so it looked like we were on fire." I shuddered. Burning to death was *my* greatest fear. "But then we all just stepped out onto the tarmac."

Amanda and I hadn't discussed 11–11 since that first conversation. I didn't even know if it was still happening. "Do you think that was the 11–11 thing?" I gingerly inquired.

"What? Oh." Long silence. "Nah." But there was an edge in her voice and I knew that 11–11 was still throwing a long shadow over her life.

Not long after Amanda's "crash," James returned to Sussex for a visit, and our group of friends all arranged to meet at the Lambs Inn. When I arrived, Amanda was sitting alone in the golden light of the early summer evening, her small frame hunched over the wooden picnic table.

"James and I had it all out," she moaned, as I plunked myself down next to her.

"And?"

"Tell you later." She cast a glance at James, who was approaching the table with drinks.

"How's work?" I asked.

"They're laying me off at the end of the month." As if some invisible force had pulled the plug on her energy source, her body suddenly deflated and she slumped in defeat.

"I can't go through it all again with another airline, Kate. I just can't."

"I know," I offered helplessly. "Let's get together this week."

"Can't. I'm going away for a few days." She brushed her fine red hair out of her eyes. "I'll ring you when I get back."

Amanda never did call me. On July 24, 1980, at 3:10 p.m. that black MGB carried her to her chosen outcome. On a narrow, winding country road, she barreled through a changing traffic light and went straight under an oncoming milk truck. It took the firemen four hours to extricate her body from the wreckage.

Amanda was, indeed, too fragile for this world. Though devastated by the loss of my friend, I felt a sense of peace for her. She had finally got her wish, her own death.

Was 11–11 a warning to Amanda to make healthier choices? An unavoidable sign that death was approaching? Or, as some might believe, a gateway, an invitation into another, kinder dimension? Years later I would have a wider interpretation of 11–11. To this day, whenever I see those numbers, I think of Amanda.

Metaphysical Endnote 12

The Final Choice

Mrs. Tinsley was reading my friend, Maria, while I sat on the couch looking on. It was just two months prior to Amanda's death. Suddenly, the psychic glanced up and stared straight into my eyes. "Someone's tired of living," she said. "They're talkin' about ending it all. But you know if you do that, you 'ave to come back and do it all over again." Was she lecturing me or referring to Amanda? When I had been depressed the previous year, my friend and I had often joked about "ending it all." But I sensed Amanda had been more serious.

As I discovered years later, Amanda was not the only one to have the 11–11 experience. The constant 11–11 presence shows itself to us at crucial times in our evolution, usually a turning point, a time of choice. 11–11 represents an opening, like a rip in the fabric of consciousness. 11–11 is a time when, by facing our challenges and making changes, we can accelerate our own spirituality by stepping through that rip into a higher vibration. Or not. To grow or not to grow. That is our choice.

So when Amanda came around that corner and saw the traffic light changing from amber to red, she made her choice. Death, after all, is a transformation into another consciousness. She had always said she would make her death look like an accident. And she had. She had committed suicide.

Some of my clients' hands indicate a strong potential for suicide, similar to those of someone who suffers from manic depression. The head line doesn't merely slope down into the Mount of the Moon, it takes a huge dive through the center of the palm sometimes meeting and becoming the fate line. Remember though, just because you have this line in your hand doesn't mean that you *will* do the deed. But you might be severely tested.

Is suicide, for some people, therefore, a life-long challenge, a test to be overcome? Or is it part of the Agreement, to leave the life early and voluntarily. As far as I am concerned, the jury is still out on that one.

Don't get me wrong. I am not a proponent of suicide. Actually, the opposite. But I *do* have great compassion for those who experience so much depression or desperation that they feel they have no other choice. Anyone who says it's a coward's way out should throw themselves into that black hole of depression some time. In readings, through my clients' energy, I have had a taste of the absolute darkness in which they live. In that black pit, choice is just a word.

But Mrs. Tinsley was correct. If we commit suicide or we otherwise fail to complete our Agreement out of fear, stubbornness or sheer laziness, we all have to come back and complete unfinished business. Whether ending one's own physical life *is* the Agreement, a challenge or a preference, I am in no position to judge. According to the energy of the 11–11, though, the final choice is ours.

And though I missed Amanda, I could not be sad for her. She was, indeed, "not strong enough for this world." I *knew* she had found peace. After all, she wasn't dead. She had merely migrated to that gentler dimension to continue her growth at her own pace, a dimension where, one day, I know I will meet her again.

I SEE! I GET THE PICTURE

$\mathcal{I}$t was 1982. I was sitting in the last row of seats of an empty Boeing 707 on the tarmac at Tripoli Airport, Libya. My friend, Bonnie, also a flight attendant, and I were waiting in the dry heat of a Saharan November for our Captain, hell, any Captain, to make an appearance. Then we could board our 189 Moslem passengers and fly them on their once-in-a-lifetime pilgrimage to Jeddah, Saudi Arabia.

What was I doing in Libya, you may ask? Good question. Some of my relatives believed I had suicidal tendencies. They could have been right. But after the British airline I was working for went bankrupt, then my oh-so-loving boyfriend left...and then...my fascinating new job was axed, I figured it was time...well...to leave town, the country or even the planet for a while. So when the ex-chief stewardess of the defunct airline called and offered me a Haj (usually a two-month stay based in any country around the world flying Moslem pilgrims to Saudi Arabia), I thought, *What's the worst that could happen? Well, actually, I could die. Oh, well.*

Although Bonnie and I had now been waiting, along with the rest of the crew and the terminal-bound passengers, for more than an hour, we were patient. After eight weeks in this very different and fascinating culture, we had learned to surrender and actually enjoy our lack of control over our immediate circumstances.

"You read hands, don't you?" Without waiting for my response, Bonnie grinned mischievously and offered me her fleshy, open palm.

"You're so subtle, Bonnie." I smiled as I started to examine the lines. "But I'm not that good."

Not good like Maggie Cullen, the palmist I had visited in Brighton the day before the airline went down. I had seen Maggie first on television. Her claim to fame was as a psychic animal reader probing horses' hooves, leopards' paws, snakes' eyes and their underbellies. (The English are known for many eccentricities but especially their choice of pets.)

"Yes," she told the anxious owner while holding the leopard's paw, "your pet has stomach problems because he is sympathizing with your stress." Reading animals was a little too far-fetched, even for little ole believe-absolutely-anything me. But her theory about reincarnation, that these pets could have been the spouse or child of the owner in a previous life, was fascinating.

And many of the things she had told me had already been ticked off the list: losing something small (my brown gloves that same day), a job ending soon that I wasn't bothered about (the next day), marriage not on the horizon (nice way of telling me my boyfriend would soon leave), going to a country like Africa (here I am!), someone going across the American border into Canada with a suitcase (not yet), having a reunion with people (I met my ex-colleagues in Tripoli) and finally, someone with the name Bonnie becoming significant (and here she was!).

I didn't have to be a palmist to know that Bonnie's strong, flattish-topped fingers denoted a practical and stubborn personality. Bonnie was also hilariously funny. She and I often looked at each other and collapsed into giggles. But when I studied her lifeline, she became serious. Especially when I jerked back suddenly.

"What is it?" Bonnie asked, worried that I was witnessing a horror show.

"Just a sec..." I replied, not wanting to interrupt the experience.

I was not seeing the static images of before. Instead, in the center of her hand, between the lifeline and the headline, there were pictures... *moving*...like a film clip in full technicolor.

What I was "seeing" was a tall, young, dark-haired man walking across a small garden. He was moving dirt, building something. I knew the garden was located in England and it was *his* garden. Then Bonnie appeared at the back door, which was covered by a sloping slate structure. She, I could sense, lived in the house with him. I realized she was the man's wife. I was then "shown" the house, a small cottage with a gray brick patio at the back. I watched, like a voyeur, as Bonnie started to trowel flowering plants into large containers on that back patio. It seemed that she and this man were building a home together, and I felt their contentment.

Bonnie wondered if the Saharan heat was finally getting to me as I jumped up and yelped with delight, "I can see! I can see!"

"What? See what?" she frowned, still concerned.

"Everything's going to be all right," I reassured her as I reclaimed my composure. Excitedly, I described all the details of the scene I had just witnessed. "You are not meant to worry about the future." Her eyes conveyed part cynicism, part hope. Whether she believed me or not, I knew, *just knew*, that seeing that clip of the "movie" was not only an accurate projection into her future but also a graduation for me, as if I had somehow passed a test and could now go to the next level. An honor had been bestowed upon me.

I had made out images before, but not like this, as if I was peering through a hole in the fabric of time and glimpsing a future while it played itself out in front of me. At that moment, I was certain that I would never regress to mere "feeling." I was now not just sensing what was and what had been, but also *seeing* what would be. Not just clairsentient but also clairvoyant. It would be some time before I understood *how* I saw.

Before I could revel in my newfound elevated status, a Turkish Captain materialized at the front of the cabin closely followed by a mob of excited *Hadj* passengers. At 30,000 feet over the Sahara, as we dished out rice and unidentified meat objects accompanied by warm cans of Seven-Up to our passengers, I wondered why this was happening now, in Libya.

But it made total sense.

With no television to watch, absolutely no decisions to make, no alcohol to consume, no phone contact (ergo protected from highly emotionally charged family histrionics), while copious amounts of thick Libyan coffee were consumed and endless games of backgammon were won and lost, a strange and wonderful thing started to happen. My conscious mind emptied of all its cluttered minutiae, and I started to relax. Because there were so few distractions, I also enjoyed a closeness with others I had never known before. And I paid attention to my inner voice.

So when, one lazy day, while sunbathing under a clear blue sky by a swimmer-less aquamarine pool, a strong voice whispered in my intuitive ear, *Move to Canada*, I listened.

Metaphysical Endnote 13

Living in the Moment

Even twenty years later, I am grateful for my time in Libya. The absence of dilemmas, dramas and decisions, a daily part of life in western culture, allowed me to graduate to the next level as a palmist. And having no control over my environment taught me a) to practice the art of surrendering, b) not to be attached to outcomes and c) to live in the present. I learned to expect the unexpected. Of course, being safely out of reach of my mother's harassing phone calls also helped me to breathe a huge sigh of relief. Gradually my mind cleared. A still mind allows the voice of a higher intelligence, intuition, to filter through.

But not everyone needs a stint in Libya to realize that the moment we surrender and give up our will to that higher power is the moment the magic begins.

Even though I had no control *over* my circumstances, I realized I could at least choose my feelings *about* my circumstances. Nor did I have to try to do or be anything (except stay out of trouble, which, being a young, blonde Western female in Libya, could be a little tricky). There was no use thinking about the past. I couldn't do anything about it anyway. Especially in Libya. And the future? Well, who knew if I even had a future? So I relaxed.

When we landed in Kufra, an ancient society in the middle of the Sahara, and greeted these desert people as they boarded the plane with their child-like awe of the gray metal bird that would fly them to Jeddah, their impenetrable faith in Allah inspired me. They refused to wear seat belts, chanting, *"Malish, Inshallah!"* (It doesn't matter, Allah will take care of everything.) So when the aged 707 flew, shuddering and bumping through the luminescent purple skies of those violent Saharan hailstorms, with jagged lightning crackling all around us, I was convinced that it was the pilgrims' belief and not aerodynamics that kept our plane aloft.

It soon became obvious that although the twenty contracted flight attendants lived under the same conditions in Libya, ten of us were grateful for this experience of a lifetime while the others complained, rebelled, and eventually railed against the circumstances that they claimed were imposed upon them. Sure, some situations got a little hairy but we knew that they might before we agreed to come. Well, kind of. So when the two-month contract was up, the complainers returned to a wet, cold, rainy November in England, while we keeners were invited to stay under blue skies and dry heat for another month.

One day I encountered three British engineers who had been in Tripoli for over a year. We were discussing the challenges that some Westerners encountered adjusting to the Libyan ways.

"Ach," the Scottish engineer shrugged, "when you've been here a wee while, you just adopt the IBM philosophy."

"IBM?" I frowned. "What's that?"

"*Inshallah, Buccharah, Malish.*" He grinned.

By then I understood basic Arabic. *Inshallah,* Allah's in charge, *Buccharah,* tomorrow and *Malish,* it doesn't matter anyway.

I smiled.

In our frenetic Western culture, where we are surrounded by dysfunctional fear-mongering and angst-provoking messages, living in the moment is akin to walking up a downward escalator. To avoid being sucked into what author Stuart Wilde calls tick-tock mentality, we must consistently and diligently choose a higher path, a process which requires discipline and practice. But the rewards are immense. In the moment, nothing else matters and the future has unlimited potential.

Then life *is* an adventure. *Inshallah!*

AAAGH! I THINK I'M PSYCHIC

*A*s it says in the *Book of Runes*, once the decision is clear, the doing becomes effortless. And so it was. Once I had decided to emigrate from England to Canada, the universe propelled me unfettered towards that goal. Six months after leaving Libya, and six days before my 30th birthday, accompanied by my younger brother Luke and his wife Lisa, I crossed the US border into Vancouver. And another of Maggie Cullen's predictions was ticked off my list.

The only way for me to gain landed immigrant status into Canada was either through marriage or through work as a nanny. Having had more success with little people than romantic relationships, I chose the latter. I have always loved (most) children and after the many responsibilities and rigors of flying, looking after two adorable little girls in an exclusive area of West Vancouver would feel like a holiday.

Being bred in the class-delineated, don't-tell-any-secrets, scathingly funny English culture where, in some circles, if you didn't hold out your pinky when drinking tea, you were silently and snottily banished, I could finally exhale in the openness of Canada. I could be me. I soon discovered that Vancouver is, comparatively speaking, not only a less judgmental society but also a place where people actually talk about their feelings. What a concept! Some Canadians spoke openly of their dysfunctional families, their emotions and their search for spirituality. I had found a spiritual home.

Though still cautious about touting my palm-reading abilities, I quickly noticed how many people were more receptive to psychics. As in California, spirituality was burgeoning. Banyen Books was a regular haunt of mine with its abundant choice of metaphysical how-tos and literature. I was like a chocoholic in a Cadbury's factory.

Maybe it was this new level of comfort that facilitated my opening up psychically. My fear of discovery wasn't as chronic. My palm readings, I noticed, flowed a little more freely, the information was expanding, encompassing deeper aspects of the person's buried feelings. My sister-in-law, Lisa, promoted my palm reading talents to all her friends, introducing me jokingly as "the witch." In social situations, I became a conversation piece. But I still wasn't taking it too seriously, believing it was just some kind of fluke that what I could "see" and "feel" matched the intimate details and truth of the person's life at the time.

One night in May, just one month after my arrival in Canada, Lisa introduced me to her friend, Charlotte. The three of us were enjoying a late night dinner at The Keg. Over coffee, Charlotte suddenly splayed her open palm on the table. "Why don't you read my palm?" she challenged as if it was some kind of honor for me to do so. I obliged anyway.

Seeing pictures in the center of the hand was now commonplace for me and they soon emerged.

K: *Do you know a man named Steve?*

C: (Laughs) *Nope.*

K: *He is coming into your life. Not yet. July of this year, I think.*

C: *Okay* (smiling cynically).

K: *He is not around all the time. He's in and out, comes and goes, whether for his work or whether he lives somewhere else, I'm not sure.*

C: *Ah-ha.*

K: *I see you being driven in a light blue Mercedes convertible down a long, straight, narrow road with tall poplar trees on either side. Steve is driving. He wears glasses but not all the time, just for driving and maybe reading.*

C: *What does he look like? Really ugly?* (snickers nervously)

K: *Well, let's put it like this. He's not Quasimodo and he's not quite Robert Redford. His hair is brownish-red, curly on one side, straightish on the other, nice strong build, about 5' 11". You are very in love with this man. It feels as if it will be serious. I can see a possible marriage. I like to stress "possible" because what happens between you is up to both of you. He is taking you to a farm. It's not his farm but it is connected to him somehow. And it's not in Canada. The States, feels like Washington.*

C: *But I don't know anybody called Steve.*

K: (Repeating) *You won't meet him until this July.* (People don't often hear the information the first time!)

While I was absorbed in Charlotte's palm, a line-up of waiters with eager expressions had formed behind me. Our waiter was the first in line. When he pressed his flattened palm almost on my nose and demanded that I read his palm, I politely told him we had to go. Behind him, his disgruntled co-workers shuffled off to their respective chores.

On a hot and steamy July day, just two months later, I was enjoying lunch al fresco with my two little charges. From my employer's sloping lawn, I was admiring the hazy view of distant, downtown Vancouver when the phone rang inside the house.

"You really are a witch!" the woman said and then chuckled.

"Who is this?"

"Lisa!" She sounded amused that I didn't recognize her voice. "What kind of psychic are you?"

"I'm not...."

"Remember what you predicted for Charlotte? About a guy called Steve?"

"Vaguely."

"Well, she just met him. And he's in the navy so he goes away a lot. He's American and his parents own a farm in the States and a blue Mercedes. He took her down there to meet them last weekend! Down the long, straight road, just like you said."

"Really!" An eerie feeling of déjà vu flushed through me. "Really?"

Lisa babbled on excitedly but I was too stunned to listen. I had seen things around people before, accurately described what was happening in their lives at the time, picked up on their Aunt Mabel's arthritis or their husband's new job. I had seen and predicted futures, but this was the first time someone had come back to me and told me the scene had unfolded *exactly* as I had witnessed it. Strange, weird, eerie. All those words floated through my mind. For a vision that I had foreseen to actually materialize so...precisely. I knew that I had not been making this stuff up but.... My God, it was real. I'm not crazy. *Aaagh! I think I'm psychic.*

Metaphysical Endnote 14

The Responsibility

We know that every gift or power that we possess comes with a responsibility. Sometimes the responsibility is merely to make sure we use that gift wisely. Accountability for our words and actions has a habit of keeping us balanced and our egos in check. This doesn't always happen, of course, but in the world of the spirit, that's the general idea. Those who intentionally abuse their power will find that negative karma comes back at some time to haunt them.

It is the same with the gift of being psychic. There are responsibilities that go with the territory. The following are some strategies that keep me accountable:

- ❖ I impart bad news in a compassionate and constructive way that leaves the client with a choice, still empowering them to follow their highest potential.

- ❖ I remind clients that the timing can be off or that the energy can be inadvertently misinterpreted. I also remind clients that they are creating their own futures with their consciousness and that they have free will. (Unfortunately, some still sit there, with eyes large, soaking up every word into their belief systems. So I verbalize my readings v–e–r–y carefully.)

- ❖ I don't believe that there is any point in telling a client of a loved one's or his/her own death, *unless* something can be done to change the outcome or his/her consciousness can be enlightened before he/she goes. Again, my interpretation of the energy just might be *out of context*.

- ❖ When I do see something traumatic happening, I pull back and try to understand the vision symbolically. This allows me to tell the truth, in more vague terms but still with integrity. It also prevents me from giving out damaging and incorrect details. (Trust me, I have had to help many traumatized clients recover from horrific predictions dumped on them by other psychics.)

- ❖ If, however, I do see the imminent death of a client's loved one, I will phrase it in terms of the action that needs to be taken. For example, "Your father needs to speak with you." Or, "I feel a sense of urgency." I do not express the vision boldly as the end result—"Oh, look! Your father is going to die."—because we can overcome our own destiny and I could be *misinterpreting the signals.*

❖ If in doubt, I always ask for spiritual guidance. As part of the preamble to the reading, I sit with the client, close my eyes and either silently or out loud ask my angels and guides to speak *through* me. Then I allow what is to be known at this time to be known for the highest good of all concerned. That way I am just volunteering to be a channel and my ego can take a nap!

❖ I do know that, as well as being compassionate to others, it is also my responsibility as a psychic to show compassion for myself emotionally, spiritually and physically. Some metaphysicians will allow themselves to be run ragged (I have been guilty of this) or, when their boundaries aren't firmly in place, let their psychic energy "bleed." For psychics it is especially important to consume healthy, clean, nutritious food, to exercise—as it is a sedentary profession—and to diligently protect our own energy. To be channels, our pipes need to be in good working order and clean!

❖ I also remember what I am *not* responsible for. And that is other people's happiness. As long as I am doing no harm and my intentions to heal are for the highest good, I have fulfilled my responsibility. The client will decide whether to follow, or not follow, the given guidance.

Though I try to adhere to my own wisdom and walk the walk, I do fall off center occasionally—but hey, that keeps me here on the planet. And human.

RINGS 'N' THINGS

*I*t was a rainy Saturday in November, my first experience of winter in Canada. It was not the frozen North, as some of my English friends had assumed it would be, but more like not-so-jolly-olde-England with its unrelenting rain and a heavy ceiling of gray closing in on us, crushing the sunlight right out of our spirits.

My weekends off from my nanny job in the British Properties were spent in the West End where I regularly imposed my company on my dear brother and his wife. Even after six months, they didn't complain about my showing up at their apartment every Friday night, black world-travelled suitcase in hand. I offered to stay at my employer's or go elsewhere, but Luke would just shrug and Lisa would say, "We like having you around."

Not that my host family beat me, made me do laundry on weekends or were otherwise objectionable but after constantly traveling for the past eight years, I found being confined to one house was akin to being a butterfly trapped in a jar.

This Saturday was different. Lisa and I were attending a workshop, a psychic development workshop. What better way to spend a cold, rainy day in Vancouver?

The tall, willowy teacher with wispy, red-brown hair flaming out and down past her shoulders in fine brittle strands suited my limited preconceptions of what a genuine psychic crone should look like. Maybe because she reminded me of Maggie Cullen, my palmist back in Brighton, I trusted her.

Anyway, here I was finally in a workshop where I could learn about what was *really* important: metaphysics, energy, finding a pulse to the

Universe, that rhythmic pattern that I knew existed somewhere hiding underneath or inside the chaos of the world.

Like a waitress citing the specials of the day, Margaret fired off a list of her psychic abilities: clairvoyant, spirit medium, numerologist, astrologer, assistant to the police in locating missing children. She sounded slightly bored by her own accomplishments. I was fascinated by them, wanting to steal her away, bombard her with my questions and greedily soak up all that she knew until *I* knew it all, understood it all.

And while I was congratulating myself on being here, it was Lisa whom I had to thank. She had registered me for the day. And to think that when I first met my younger brother's green- and purple-haired wife I was apprehensive that, except for the love of my younger brother, we would have nothing in common. So much for being psychic.

I scrutinized the large room and other students. They were a motley collection of down-to-earth thirty-to-forty-something women all as hungry as I was to know the mysteries of the Universe. No weirdos here. But then what did I know? And could we be actually *taught* to be psychic? I had always believed that one either had "it" or one didn't. I supposed I would find out.

Our teacher was asking us to split up into pairs because we were going to do something called Psychometry. "And for a partner, pick someone you *don't* know," she stressed.

As chairs scraped on the wooden floor, Margaret continued, her voice elevated above the noise, "Psychometry is the science of reading residue energy left on a person's belongings like clothes, jewelry, car keys or glasses. We all leave traces of energy everywhere we go, in the car, in our homes, on our clothes. If possible read something metal and something that the person wears because it emanates more of the owner's energy. Also read something that they have worn for at least a year."

"But what if I can't pick up anything?" one bespectacled woman piped up, giving voice to my own question.

"You will," Margaret responded tonelessly. "We all can. Just say the first thing that pops into your mind even if it doesn't make sense to you. In fact, expect it *not* to make sense. What you see may or may not have any meaning to your partner either but just keep speaking it out loud."

I turned to the younger, blonde-haired woman on my left. "Do you want to...?" I didn't finish the sentence. This was a psychic workshop, after all. We shuffled our chairs into position until we were facing one another, knees almost touching.

"Five minutes each and then we'll discuss what you see afterwards," Margaret added.

"I'm Sherry." My partner smiled coyly.

"Hello. Kate. What do you want to read…?" I extended both arms and showed her my jewelry. "I have a watch, a ring, a gold chain."

Sherry surveyed her options and then pointed. "The watch, I think." She took the gold-plated piece in her hands and closed her eyes. Before long, her eyelids were twitching, eyeballs swiveling from side to side, as though she was in a deep REM sleep. What was happening?

"I'm not sure but…" she started.

"Just say it out loud," I urged, echoing Margaret's instructions.

"Well…I am seeing you alone in a strange country. You have money but you're alone."

Great! I thought. *Well, I am in a strange country and I am alone but I certainly don't have any money. Not in the bank at least.*

"I see you walking across a field by yourself, you are somewhere in the countryside," Sherry continued.

I shrugged. What could that mean?

"It feels like you are pining for someone with the initial 'J'."

James! Bingo! Amazing for a so-called amateur.

Her eyes suddenly popped open. "That's it. That's all I can see."

Slightly disappointed that there wasn't more, I told her, "My ex-boyfriend in England was called James, and I suppose I am still missing him."

"Oh." Sherry beamed at me suddenly, thrilled that she had something right. "What about the other…?"

"I just came to Canada about five months ago so I am in a strange country but I can't say I have lots of money."

"Maybe you will," she offered.

"Maybe."

Now it was my turn to read her.

When I held her ring in my hand and closed my eyes, I was surprised at how quickly and vividly the imagery popped into my head. Despite my lack of confidence that I could actually *do this*, I followed my teacher's instructions and just spoke the pictures out loud.

"I see an elderly couple traveling in a horse and buggy cart down a dirt track," I told Sherry. Once I had said the actual words, the screen in my mind emptied and was promptly filled by other images. "I am watching them from behind and their bodies are slumped over, as if they have just had some bad news and are dejected."

And so the process continued. As soon as one picture showed itself to me, I described it to my partner as if to a blind person. Then another would fill the space. Is this what they called flow? And where was this all coming from? The energy on the ring or my imagination? With palmistry, I could rationalize the source of the pictures but this…? So I reserved judgment and just relayed the details.

"The area around them is flat, it's not here, maybe it's in the States. The land is quite barren."

Then, like switching TV channels, I suddenly saw Sherry standing in front of a brick wall clutching a baby boy. Words of a song invaded my mind. What was it? Oh, yes. "Danny Boy." Then a huge wave of love flooded through me but it wasn't intended for me. Merely the conduit, I relayed to her what I was hearing, seeing, feeling.

It was like being in Switzerland when I was learning to speak German. Was becoming a psychic like learning a language in a foreign land?

My mind then went blank, the TV turned off, leaving me with a black empty screen. I opened my eyes and saw tears on Sherry's pale cheeks. Slowly her lids fluttered open and she stared at me with sad eyes.

"Sorry, did I upset you?" I said, feeling awful that on my first psychometry reading, I had reduced someone to tears.

She shook her head while groping for a tissue in her jeans pocket. "No," she finally whispered. "That was amazing! My grandparents were farmers who lost everything in a drought. They lived in Minnesota. My grandfather killed himself soon after that. That is my grandmother's ring."

"I'm sorry."

"It's all right. I didn't know him."

Oh, my God! I can *do this.* "What about the baby? Did that make any sense to you?"

"Not really. Except that I'm dying to have a baby but my boyfriend doesn't want to get married yet."

Maybe the brick wall was symbolic of her feelings about her lack of options. But I could be wrong. I didn't feel confident enough to voice my interpretation out loud.

" 'Danny Boy' is my father's favourite song though," Sherry murmured. "He died ten months ago."

There was her grief. "I felt he was sending his love to you through me." I touched her lightly on the arm. "He really loves you a lot."

Even after we had pulled our chairs back to face the class to discuss our readings, Sherry was still quietly sniffling.

"Some images are symbolic, just like your dreams," Margaret explained and then went on to give some examples of interpretations. "You might see a road representing the path ahead. Or you might envision a busy city that you know but which is merely symbolic of another similar place. What we see is still seen through our eyes and often reflects our own perception and experiences of life." Yes, when I felt stuck, I often imagined the inescapability of a brick wall in front of me so I had projected that onto Sherry's frustration about her baby.

My compassion for Sherry's sadness though was mixed with a sense of triumph. I can *do* this! I *can* do this! The pictures, like watching film clips or peeping through a hole and seeing a microcosm of strangers' lives—feeling their feelings, being in them but not of them—were not unlike the quality of energy I felt when reading palms.

But there was a difference. Reading jewelry was a little more remote, less personal than feeling someone's hand. Isn't that what had attracted me to palmistry in the first place over and above Tarot cards or astrology or numerology or the I Ching? Palmistry is personal. I can feel the person's energy, what they are thinking in their subconscious minds, their hearts, their heads and sometimes in their souls. And already I could tell the difference, I could intuitively know, although I didn't understand *how* I could know, from which part of their being those thoughts were emanating. Those other means of divination were to me somehow cold, calculated, all to do with numbers and phases of the moon, something out there, not in here. Missing heart. But palmistry, and to a lesser degree psychometry, was about the real live person sitting right in front of me.

As Lisa and I wove our way back to the West End through early Saturday evening traffic, we shared the enlightenments of the day. My sister-in-law was elated. Two years ago when I had first read her, I took one look at her hands and exclaimed, "Lisa! You should be reading me! You are far more psychic than I am." Maybe it was her part-Native-part-Italian-part-Scottish-part-French heritage that bequeathed her the sight. When genes of different races are mixed, apparently it stimulates the brain and makes us more intelligent. And I was pure Anglo-Saxon stock. Whatever it was, Lisa was a very potent psychic who, I suspected, was probably terrified of her own power. She had just laughed, shrugged and responded with a "Maybe." She had also laughed when I told her she would be a famous artist one day. That remained to be seen. Today, she had discovered that I was right. She did have a psychic ability and it came easily to her.

The most valuable education I absorbed that day, over and above the color of auras and their meanings, past and future lives and the difference between the various levels of consciousness, was that we are all, if not psychic, inherently intuitive. I was not special or different nor did I have any otherworldly powers. If we trusted, if we suspended judgment, if we were willing to keep an open mind, we could *all* read energy. Every one of the fourteen students in that class, especially Lisa, was able to pick up on something: feelings, pictures, sounds, even smells, which were mostly validated by the owners of the auras, keys, rings or glasses.

Part of me was relieved by that and part disappointed. If everyone could do it, then that made me normal, whatever normal is. There was no great gift that I possessed, ergo no great responsibility I had to bear. In some vague way, I felt I was off the hook.

Yet something inside me felt let down. I wasn't here to learn how to be a professional psychic anyway, I told myself. I had neither the talent nor the desire. Then why was I disenchanted? I had felt special, different, when, as an English person, I surprised Norwegians with my ability to speak their language. I had a modicum of control over my circumstances in an alien culture. Was it control that I wanted then? Did I need to feel special, separate from the crowd? What *was* my motivation?

In the beginning my search had been to understand my mother, but now it appeared that she had motivated me to understand the Universe. Putting a label on it didn't matter. Nor did it matter whether I was more or less able as a psychic than others. It was my own very private, individual journey, and all I really wanted was to be master of my own life.

Metaphysical Endnote 15

Are You Psychic or Intuitive?

The dictionary definition for the word "intuition" is "the immediate apprehension of truth or supposed truth in the absence of conscious rational processes."

And the definition of "psychic" is "being able to see and feel things of a non-physical nature." Well, sorry, but psychic or not, we can all do *that*.

I would elaborate on these definitions as follows:

Intuition: An inherent sense and form of logic. The ability to experience vibrations of energy through sensory perception and, therefore, feel, sense, know, hear and receive protective guidance without visible physical evidence. Intuition can be developed into a psychic ability.

Psychic: The ability to feel, see, and hear a very wide range of vibrations of energy through extrasensory perception and to translate that energy into detailed visual, emotional and auditory information manifesting in the physical plane. The capacity to identify the present, past and future potential of body, mind and spirit by scanning different levels of human and universal consciousness.

We are all intuitive to some degree. And while being intuitive is a prelude to being psychic, and the lines between the two categories are so murky that they are almost non-existent, it is healthy to acknowledge the level of your own abilities so you know how to progress. To illustrate the differences between intuitive and psychic, I have defined exactly how each level of ability manifests.

With intuition, we can all do the following (to varying degrees):
- ❖ Empathize with others' feelings.
- ❖ Practice telepathy. (We think of someone or something and it shows up.)
- ❖ Predict the future in our dreams. (Up to 75% of our dreams are precognitive.)
- ❖ Sense when someone is looking at us, thinking about us, without physically seeing them.
- ❖ Have invisible friends when we are children. (We have them when we're older too, but as adults we shut down our ability to see.)

- ❖ See the color of auras.
- ❖ Sense who is on the phone.
- ❖ Know what others are thinking. (Only 7% of our communication is verbal.)
- ❖ Have premonitions.
- ❖ Sense danger before it is physically apparent.
- ❖ Know when someone close has died without being in his or her presence.
- ❖ Send positive energy (love) or negative energy (fear) to anyone we choose. (Remember it comes back ten fold!)
- ❖ By thinking of something or someone, magnetize them to us.
- ❖ Create and direct our own future.
- ❖ Receive gut feelings (for the guys) or intuitions (for the girls) about a business, relationship, person or event.
- ❖ Astral travel. (When we are sleeping our spirit can go "flying" anywhere in the world.)
- ❖ See ghosts.

If you are psychic, you can also do some of the following:
- ❖ Experience extreme sensitivity to energy: the weather, electricity, people, natural disasters and world events.
- ❖ Empathize with other people's feelings to a point where you feel you are inside their skin. (If your boundaries are not in place, you may feel that you don't know where you stop and others begin, as if you are meshing with their energy.)
- ❖ See the colors in people's auras and the people, events or spirits in their energy field.
- ❖ Experience overload sometimes when in crowds of people or cities. (Combinations of intense energies can bombard your energy field.)
- ❖ Hear another dialogue in your mind when in conversation which differs from the words coming from the other person's lips. (Because you are consciously/unconsciously aware that they are not speaking the truth.)
- ❖ See ghosts, spirits and spirit guides, angels, fairies and communicate with them telepathically.
- ❖ Identify illness, energy blocks and stuck emotions in others.
- ❖ Have conscious out-of-body experiences, where your body is in one location and your spirit is in another.

- ❖ Receive conscious or "in trance" visions of global or community events.
- ❖ Experience communication with other-dimensional beings.
- ❖ Be the recipient of psychic attacks (oh, joy!) in your dreams or consciously during which you feel dark entities are toying with your energy.
- ❖ Attract other psychics (or crazies) into your circle.
- ❖ Attract some who will try to take advantage of, manipulate or rob you of your psychic energy. (Once you have mastered your psychic boundaries, you will not attract this "vampire" energy.)
- ❖ Find fascination in all things metaphysical and be drawn to study that subject.
- ❖ Often feel the need to be alone, away from other people's dysfunctional energy.
- ❖ Offend people just by looking at them. (They sense your psychic power and are afraid that you are boring into their souls even though you might be merely thinking about tomorrow's dinner!)
- ❖ Discover that others experience you as quite intense.
- ❖ Rise above a highly dysfunctional background or overcome heavy trauma experienced in childhood.
- ❖ Descend from parents or grandparents who are psychic, even if they don't admit it.
- ❖ Experience déjà vu frequently.
- ❖ And of course, read people, their personalities, their fears, and what they are potentially creating in their futures.

All of us can work towards heightening our sensitivity to energy. Just as you would go to the gym to strengthen your glutei, you can build trust in your own senses to whatever level of intuitive or psychic ability your little heart desires.

After all, isn't the meaning of your life about waking up to your highest potential?

DUMBBELL

$\mathcal{B}$efore my first year was up, even working as a nanny I had decided Canada was the place I wanted to be. Sure, I missed the English pubs, the coziness of the Sussex countryside on a golden summer's eve, my friends with their wicked sense of humor, but I certainly didn't miss my mother's regular character assassinations of me or the gray oppressive dullness of November Sundays. In Canada there were so many interesting things to do, such as studying metaphysics and meeting new people. The locals were welcoming and I was rapidly making new friends.

Exactly one year to the day of immigrating to Canada, I was back in England, finalizing the sale of my house, selling off some of my possessions and preparing a shipment of special belongings to Vancouver. I made sure I had time to visit those precious friends I had missed.

Wilma, my former neighbor and friend, had left White Hart Court soon after I had departed for Vancouver and purchased one of those beautiful Victorian flats close to the waterfront in Brighton. After the excitement of our initial reunion, she ushered me into the living room where two other close friends, Marilyn and Georgina, greeted me.

Wilma was habitually pensive so when I first saw her I didn't sense immediately that anything was wrong. The women oohed and aahed about how healthy and happy I looked. Then came a barrage of questions about Canada and my new life. When I finally came up for air, I turned to Wilma.

"So…how are you doing?"

A shadow of something passed across her face and she exchanged a weary smile with Marilyn and Georgina. Her long, slim fingers reached for her Dunhills lying on the coffee table. She chuckled, that familiar, deep, gurgling sound which had warmed me to her in the first place.

"Well, chuck," she started, inhaling on her cigarette and then blowing the smoke out as if wishing she could drive away this thing she was about to tell me. "Where do I start?"

"Must be to do with a man," I ventured, grinning at Marilyn and Georgina.

Georgina snorted, not smiling, and sat back in her chair.

Oops! It was serious then.

Wilma sighed wearily. "I 'ad a relationship with this bloke. 'E came to live 'ere."

"Live here?" I repeated inanely, looking around the sun-filled living room as if I might find him.

Wilma had been my neighbor, co-worker on the same airline and friend for over seven years. I had never known her to have a relationship for longer than a month, let alone a live-in boyfriend. I had always suspected that she was still in love with someone who was unavailable to her either through marriage or unrequited love. Being a very private person, she remained a mystery to most of her friends.

"Yeah," Wilma took another puff, remembering, "a whole seven months." For a moment, she appeared to be awkward in her own skin. "Anyway," she said, flicking ash into the ashtray and studying it, "to cut a very long story short, he's run off with me car an' seven thousand pounds of my money."

I stared at the others. Georgina nodded solemnly while Marilyn rolled her eyes in confirmation.

"Have you told...?"

"The police, yeah. They were over 'ere yesterday. Bluddy embarrassin'."

"Do they have any idea where he is?"

"No." She stubbed out the cigarette. Poor Wilma. She always seemed to be suffering. The hunch in her thin shoulders begged protection from whatever would fall next from the sky. But it hadn't worked. And now this.

"Do you have anything of his? Something personal."

"Why?" Wilma gave me one of her what-are-you-talking-about-now? looks. All three women were aware of my budding talents as a palmist and my fascination with metaphysics but would often appear bewildered by my psychic theories.

"Well, maybe I can pick up something," I offered more confidently than I felt. "I learned to do it in Canada. It's called psychometry."

Suddenly there was a flurry of activity. Marilyn and Wilma went searching while Georgina told me in her low conspiratorial voice about the hell that Wilma had recently been through.

"Preferably something metal," I called after them, "like a key ring or jewelry."

Wilma appeared at the living room door, a five-pound dumbbell in her hand. "How about this?"

"I'll try," I said, wanting desperately to help my friend.

The three women sat on the edge of their seats while, with eyes closed, I prayed that the cold, shiny, metal weight would "speak" to me.

Immediately, the images came. "I'm seeing a tall, blond-haired man, very blond."

I heard a collective gasp.

"Is that him?" I asked.

"Yes." It was Marilyn's voice.

"I feel like he's got something in his body, like pins...as if he's been in a bad motorcycle accident."

"Bluddy 'ell!" Wilma spluttered, her Nottingham accent always more pronounced under stress.

"There's one in his left leg and one in his foot, I think. I also see scars on his stomach area and one..." I pointed to the right side of my brow, "just here."

"That's amazing!" Georgina whispered. "I think we should write this down in case the police can use it." I heard sounds of Georgina rifling through a drawer.

"Did he like to watch a lot of TV? I see him lying on the floor with his head resting in his hands." I let go of the weight and cupped my head in both hands. "Like this...and *really* studying people. Oh...I get it...he's a professional confidence trickster."

Wilma was quiet now, listening intently.

I could feel the stony coldness of this man's energy, as though the connection to his heart had been amputated and his soul was devoid of any emotion. Any feeling he showed had been calculated, carefully studied and mimicked. Maybe he was a psychopath? I shuddered.

"I hate to tell you this, Wilma, but it feels as if he regarded this time here with you as a kind of resting place, an in-between job. He's done this before, much bigger stuff, so don't feel bad about being taken in. He's wily, very good at what he does."

"You got that right!" Marilyn huffed. "Can you see where the car is?"

"Just a sec..." The interruption had thrown me off balance for a while, and it took me some time to regain the flow of images that were coming to me. I realized I was now in this man's head, able to feel his thoughts, see his plans.

"I'm seeing a place in Newcastle. It's his base, where he always goes back to. But it's just a safe in an old derelict red-bricked building like an abandoned warehouse, factory, something like that."

"Got an address?" Wilma probed, only half-joking.

"Sorry, I'm not that good. This place is where he keeps all the money that he's stolen." My mind showed me an image of the man stuffing a brown padded envelope into the safe with his other spoils. "But he's not going there straight away."

The letter "B" then loomed large in my mind. "He's going to a town...Bristol or Bournemouth, west of here. No...wait a minute, it's on the coast...it's Bournemouth!"

"Is he there now?" The suppressed rage in Wilma's voice revealed her desire to strangle this crook if she could just get her hands around his neck.

"Not yet." Like watching a movie, I waited for the next scene. "He plans to carry on down to Devon, Cornwall area. There's someone there, an older lady. He knows her already. It could be his mother or someone like his mother, but he steals from her, too."

"The cad!" Georgina hissed.

"Wilma, I know he's humiliated you, but it's good that he's gone."

"Yeah, but will I ever get the money or me car back?"

"The car...yes. The money?" The screen in my mind went suddenly blank. "I'm not sure." No more images. I opened my eyes.

All three women were staring at me in awe.

"That was incredible!" Georgina exclaimed. I smiled, pleased and amazed at how much information had come through. And the detail! Had those images just emerged out of my own imagination or were they the truth? I felt they were the truth but.... And I had *felt* his energy as if I had been inside his skin.

"You know, he *was* in a motorcycle accident and 'e *did* 'ave scars right 'ere." Wilma pointed to the side of her stomach and then her thigh.

"And I was always telling him not to get so close to the TV, wasn't I?" Marilyn added. "You're spooky."

Thanks.

Later that week, I visited one of my very proper, stiff-upper-lip aunts. Over high tea served promptly at 4:00 p.m., I sheepishly confessed to her that I suspected I might be psychic. I was stunned when she responded matter-of-factly, "Well, you always were, dear."

I was? Why didn't anybody *tell* me?

It was getting close to the date of my return to Canada, and I was packing mementos into a crate. Marilyn called me at my soon-to-be-sold home. She sounded breathless.

"Has Wilma told you yet?"

"Told me what?"

"I just thought you should know, the police have just rung and they've got the car."

"And?"

"They found it abandoned. In Bournemouth."

Bluddy 'ell!

Metaphysical Endnote 16

Cops and Robbers and Psychics

Probably a victim of his own limited thinking, Wilma's ex-boyfriend believed that conning his way through life was the only way he could survive. Or the only way he wanted to. He was also addicted to the adventure of it all. Where did that conditioning come from? Maybe he was left to his own devices to survive as a child and it became a habit, a way of living. Or maybe the synapses in his brain had shorted and he just saw the world differently. I, for one, didn't want to get too close to him physically to find out.

This man lived totally on his instincts because to survive he had honed his ability to mimic and live inside other people's heads. Though it wasn't a pleasant experience, he had made it easy for me to get inside his. What is a con artist but just one application of a focused psychic ability? Perhaps he was also a psychopath, having no conscience and not acknowledging any boundary between right and wrong. Anyone was fair game, even little old ladies.

There are many people who are already using their instincts at a heightened level because they have to, either to survive or to function in their line of work. Street kids, social workers, criminals, police, nurses and anyone who works with people on a regular basis, especially in crisis situations, all do it. The shame is that their intuitiveness could be even sharper if they acknowledged its existence, if they learned *how* to master this inherent talent and then used it to its full potential. It is often fear of the unknown that keeps people away from developing this instinctual drive.

My hope is that the police will in the near future be more receptive not only to integrating more psychics into their detective functions, especially with missing children, but also to developing their own intuitions to a point where they don't need outside help. Like the criminals they pursue, law enforcement officers are already working and living by their wits. It wouldn't take very much more training for them to understand and harness this talent to an even more efficient level. Wouldn't it make sense that they, the good guys (well, most of the time), have the upper hand and not the criminals?

On three occasions when I have picked up on the whereabouts of an abducted woman and telephoned the police, it was evident by the weary response at the other end of the line that the poor police officer had been inundated with psychics and their visions. How do these officers, not trained in deciphering psychic energy and symbology, sort through all that information? It's not just a matter of putting all the data into a computer database and pulling out the most literal common denominators, although that's a start. Deciphering psychic images can be like dream interpretation: sometimes it is literal, sometimes symbolic. You have to know the difference *and* be able to translate the symbology before it makes any sense. Like the ancient Greeks did, maybe the police could employ a psychic interpreter to analyze and make sense of psychic information supplied to them.

In the summer of 2002, when "The Sniper" was loose in the United States randomly shooting people, I contacted the police there. After I had given the officer my intuitions—that this man was not acting alone but was part of a father and son team—I was met with a disbelieving "Uh huh."

"Are you using psychics to help in this case?" I asked, curious.

"Oh, no," the woman responded lazily, chomping on gum. "We wouldn't do th–a–a–t."

"But couldn't you take twenty psychics from your area and see what they all come up with? Their readings might all be varied but there might be five clues that are common denominators. It's better than no clues at all, isn't it?"

"Yeah," she droned. "I guess we could do th–a–a–t."

I know you won't, I thought. *But what exactly do you have to lose, except people's lives?*

LET ME IN!

*A*fter a hectic month in England, finalizing the sale of my house and its contents, visiting family and friends, and hurriedly collecting the house funds from the bank just outside the airport departure gate, I had come back to Canada on a four-month visitor's visa. I intended to find a way to immigrate legally without having to subject myself to being a nanny for another year, two years being the requisite. The first twelve months had been a pleasant sabbatical, but long enough.

I had until the end of August to find a way. Until then I was free. So I rented a ground-floor apartment on Vancouver's Pender Street and treated myself to a TR7 convertible. Okay, so it was second-hand and it shuddered violently at any speed over 60 mph, but hey, I, Kate, now had my very own sports car. Then, for the first time, I went solo on a two-week holiday to Hawaii.

What awaited me on my return was a long and arduous communication with Canada Customs and Immigration, first by mail, then by phone, then in person. Finally, after too many visits to immigration offices where they began to greet me by first name and hand me coffee in my own cup, I learned that, despite having the funds and the ability to start my own business, knowledge of not just English and French but five additional languages, and two gainfully employed and successful brothers in the country who had offered to sponsor me, I was not a desirable candidate.

My brother Luke made suggestions of marrying me off to one of his car dealer buddies. "But I thought you loved me," I responded.

In desperation, I enquired at one of my regular visits to Immigration what it would take, apart from feigning a complete ignorance of French and English, to claim refugee status.

"All your family in your home country have to be dead," the officer informed me, stony-faced.

"This could be arranged," I quipped, smiling.

She didn't think it was funny.

So I resigned myself to the possibility of doing another year as a caretaker of children, but not until I absolutely had to.

August rolled around very quickly, too quickly. Despite offers of marriage from various quarters, I opted for the simpler but longer route, another nanny job. One of my allies at Immigration had told me to apply nine months prior to the end of my two-year term so I could step from the nanny position into a "real" job. Whoopee! I wouldn't have to subject myself to slave labour for a single minute longer than necessary.

I must have had "sucker" written all over me as the nanny agency placed me in a monster of a house at the top of the British Properties. The 6,000 square feet rambled off in various directions complete with wall-to-wall brown carpets (shows everything, don't you know, dahling), windows from floor to ceiling and skylights (a–a–always needed cleaning), white furniture (aaagh!!) and four delightful but extremely messy children who attended four different schools and at least four different extra-curricular activities. The Baileys were lovely, but I was running in circles even before I woke up. In three months, I lost eight pounds without dieting. For this privilege, I would normally have paid *them,* but as I told the mother when I gave notice, "This is a job for two people."

"Oh, I know," she responded blithely, perhaps surprised that I had lasted so long.

No wonder the Bailey children barely gave me a wave goodbye as I tossed the last of my belongings into the back of the TR7 two weeks later. I found out from the agency that I wasn't the only nanny who had resigned after such a short time. The children were, I now understood, suffering from "nanny fatigue." Just how many young women had been their surrogate mothers I wasn't sure, but I felt very guilty adding to their long line of abandoners. Although they had the consistency of two sane and caring parents, I still worried that this revolving door of nannies would leave them with a life-long expectation of rejection.

For my next job, I was very specific with the agency about what

I was prepared to do and not do. No more twelve-hour days running ragged for yours truly.

"You're crazy," Joanne, the gregarious redhead at the agency, boomed. She was offering me a job as an executive housekeeper and I was turning my nose up at it.

"Just go and find out," she urged. I was aware of my tendency to refuse what was really good for me. So this time I listened.

The 11,000 square-foot mansion sat back from the corner of a quiet residential street in Point Grey. I was already intimidated by the size of the place and the iron gates so when two mean-and-lean German shepherds bounded up and snarled at me, I didn't exactly get a sense of the warm and fuzzies.

"I'm here to see Mrs. Helman," I muttered into the gate intercom.

"I'll call off the dogs and you can just drive in," a warm voice responded.

Phew!

Instead of the baronial front door in the center of the mansion opening, a single narrower door at the far end of the house was flung open and the two dogs obediently slunk back into the house. Then a buzz, a click and the gates opened and I felt like Ali Baba, without his thieves, as I drove into the massive paved courtyard.

They say the job interviewer makes up his/her mind about the candidate in the first seven seconds. It didn't take me that long to decide that I wanted to be Mrs. Helman's Executive Housekeeper. I warmed to her immediately, not because she was elegant and pretty and exuded motherly warmth (not that I was any expert on motherly warmth), but because there was a twinkle in her eye. We recognized the humor in one another. She reminded me of Grandie, the pride without the snobbery. And though Mrs. Helman was obviously used to wealth, there was a down-to-earth compassion in her that allowed me to relax in her presence. I knew I would enjoy working for her.

But first, I had to lay down the rules.

Mrs. Helman ushered me into a somberly lit dining room where none of the light from the crisp, sunny January day poured in. She sat there, her back to the window, slightly bemused as she listened to my litany of conditions on what I would and would not do. Graciously, she waited until I was off my soapbox.

"Would a split day be okay, four hours in the morning and four in the afternoon?" she asked.

Really? I nodded.

"You would be in charge of coordinating the pool man, the gardener, the housekeepers, the plant man. We would want you to make sure the children get to school, and make breakfast and dinner for us."

You mean, there's no playing mad taxi driver in between cleaning four bathrooms, making five beds, cleaning massive windows, lugging fourteen bags of groceries up flights of icy stairs and vacuuming thousands of square feet of carpet every day?

"You will have your own apartment, separate from the house, above the garage. And you can park your car in that garage. There's a Bentley in there now, but we can move it over."

Own apartment!

When Mrs. Helman gave me a tour of the cozy one-bedroom apartment, which consisted of a quaintly furnished living room with fireplace, a sunny kitchen, a large comfortable bedroom and a million-dollar view of Vancouver, I felt a flash of déjà vu. Then I remembered. At 17, on my first job as a shorthand typist for an engineering company, stuck in a claustrophobic office, I had been trying to decipher my own spidery shorthand—something about "bleeding nipples"—when I spotted a postcard on the wall. I went over and peered at the picture of the modern city. It was Vancouver. *Some day, I'm going there*, I had promised myself. And now here I was, staring over the bay at the downtown core glistening in the sun, at that very same postcard scene.

I got the job. And though it was never really spoken out loud, Mrs. Helman knew that as soon as I had my walking papers, I would be running out of there. But that was nine months away.

Metaphysical Endnote 17

Deservability

There is a myth afoot in our culture that life is hard...and then we die. Yes, life is hard...some of the time, often because we make it so. But by the time we shed our mortal coil and return to spirit, let's hope we have learned a thing or two. Let's hope we have realized that we deserve all the good the Universe has to offer.

Depending on your age, you might have been brought up in the old cultural myth that if you work hard and are a good person, you will be justly rewarded. This is only partially true.

Missing from this formula is the key to it, that you will only receive what you *subconsciously believe* you deserve. The subconscious does not judge or decide whether you deserve good or bad. It simply draws to you according to your beliefs. Sometimes nasty people enjoy great wealth and innocents go to jail. The reason that happens is that you *will* get back the same or complementary energy, that is, you will get back whatever you put out or believe you put out, and ten fold. While your ego mind may emit happy thoughts, it is your subconscious that is the driving force, the bigger magnet. So it doesn't matter how many hours you put in or how saintly you are if deep down you are carrying some guilt, or feelings of low self-esteem, or negative expectations or other thoughts of "undeservability." What you do in the physical will be irrelevant. You will still only receive what you believe you deserve.

The other part of the myth is that in order to have, first we have to get. In Western culture, we tend to work from the outside inward, as if everything we need originates in the physical. But, in fact, everything made up of physical matter is first conceived in thought, in the ether. So the converse is true. A builder first lays the foundation, not the roof. When you throw a pebble into a pond, the ripples start at the center and flow outward. It makes sense, then, to start at the core. First we have to conceive and believe and only then can it become a reality.

For example, I recently believed that I deserved a new car so I used my mind to bring it to me. (Partly because I didn't have time to shop.) The fact that I didn't have the financial means to buy one was also immaterial. I visualized the color, the sensations, the new car smell and how I would feel when I drove my new vehicle. I just sat back and waited with faith and knew ultimately that what I felt I deserved *would* show up. Two months later—this really did happen—my ideal brand

new car was presented to me as a gift. (See Chapter 32 on Manifesting.)
The truth is we are surrounded by the good. It is our beliefs of undeservability (and GUILT!) that repel our natural flow of abundance.

So when I was working for the Baileys, I was in a situation where I
was being a "good" person but still wasn't getting the results I wanted,
because I was working too hard for too little reward. It's all a question
of balance. So I reviewed my expectations for myself and decided I deserved something better. While the final details of my picture weren't
filled in, I had a strong sense of what that something better was. I
changed my Mind. In my revised mindset, I decided on new boundaries,
circumstances I definitely wanted, tasks I was absolutely *not* willing to
do, and areas where I was prepared to compromise. In my new position,
the Universe rewarded me for finally taking action by giving me even
more than I had asked for, as if congratulating me on my elevated level
of deservability.

Whenever I have raised my deservability quotient—such as giving
myself time out from an intense period of work, going for a massage
or booking a trip—the "good" has multiplied ten-fold. I have returned
home to a new contract, received a gift of a massage and found an unexpected cheque in the mail the day before my trip, as if my angels
were cheering, "By George, I think she's got it." While some rewards
are more spectacular than others, the message is always there: *Do unto
yourself as you would do unto your most cherished friend.* Then allow
the Universe to bring you, magically, whatever your little heart desires
because, as a spark of the divine, you *do* deserve the best!

18

DON'T SHOOT THE MESSENGER

"*H*ave you found what you're looking for?" He grinned, nodding at the magazine in my hands.

"Oh, hi, John." I smiled, happy to see this bespectacled, olive-skinned man. We had met a week earlier at a multi-level sales seminar and had quickly discovered we were both lost souls searching for something. But it wasn't multi-level marketing.

"How about going for coffee?" He tilted his head towards a restaurant across the other side of busy Robson Street. I gladly accepted.

The coffee shop was lively with people chatting animatedly at elegant formica tables. After the coffee was placed before us, John picked up the thread of our last conversation.

"I made a decision this week," he told me. "I'm going to see a career counselor."

"Good idea." I sipped my coffee and smiled. "I'm going to see a psychic tomorrow."

"You believe in that stuff, then?"

"I'm addicted."

"So what do these psychics tell you?"

"Oh," I groaned, "that I'm psychic, too."

"Is that true?" John sat back in his chair.

"Well, I do read palms...."

"There's your answer then."

"But I don't want to be a psychic," I whined. "People will think I'm weird."

"I see...."

Just then my attention was drawn to a trio entering the restaurant. Maybe it was because the slender young woman was lolling in a wheelchair that she caught my eye or because she and the two young men accompanying her were wearing the sunset colors of the Bagwan Rajneesh sect. I knew I was staring to the point of rudeness, but I continued to observe them until they were seated. The woman had her back to me while the dark-haired man and his blond-haired companion sat on either side of her, facing me.

"Sorry, John. What were you saying?"

"I see you as being very powerful."

"Please...I hate it when people use that word."

"It's a compliment." He sounded hurt.

"I know...and thank you. But it makes me nervous."

"Why?"

"It's like...people, even strangers, can see some great potential in me that doesn't exist. I'm afraid they'll have expectations that I won't be able to live up to. And anyway, how can I be powerful when I don't even have a direction for my life?"

I glanced again at the trio in red. The woman's head was flopping to the right. I realized she must be drooling as the blond man leaned forward and, with a scrunched up napkin, solicitously wiped her mouth then gently propped up her sagging body.

I became transfixed by her back, as though a magnet was implanted between her shoulder blades and she was pulling me to her. I was vaguely aware of John's voice but another voice was louder in my head. *Go and give her a message*, the voice commanded.

A mental battle began. *I can't just go over there. I don't know her*, I reasoned.

Go, the voice urged.

But she'll think I'm crazy.

Just do it.

My whole body was shaking with resistance and fear, but I knew the force that was urging me to deliver this message was more potent than my frail ego.

"What is it?" John inquired.

"Excuse me," I said as something pushed my chair back and, as if in a protective bubble, I was propelled towards her wheelchair. Even as I approached their table and the two men glanced up puzzled, I had no idea what I was going to say. The bubble I was in must have exuded some gentle force because, although taken aback, they seemed assured that I would do their friend no harm. They sat back and watched, curious, while I knelt down on the left of the woman's wheelchair and took her slim, gnarled hand in mine.

The woman's head lolled towards me, the eyes sliding from side to side, unfocused.

"You have MS, don't you?" I probed gently.

Her eyes blinked a "yes." The pain of being trapped in an out-of-control body was evident.

"Something happened in your life and you got really mad at God, didn't you?" There was a twitch of a wry smile at the corners of her mouth.

"Is that when this disease started? When you decided that God had abandoned you?"

Her head inclined in a slight nod.

"But he didn't leave you, you know. *You* left *him*. That's when you got sick."

There was a dawning revelation in her eyes. And astonishment. I was astonished myself. How could I know that?

"Are you still very angry at God?" I continued, the words just tumbling out of my mouth.

A sound like a small groan came out of her. Her head stopped rolling, her eyes focused steadily on me now. Our eyes were locked. "You *will* get better," I said, not knowing where this information was coming from but feeling its truth in every cell of my being. "First you need to forgive yourself. Then God," I continued. "You will get out of this wheelchair and walk again, and then you will show others who have the same disease how to heal themselves."

Another small noise escaped her lips. "How?"

An image exploded in my head. I could feel the power of it in my own body and attempted to describe it to her. "Let the earth give you back your strength. Place both your feet firmly on the ground and feel your strength coming up from the earth and filling your body with healing and power. Keep visualizing that until you are strong again."

Unexpectedly she sat up in her chair and gave me a huge bright smile. Her claw-like hand squeezed mine tightly. We exchanged a look of recognition, not of each other, but of the truth. There were tears in both our eyes.

Then the spell was broken, the bubble gone, and I stood up. I glanced at the two men, afraid that any minute they might have me arrested. The dark-haired man—was he her husband?—glared at me. I saw fear, resentment, anger in his eyes. Maybe he was afraid she would heal and then have no need for him. *Don't shoot the messenger*, I thought. The blond man merely appeared stunned.

"Hank oo," the woman whispered, peering directly up into my eyes.

I touched her shoulder and then returned to my table where John had been watching the whole scene.

"What was all that about?" he asked.

Before I could answer, the blond man was standing over me.

"Thank you for what you just did. That took a lot of guts."

I wanted to tell him that a higher force used my vocal chords, but still shaking I just stammered, "You're welcome."

As John and I resumed our conversation, I noticed that the three had paid their bill, and I watched gratified as the woman rolled herself out of the restaurant, her back straight, her head erect.

Years later, I realized that the message that day was just as much for me as it was for her. Unlike me, she wasn't intimidated by that vision of her future because on some level she knew she had the power within her to change. She had already envisioned being whole again. Those channeled words from me were light and water for seeds of hope that were already planted within her. The reason we understood one another, and in those brief moments bonded, was that we both had a power inside us that we weren't using.

That was eighteen years ago. I often think about her now. I wonder where she is and if she chose her higher path. As for me, though I mentally kicked and screamed, I finally surrendered to mine, my psychic gift. The word "powerful" doesn't give me the heebie-jeebies anymore. I know I am not the message, merely the messenger. Just as long as nobody shoots me, I can live with that.

Metaphysical Endnote 18

Establishing Psychic Boundaries

When I was first in Norway, fumbling my way through the Norwegian language and learning its singsong intonations, I often made mistakes. But my intention was to master fluency, so I persevered. After two months, I spoke limited, grammatically incorrect, but fluent Norse.

In order to get what we want, sometimes we have to be willing to make mistakes, to take risks, to appear the fool. In the Tarot, The Fool represents the open-minded person who believes anything is possible. The trick is not to take yourself *too* seriously along the way. When I made linguistic mistakes, my Norwegian employers and I just chuckled, they corrected me and we moved on. But it took me a lot longer to develop a sense of humor about mastering my psychic ability. And this happened only after I had established my boundaries.

When I was first cognizant of *really* being psychic, I was only aware of being surrounded by a chaotic energy, like being at the center of a whirling dervish that wreaked havoc in every area of my life. It didn't help that my mind was also in conflict. I wanted to know everything *about* the psychic but I didn't want to *be* one. After all, that would mean not just appearing the fool but also being branded as crazy. Even though I didn't have to worry about fundamental Christian parents, a devoutly Catholic uncle or an I-don't-believe-any-of-that-stuff husband having me committed, *being* a psychic was still scary.

I believed I had no control over this turmoil. I realized later that this chaos was due to a combination of things: a) not being grounded, b) having a surplus of psychic energy that needed to be channeled and, most of all, c) not knowing my boundaries.

I am not saying that you have to be old or perfect to be a psychic—I am neither by the way—but while this book promotes the idea of limitlessness, it is also important to know where you as a psychic stop, and the other person begins. Being master of your own energy is not only good for your sanity, it is essential to your psychic health and to the mental health of those around you.

Having boundaries:

❖ Allows you to function within healthy parameters.
❖ Ensures that your intention is for the highest good and not merely to placate your ego.

❖ Ensures that your energy cannot be sucked dry.

❖ Protects you from lower vibrations and their nasty intentions.

❖ Keeps you in balance.

❖ Promotes staying grounded (more on that in Chapter 24).

❖ Allows you to switch the psychic you "on/off" at will.

❖ Teaches you when you do have power and when you don't and how to know the difference.

❖ Validates your strengths but reminds you when it's wiser to delegate.

❖ Lets you know where you are in your process so you don't go beyond what you know.

❖ Gives you permission to say, "I don't know."

❖ Reminds you to ask for guidance, strength and wisdom every day.

❖ Advises you when to act and when to surrender.

❖ Affirms that you are merely the messenger, not the message.

❖ Keeps you in perennial student mode and humble!

How do you become cognizant of your boundaries? The easiest way is to simply surrender your will to your higher power. Imagine a little trap door in your crown chakra at the top of your head. Open up that door and visualize a beam of light going from your head all the way up to a brilliant ball of white light way up in the Universe. Know that you are now connected to Divine Intelligence, God, Allah, Buddha or another higher power. Be assured that they are guiding you, protecting you and even channeling the words that come out of your mouth. With that guidance, you are always safe within your boundaries.

"In the life of the spirit you are always at the beginning."

— *Book of Runes.*

INITIATION?

*T*he summer of '85 was the beginning of something that I didn't understand, something overpowering. I felt as if I was being swept up into a vortex of swirling psychic energy, and it was soon evident that this force was much bigger than little old me. I had no choice but to hang on for dear life and pray that I would be all right in the end.

There were just nine months to go before I could have my freedom and give birth to myself as a bona fide landed immigrant, but only having one foot in the door of a country made me feel "less than." The constant reminder of my conditional and servile position detracted from my already precarious confidence. But it wasn't just my present status that was chipping away at my sense of self. There were other factors.

In the early '80s, behavioral modification was a popular process to make people wake up to who they really were, breaking them down in order to break through. The Mastery, which I had done in 1983, was an actor's workshop loosely based on Werner Erhard's EST concept. While the weekend workshop had done me some good (I think?), I also felt as if I had been stripped of the foundation of my being. I had learned a lot about people and their pain. How much agony, abuse and anger we as human beings can survive amazed me. At the same time, I also developed another less flattering awareness of my Self.

The facilitator, I noticed, handled others with kid gloves but seemed to think I would benefit from a more brutal approach. He assessed accurately that I was independent (what choice did I have?) and strong (Hello! I'd had to be!). So he decided I needed to be humiliated (or that's how it felt) to break through my iron shield of protection. I took it personally. Just because I have a persecution complex doesn't mean I wasn't being persecuted.

From the time I was 13 years old, my mother had screamed at me that I was "a whore, a slut and a bitch." (The whore bit was very funny as she hadn't even deigned to explain the facts of life to me, and on that topic I was pathetically naïve.) In addition, my older brilliant sister (brilliant academically at least) had constantly told me how "thick" and "stewooopid" I was, while my brothers teased me about being "fat and ugly." Normal sibling rivalry? Maybe. If, on rare occasions, I revealed my hurt, apparently I was also "too sensitive." As a teenager, I wondered what I could possibly have left to contribute? I decided on humor. At least I could make people laugh. That felt good, and bringing a smile to others' faces gave me a sense of esteem I didn't otherwise feel.

According to the facilitator, humor had been my cover, and I was told it was fraudulent to be funny, to use humor as a defense and a reason to belong. What had been uncovered about me was found to be deceptive; therefore I was not being real. I was a con. Always having prided myself on my truthfulness, I was horrified at this interpretation of my behavior.

Now that humor had been taken away from me, I felt denuded. Being funny had always been my fallback tactic and I was being told it was wrong. I was like a child deprived of my one and only toy. Like a small raft on a vast ocean, without humor, I was lost.

So I had to start again with nothing...but truth.

Who I had become after the Mastery was definitely not the "me" I preferred, or even liked. I developed an ultra-serious, intense personality, seeing behind others' fronts or social personas. Maybe because I was suddenly naked of my humor and conscious of being absolutely truthful with myself, I was able to see the truth in others.

But I made the mistake of speaking it out loud. The feedback I elicited was a mixture of outrage, indignation, curiosity and sometimes blatant rudeness. I didn't understand why all these people were so offended by me and my words. It hurt. I was telling the truth now and still I was wrong. But wasn't being honest what I was supposed to be doing? I was only trying to help, wasn't I?

Although I was not aware of it then, I suspect that this is when my clairvoyance began to make itself really known. But unfortunately for those people, and myself, there was no banner, barrier, veil, film or neon sign to let me know that what I was seeing in others wasn't out there to be seen. Like telling your friend the end of the movie while they are still at the beginning, I was seeing the whole plot, the one they had yet to discover about themselves. While they felt that their innermost sanctums were being invaded by moi, I was hurt and confused by their angry reactions to me. Wasn't what I was seeing out there for everyone to see?

Apparently not.

One morning in my apartment, I popped two pieces of bread into my temperamental toaster. Two minutes later, the smoke alarm at the top of the stairs went off, and despite my frantically waving a tea towel at it, the ear-piercing shriek didn't stop. Away in the distance, in another part of the suburb, I heard sirens blaring. It briefly occurred to me what a coincidence it was that someone else had started a fire. The sirens got louder and louder and louder, coming closer and closer until I saw, with some horror, that the large yellow truck was sitting outside the baronial iron gates, lights flashing. Before I could move, three hulking and handsome firemen were clambering up my narrow staircase.

"Are you all right?" the first one asked.

"Uh, uh…" (Firemen always had an embarrassingly paralyzing effect on me.)

Not getting any intelligent response, he inspected the whining round white thing in the ceiling.

"You have an oversensitive alarm and it's hooked up to our station."

"Oh, I'm so sorry," I finally managed to say. "Is there anything I can do about it?" I gleefully envisioned the hunky firemen showing up every morning at breakfast.

"We don't want to disconnect the smoke alarm," he responded still staring up at it. Then he gave me a disarming smile. "Just don't burn your toast."

As they trampled back down the stairs, I wished I could have summoned these heroes for my oversensitive self but rescuing lost souls wasn't in their job description. I was on my own. Well, kind of.

One thing I did get out of the Mastery was an eclectic group of great friends. Graham was one of them. By the summer of 1985, he had become my constant companion. He was a tall, lean Englishman, reminiscent of a philosophy professor but in actuality a struggling artist of the painting variety. Through the workshop and the subsequent work we did on ourselves, we had recognized in each other two repressed English people looking for a way out of our damaged psyches.

Another gem I had met through the workshop was Grace Young

whom I half-jokingly called my guru. Ten years my senior physically, but light years ahead of me spiritually, she would invite me over for tea once a week where we would discuss metaphysics, philosophy, spirituality, psychology and other areas of mysticism. Actually, it was more a question-and-answer period with me, the interrogator, thirsty for understanding. Without even knowing what my next flood of queries would be, Grace would regularly present me with a book, which, when I read it the following week, would eerily respond to my specific enquiry.

Grace suggested that I pay a visit to Rose McDonnell, a psychic she respected. When I look back now, it seems the subsequent events were set in motion as a result of the psychic reading I had that summer with Rose. But who knows for how long the force had been silently building? In retrospect, this point in my evolution felt like a culmination, the end of a cycle, and the beginning of something much greater. It felt like an initiation.

The appointment was on a Saturday in June.

I phoned Graham that morning before the reading. "I'm thinking about taking a drive down to the Oregon coast leaving tomorrow for four days. I need some time to think. This sounds rude but I can't decide whether to go alone or to invite you to come with me. If I did invite you, would you like to come?"

"Sounds like fun," he responded.

"I'm going to see Rose, a psychic, this morning."

"Maybe she can help you make up your mind." I could hear the smile in his voice. "Just let me know. Doesn't take me long to pack a toothbrush."

Rose was a lady of 81, who, Grace had told me, was very good and didn't charge for her readings. The white-haired psychic opened the door wide into her pristinely clean West End apartment. If cleanliness was next to godliness, I was in the right place. Without any ado, she pointed me to a green-baize-covered chair where I obediently sat. My back was to a splendiferous view of Beach Avenue and a sparkling ocean dotted with Saturday afternoon boaters.

Across the room, Rose settled herself into a Queen Anne chair, crossed her ankles, rested her arms in her lap and studied me. No cards, no crystal ball, nothing. And then she began.

"Your grandmother has come in the door with you," she said. "She is pushing you to do something. You have a lot of great ideas but not the ambition to follow them through. The letter 'R' is all around you. It could be Ramtha."

Ramtha was a twenty-thousand-year-old soul who channeled through J. Z. Knight and was well known in Vancouver at the time for spouting great wisdom.

Neat.

"A spirit, a Dr. Leonard, is also with you, guiding you. You have to overcome rejection which is your big issue and is holding you back."

Yes, I thought, *it's not easy to grow up in a home where the sport is let's-see-how-much-we-can-really-hurt-each-other, and emerge unscathed.*

"You are pretty and still young enough to go on camera. You possess a strong psychic force which, if you let it go, could be very powerful."

I knew *that* one was coming sooner or later. Only this time when I heard the same old prediction, I felt a murmur of something else. Excitement? Acceptance?

"You will be involved in the human potential field but you have a lot of talent for becoming a good trance medium."

Excuse me, do you mean seeing dead people? Aaagh! I don't think so.

The time went quickly and soon the reading was over. "Do you have any questions?" she asked.

"Yes." I remembered the vision I had in the British Properties last year. At the end of my day with my two charges, I would often drive right to the top of the steep, narrow roads where I could smoke my one cigarette in peace and contemplate the fabulous view of the city. Early one summer evening, I was admiring the tableau of the downtown core, its tall elegant white towers glistening in the evening sun, stretching upwards into a deep blue cloudless sky. Suddenly, before my eyes, the scene cracked down the middle and split as if I was looking at a photo being ripped down the center, leaving jagged edges. At first I hadn't trusted my eyes. I blinked and peered again but the torn image remained. Then an inner voice told me that, one day, when the earth shifted, downtown Vancouver would just sink.

At that time, I had no knowledge of the geological structure under the city and was blissfully unaware that Vancouver, as well as Los Angeles, was affected by a major fault line. I didn't have to ask too many locals to discover that the Lower Mainland was just waiting for "The Big One."

"Do you get a sense there will be a big earthquake in Vancouver soon?" I asked.

"Yes." Rose cast a tragic look towards the window and the view of Granville Island spread in the distance. "There's going to be some kind of mass destruction here," she said, repressing a shudder. "I'm not sure…."

"How much would you like me to pay for the reading…?" I wanted to make sure that I had not been misinformed.

"I don't charge for my readings," she confirmed.

"Can I be rude and ask how you survive then?"

"They take care of me." She inclined her head heavenward.

I wasn't sure who "they" were but surmised they were not of the physical plane. "I only have to think of something that I need and it appears," she added, smiling.

Oh, to have that kind of faith!

I thanked her and despite her protestations, laid a twenty-dollar bill on her highly polished dining table. As I walked out of her door, she said from behind, "Remember to go for it."

"Yes, I will," I replied, turning to thank her, but the door was already closed.

Maybe it was the reading with Rose that had put me in a tizzy but I still couldn't decide. Did I want Graham to come with me to Oregon on a four-day mini-holiday? Or, like Greta Garbo, did "I just vont to be al–o–o–o–ne"? My increasing desire for solitude was ruining my image as a social butterfly but I didn't care. It was about ten at night when I finally called him to say, "Please come."

The next day, my trusty but vibrating TR7, with me at the wheel, carried Graham and me along the straight gray monotony of the #1 highway towards the US border. As my long, thick hair whipped my face and Graham's wispy locks reached skyward in thin strands, he said, "I almost feel like I was meant to come with you…to protect you."

I nodded, understanding. I felt different now, as if since that reading, something had opened up within me. And we were not alone. There was someone else with us, of the invisible kind, like a spirit sitting atop the back of the car. The presence was comforting and unsettling at the same time. Though I knew the spirit was here for a very specific reason, I couldn't sense what exactly.

I was also a little apprehensive driving into the States. Whenever I crossed the border at Peace Arch into the US, I felt an ominous tension in the air. We were, after all, entering the land of trigger-happy gunslingers. And though I was even more vulnerable in an open convertible, that wasn't the reason I had asked Graham to come.

"I'm glad you're here," I shouted over the deafening noise of a bypassing truck. He was like a brother to me. Neither of us were experts at intimate relationships with the opposite sex, and we often bemoaned the fact that there was no physical attraction between us since we got on so well. Graham and I also shared a sense of the ridiculous that the English are known for. Laughter constituted at least half of our communication and it felt good.

"Did you need to get away, too?" I asked him now the truck was ahead of us.

"I always need to get away," he chuckled, "even when I'm away."

I smiled. It reminded me of the time I was in Libya, sitting at the overwing and talking to Bonnie on the other side of the aisle as the engines wound up power for take-off. The male passengers were chanting their praises to Allah, while the women interjected with their ear-piercing and shivers-down-your-spine ululating, their tongues flapping against the roofs of their mouths. The pitch of their chants rose with the increasing revving of the engines as if they had to outdo Rolls Royce technology. With the whole scene redolent of a Monty Python sketch, Bonnie and I were trying to have a meaningful conversation above the racket as if we were actually sitting in our living room enjoying a nice quiet cup of tea. "You know, Kate, I've come to the conclusion that airline people are all messed up. We are always running away from something. Or running towards something." It was true. The flying life did seem to attract the young and the restless and the confused. I was definitely in that category. But at least we had fun on the run.

As Graham and I veered off the highway to take the more scenic route along Chuckanut Drive, I gave him the quick version of the previous day's reading. He was always interested in my soul-searching exploits. "And of course, she told me I was psychic," I concluded.

"Do you think all these psychics might be trying to give you a message?" Graham smiled wryly.

I nodded. "Normally I cringe. But this time, it felt okay."

"Ach," he jibed, "yer just gettin' old."

Or maybe I am finally ready to accept it, I thought.

Metaphysical Endnote 19

Timing

Definition of time: A human-made device to measure the space between, or the duration of, events.

Part of my preamble to my readings is to request that my client not sue me if my predictive timing is off. The weather forecaster sometimes predicts rain, and sunshine appears. The rain *does* come, just not on the day he predicted. While I can see *what* is going to happen, it is often up to the client as to *when* they are ready to experience that particular event. Astrologers and numerologists can be more specific as to *when* a change is more likely to occur according to the planetary influences and the client's numerological path, but they often can't see the details of *what*. Astrologers, numerologists and I make a great team.

While I have often been accurate with my timing, I still warn my clients not to pen the event into their diaries. Rather than assigning a specific date to the occurrence, I am more inclined to see the time of year, what the weather is doing. But because many of us don't trust that we live in a beneficent Universe and haven't yet accepted living in the moment, it is our fear of lack of control that drives us to ask When? When? When?

But predicted timing can vary for many reasons:

❖ Willingness. The querent's willingness to grow, to move willingly towards his highest good. On this physical plane, we often put space between us and what we are afraid to experience, including great happiness. This we call time. So I can be either off about my timing or my client is postponing the event. Believe it or not, many clients resist their highest good out of fear of the unfamiliar. So in the business of predicting, instead of committing myself to a specific time, I might say, "Whenever you are ready for the experience," or "It *feels* like this July but it might be next year."

❖ Evolutionary Process. I believe that everything that *will* be in our future already exists somewhere out there in space. And because like attracts like or complementary energy, we have to be ready before we can receive. Getting ready to receive is often a process, but it is the client's free will that determines the amount of time and space it takes to evolve through that pro-

cess. As Richard Bach wrote in *Illusions,* "There is no problem
so big that it cannot be run away from."

❖ Synchronicity. While we like to think of ourselves as individuals
with control over our Universe, unexpected events often remind
us that we are merely one piece in a very large jigsaw puzzle.
When all the other players are in their positions, then and only
then can the universal synchronicity take place. Sometimes we
call this an accident or a coincidence.

❖ Impact. If an event in the querent's life will create a huge emotional impact on him, the energy surrounding that event will
often loom large and close, giving it a sense of immediacy. In
reality, the event may take place far out in the future.

So do not expect your readings to be 100% accurate, especially
the timing, because it takes two to tango. The psychic can predict
but the querent has free will. And the client can and *will* change his
mind. Sometimes, I really hope he does, for his own good. As I told one
querent, "You will meet your birth mother within two years. I see you
getting together for a coffee and having a good chat. Once you understand what happened at that time, it will bring you some peace and a
healing of your abandonment."

Five years later, there were recriminations of "But you told me…
and it hasn't happened."

"Well," I responded gently, "I was either wrong or it is still to
come."

It would be *another* five years, and ten years after the original
reading, before the scene unfolded exactly as I had predicted. While *I*
sensed that this important reunion was delayed because my client was
not emotionally ready, she might have merely perceived that my timing
was off. She could have been right. But being psychic is not about being
right. (Not at the time anyway!)

ASTORIA

*A*t ten o'clock that night, Cannon Beach, our final destination, was only another hundred miles away, but Graham and I decided we didn't want to be searching for a bed at midnight. When we located the Sunset Inn, a motel right on the coast road just outside Astoria, the shadows had already fallen. An open-faced young Chinese man signed us in, and I invited Graham, as soon as he was settled, to my room for a glass of wine.

Even with the light on, the small square bedroom was somber. Though there was no evidence of dirt or any particularly obnoxious smells, the room still didn't feel clean.

Graham arrived and stretched out his long legs on the bed, propping the rest of his lean frame against two hard-looking pillows and a flimsy headboard. I handed him a glass tooth mug, half-filled with not-very-cold Piesporter.

Our conversation was, at first, about humor. Since leaving England, I was missing the dry wit. I found Canadian humor to be much more slapstick and some of the locals found my droll joking at best puzzling and at worst downright offensive. When one of Lisa's girlfriends had described me as "outrageous," my fear of standing out reared its ugly head. I decided it was time to tone down my personality and my ideas of "funny."

"Humor is like being able to rise above a situation and look down on it, isn't it?" Graham postulated. "Ever heard of Brain Mapping?"

I shook my head.

"Say you have a problem that you need to resolve, you know, like every day. You go forward to the future to a time when you have resolved the problem and got the result you wanted. Then you retrace your steps from the future back to the present and review how you got there. Then you have your solution, theoretically at least."

"Sounds great."

"Yeah, especially when it works," Graham grinned.

"Kind of like creative visualization, then." I had just read Shakti Gwain's thin book last year, *Creative Visualization,* and remembered thinking, *Thank God. Somebody thinks like I do.* It was like coming home. "But isn't everything really about energy?" I offered, warming to the subject. "Understanding energy. I mean if we all understood the universal laws of energy, couldn't we then apply them to all things?"

"How do yer mean?" It was Graham's turn to be perplexed.

"Pass me that pad, would you?" I asked, curling up on the end of the bed. He handed me a pen and the tattered notebook that was my journal.

"I almost feel like there is some equation to life, like Einstein's theory of relativity. And somehow it has to do with pyramids." I started to doodle on the pad, trying to get my thoughts in order and clarify exactly what I wanted to say. This had been a theory of mine for a while but it wasn't clear for me. I hadn't shared it with anyone yet, and thankfully Graham was always interested in my "non-tick-tock" thought.

"Maybe it's *in* the pyramids," he suggested, sipping his wine.

"What?"

"Well, you know how they never really knew conclusively how or who built the pyramids. Maybe the equation you're talking about represents the secret to their construction," Graham lapsed into a Monty Pythonesque accent, "yer know, and the meanin' of loife." The intense moment melted into laughter.

"It's like this...." I began to draw a rough facsimile of a pyramid. Unlike Graham, I am definitely no artist and sketched a four-sided wonder of the world with far less precision than that with which they were built. I wasn't even sure at that moment what I was trying to communicate when, suddenly, what I had been striving to express flooded into my brain. As if on automatic pilot, I drew another pyramid with a circle around it. To the side of the diagram, I wrote:

$$\text{Energy} \times \frac{\text{Love}}{\text{Fear}} = \text{Evolution}$$

Physics or math had never been my strong suit. I now regretted that at fourteen, instead of the boys, clothes and make-up that had taken up all my brain cells, I hadn't focused more on Bunsen burners and Pythagoras. I now realized that knowledge of both math and physics was essential to my growth as a metaphysician. Still, it wasn't as if I had announced to my pubescent schoolfriends, "Hey, when I grow up, I'm going to be a psychic."

"It is almost as if the bottom four lines of the pyramid, the foundations, represent fear and the sides equal four pathways to love, the highest vibration of energy," I continued.

Graham listened intently, musing on my theory.

I continued. "Or maybe the four sides represent the emotional, mental, spiritual, and physical mountain we have to climb. Then the pinnacle represents the highest point of evolution, becoming whole, on the earth plane at least," I swirled the pyramid with another circle, "and all of that is energy."

Einstein I am not, though he is my hero and despite my struggle to grasp the concept and put it into words, I felt as though the information, though stymied at first, was not coming from me but somewhere outside of me, a higher being. Often, when I have received a sudden flash of insight into a higher knowledge, I am aware of a physical sensation of becoming lighter, clearer, even cleaner. I sensed it now.

"Hmm?" Graham was contemplating what I had drawn when I froze and stared past him to the other side of the bed. "What is it?" he asked, suddenly alert.

"There's someone here."

Graham remained perfectly still, silent, as if a tarantula was sitting on his shoulder. "Who is it?" he asked.

"I'm not sure," I replied, my eyes fixed on the entity. "I just see a dark man in a white coat." Did this mean a dark energy disguising himself as a light being? I had heard of evil entities being cunning in their presentation in an attempt to fool mediums. "He is standing right by you," I warned Graham. "This sounds crazy but he's putting a laser line around the bed." And I watched as the spirit "drew" a black line two feet above the outline of the bed and enclosed us within its confines.

"Is this good or bad?" Graham inquired, shifting his weight closer to the middle of the bed.

"I don't know…." I closed my eyes to feel the energy more acutely. "It's as if he is preparing us for something."

Then I felt another presence, standing on my right. I turned and saw an older man in a dark suit and tie. "It's okay," I breathed. "Dr. Leonard is here."

"Oh, goodie. Who the hell's Dr. Leonard?" Graham giggled but there was a tightness in his voice.

"He's the spirit guide Rose spoke of. He's come to give us some information."

"Shall I write it down?" Graham offered.

"Yes, please."

Somehow and without fear, I knew my initiation was beginning. Graham was the perfect person to be here with me. His presence was unobtrusive, and because of his sensitivity and intelligence, I trusted that he was "spiritual" enough not to freak or run screaming from the room. Even though he may not have known consciously that this would happen, I especially valued Graham's willingness to embark with me on this unusual journey. It was as if he had volunteered to be present and hold my hand at the moment of giving birth, my birth as a psychic.

Dr. Leonard was letting me know telepathically that he was my guide. He was not merely a doctor of medicine but also of philosophy. He was encouraging me to keep studying, reassuring me that I was on the right path. Though I was still very much a student, he advised me to have faith in myself.

I felt honored, intimidated, mystified. I verbalized to Graham the information I was receiving and he scribbled furiously. Then just as gently as he had appeared, Dr. Leonard's presence faded.

"He's gone."

Graham glanced nervously to his right. "What about the dark dude in the white coat and the black line?"

"Him too."

He exhaled. We were both silent at first, then, exchanging smiles, we burst out laughing.

"Bluddy 'ell," Graham blurted in a pseudo-cockney accent.

"Bluddy 'ell is right," I agreed.

"More wine?"

"Maybe not!" But he leaned over and topped up my glass. I was in shock. We sat in silence, reflecting on our own thoughts. Suddenly the energy in the room changed again, as if someone, or something, had turned up the heat.

"What is it now?" Graham inquired of my stiffened posture.

"I need to write, but with a pencil." Graham pressed a pencil into my right hand but it was the left hand that was tingling all the way up my arm. Whatever or whoever was coming through me wanted to override my right-handedness and write with my left hand. As the pencil started to move across the white paper in jerky patterns, I observed as if I were merely the witness watching a child draw and waiting for the next stroke to reveal the whole picture.

"What is that?" I asked Graham to view the lines "I" had just drawn on the paper.

"My God!" he exclaimed. "It's a tsunami." When I looked down, I saw what Graham saw, the clear image of a wave crashing against the side of a building.

Earthquake, my left hand wrote in a large fluid script that was not mine. I repeated the word to Graham who sat frozen in the same position.

"When?" I asked in my mind.

July 11, came the response in the same alien script.

"What year?"

The pencil didn't move.

"In Vancouver?" I tried.

Yes.

"What shall I do?"

Tell them.

"How?"

Radio.

"Will I be there when it happens?" I was already forming plans for a move in my head. Who wanted to be in a city when a tsunami was going to come crashing through?

No. (Phew!) *London.*

"Why London?"

Radio.

"How is that going to happen?" I inquired telepathically.

Me.

But who *is* Me, I wondered. Dr. Leonard? Aliens? God?

More messages about friends and family, some of whom had passed, came through before the session ended. *We're very proud of you*, the pencil finally scrawled across the page in large loopy writing before coming to a halt.

That's nice, I thought, *but who is proud? Who are you?*

"You all right?" Graham asked, bringing me back to earth and the motel room.

I nodded, unable to speak. Such a concoction of exhilaration, honor, intimidation, overwhelming awe, fear and extreme happiness was tumbling around in my head and my emotions.

I had been initiated. Little did I know this was, indeed, just the beginning.

Metaphysical Endnote 20

The Soul Urge

An immutable law of physics states that energy cannot be created or destroyed. It merely changes form. By definition then, we as humans who are comprised of energy always exist. There is no death.

What the soul's role is, however, may be up for debate. The following version of the soul's journey is based purely on my own interpretation of what I have been shown, through my psychic readings, of the spirit world and its workings.

Before being conceived and being born again into the physical world, and according to what your soul now needs to learn, you and your spirit guides "co-write a movie" of your upcoming life. This movie might also be known as the soul path, fate, or Agreement. Just one aspect of your soul, the spirit, comes to the physical plane to act out this role and express itself through the vehicle of your physical body while much of your soul stays "home" in the spirit world.

The theme of your spirit's movie might be to focus on loving the self, compassion, humility, right use of will, right use of power, spiritual awareness, responsibility, healthy relationships, contributing to the evolution of humanity, acquiring specific wisdom or spiritual knowledge. This movie script is then embedded in your spirit and subconscious. But once you are born into the physical, you forget what your soul agreed to, on a conscious level at least. (If we did remember, we might want to bypass our movies and not do the work.)

While some spirits elect to clean up their karmic debt from past lives by repaying and/or relearning previously avoided lessons, other spirits opt to "take time out" and experience a free will lifetime where they make up their own story as they go along. In these lives, but to a lesser degree, lessons still have to be learned. They just might not be so gut-wrenchingly dramatic. Many spirits choose a combination of free will and destiny. Usually when the work is done, then the spirit can go out and play.

Each of us is given challenges and gifts in equal measure. The gifts that are given emerge out of, or facilitate, the overcoming of our challenges. And the pace at which your soul/spirit evolves is up to you (hence the difficulty of predicting timing). As you are energy, an electro-magnetic being constantly in motion and vibrating at a certain frequency, the urge of the soul/spirit is always to expand and grow. And as you are an integral part of creation and, therefore, creative in nature, you *will* eventually evolve however long it takes.

When the life is done, like a snake shedding its skin the spirit sheds the physical body and is drawn "home" to the spirit world. There you are embraced with absolutely unconditional love by previously deceased loved ones, your angels and spirit guides. After the reunions with loved ones have taken place, the review committee, your spirit guides, critique your last performance, with you as the ultimate judge. As we are Spirit/Thought/Mind/Consciousness, we create our own heaven or hell on earth, *and* in spirit. *On earth as it is in heaven.* Your soul, therefore, determines your own punishment or reward according to your belief in guilt or innocence whether in this life, the in-between life or future lives.

At some point, your soul may choose to come back to the physical plane and "do it right this time" or, having done the learning in the spirit world, move forward to a higher vibration and/or another dimension. Your soul will always strive for balance. It knows what it needs in order to grow. And being eternal, the learning and the evolution never cease.

While some of us will go through life totally oblivious of our "script," still unaware of any higher purpose or plan, the truth is always there inside us and can be accessed through listening, meditation, prayer, dreams and, of course, psychics!

CANNON BEACH

*T*he next morning, without stopping for breakfast, Graham and I checked out of the motel. It wasn't that we needed to leave Astoria or our experiences of the previous night in a hurry. But for some undefined reason, I felt a sense of urgency to reach our destination and get on with it even though I didn't know what "it" was.

By ten o'clock, we were ensconced in Cannon Beach in another middle-of-the-road but comfortable motel overlooking the ocean. While the rooms were much bigger, the K-Mart décor was about the same. The view from our patio was a huge expanse of Pacific Ocean which, even though it was the middle of June, was still a steely gray, the waves crashing onto the endless stretch of gently sloping sand in gushes of luxurious foam.

As I inhaled the salt sea air, I was not sure whether it was the protective spirit accompanying us on this journey that made me feel cocooned or Cannon Beach itself, but I felt safe there. The place offered a coziness that wrapped itself around us and a mystical quality that let me know it was no ordinary town, not for me anyway. I knew that the area was sacred to several native tribes, the Chinooks, the Clatsops and the Tillamooks. I imagined I could still hear the faint echoes of their sacrosanct rituals, haunting voices chanting to the Great White Spirit. A sense of honoring still hung in the silence as if frozen in time. *Their spirits would always be here,* I thought.

As if our psychic adventures had exhausted all our energy, Graham and I strolled over to an adjoining restaurant to enjoy a hearty breakfast. Then we returned to the motel to sit at the edge of the beach, Graham lounging on a flimsy beach chair while I sat on the sand. He buried himself in his book, and I just stared out at the ever-changing sea and ruminated over the visitations of the previous night.

Would this inclination for automatic writing come again? The whole idea of my being a channel still didn't match the image I had of myself. I had always felt (and feared) that I would do something big, but surely it would be in some kind of business. Was the idea of who I really was *so* distorted? Though I had been fascinated all my life by metaphysics, psychology and anything that goes bump in the night, I was still a businesswoman, wasn't I?

And what was I to do with this newfound talent? Be a Rose McDonnell, sit in my apartment, have clients show up at my door and charge nothing, hoping that the gods would remember to feed me? Couldn't see it. Some powerful force was definitely wanting to come through me, something huge. *Too late to turn back now*, I thought. *I'm on a road to somewhere, almost as if I'm going to be driven off a cliff into a huge abyss with terror and excitement for wings.*

"It's gettin' a bit cool," Graham piped up. A cold wind off the ocean had started to permeate our thin clothes.

"Want to go back to my room for coffee?" I offered.

"Sure."

Graham and I resumed the philosophical conversation about pyramids and humor that we had started the previous night before we had been so rudely interrupted. I was sitting cross-legged on the king bed, and Graham was in his favorite position, leaning his back against several pillows propped against the wall, when I began to get a very high-pitched hum in my right ear. Somehow I knew this was signaling another "transmission." I sat up and closed my eyes. The room became thick with a buzzing which was closing in on me. Every particle of air was humming as if compelling me to go into a trance state.

"Graham." I straightened my spine and rested my hands, palms upwards, on my knees and listened. "It's happening again."

He grappled for my pad and pen on the nightstand. And then it started. As I verbalized the images that were being communicated to me telepathically, Graham scribbled down notes. (The comments and thoughts [in brackets] are what I interjected after reading his notes and reflect what I was experiencing during the transmission.)

18 June 1985–11:50 a.m.

Dr. Leonard is present, and a lady. She is something to do with [Graham], *but her presence is not very strong.*

Is my face changing? Feel pressure on left side.

Dr. Leonard's hands around my temples—gentle—relaxing me. He is raising and inspecting the back of my hands and wrists, telling me to let energy go. I'm seeing "needles" of energy going out through ends of my fingers, very relaxing. He's preparing me for something. Dr. L. is telling me to put hands on Graham's throat. [I wondered if he wanted me to strangle him?] *He is showing me how to heal.* [Phew!]

Dr. L and the lady are behind me now. They are discussing the best way to communicate with me. Writing is too strenuous for me (or them?). [Hey, I'm new at this! What did they expect?]

As if coming out of a deep sleep in which I was still awake, I felt the room and my body clear of the buzzing again. I glanced around the room and then at Graham to get my bearings. *Thank Heavens for him*, I thought. Would this be happening if he *wasn't* here? No way. I would have been calling the men in little white coats myself and ordering a straitjacket-to-go. But Graham just smiled beatifically at me as if channeling information from the beyond was on a par with tuning into the BBC for the six o'clock news. His trust in me was both touching and unsettling.

"Can you feel the energy in the room change just before it happens?" I asked. Maybe I *was* crazy? God knows, it ran in the family. Instead of my mother's schizoid outbursts, maybe this was my way of expressing our legacy of misguided brilliance.

"Yes, I can feel something," Graham replied, leaning over to reclaim his coffee cup from the bedside table. "It suddenly goes really quiet."

"Can you hear the buzzing?"

"Nope...." He saw my disappointed expression. "Sorry. I think it's your trip, Kate. I'm just along for the ride."

"But there's a reason why *you* are here, Graham. How many men do you know who would have the courage to do what you're doing? Or women for that matter." I pulled myself off the bed, stretched and peered out the window. The sky was a pale blue but a light cloudbank was moving in over the horizon. "I think the information is for you, too."

"Thanks a lot," Graham responded with a wry smile. "Just what I need, a warning about an earthquake and conversations with a bunch of dead people."

"I think it's going to get more interesting," I responded.

"Oh, no!" he said, his blue eyes twinkling.

After a brief walk along the beach, we returned and carried on talking into the night. I was right. It did get much, much more interesting. But not until two-thirty the next morning.

18 June 1985–2:33 a.m.

Feels like something big in the room. A lot of spirits here with us, all assembled over there [I pointed to the large space on my right]. *I recognize some: Granddad!* [my mother's father]. *He's very funny—always telling jokes, Joan* [somebody known to Graham], *and Dr. Leonard—cool draughts everywhere—Amanda* [my friend who died in a car crash]—*quite strong presence but she is just one of the crowd, Grandie* [this was my grandmother but she was still alive!] *is at the back observing, looking over everyone else at me. My sister, whom I never met* [at least, they told me she was the child my mother miscarried], *and a native Indian guide. A monk stands out* [I got the impression that he was another of my guides]. *Martha* [the lady who haunted my friend's house and whom I attempted to exorcize] *needs to heal or witness healing. There are many entities—students and teachers. These spirits are attracted by our questions, and though it is a big teaching for us, they also benefit. They tell me that spirits learn unlearned lessons vicariously through us on the earth plane.*

The room is full of anticipation, good high energy. My hands are tingling.

A being has just appeared in front of me. He/she is from another dimension, much higher evolution. Extremely high vibration. [The words Divine Intelligence came to mind.] *Asexual. Human form but not human. He/she is pure light, like the sun. Difficult to describe but s–o–o–o beautiful! So much joy.* [This brought tears to my eyes.] *Pure unadulterated joy! Like unconditional love, only much, much more intense.* [I was gasping as I felt this joy, like the warmth of the sun, washing through me.]

They are telling me life on earth is really just bottom line, very primal and animalistic. We are one of the most primitive species in the Universe. [Big surprise!] *We all have to experience the physical plane. This is the only planet that lives in such dense matter. Earth is actually only on the second rung of the ladder of evolution in the whole Universe.* [You mean, it could be worse than this?] *Life only gets better as we ascend that ladder but we live many, many lives in order to evolve to that higher intelligence.* [I think I already knew that.] *Divine Intelligence's (DI's) level of knowledge is far beyond our comprehension.*

Earth is just a tiny molecule in the whole scheme of our existence. What is above earth is beyond your belief systems. Those who exist above us laugh with us. They were here once, too. Humor permeates all levels. Humor is truth.

We won't leave earth until we understand and have mastered our emotions. If humans aren't willing to rise above ego, the emotions will destroy us. There is reincarnation for some if they don't get it right the first time. Others move on quickly to a new world. Everything is timeless. Evil only exists on earth. In higher dimensions, even those who evolve to higher levels but who then regress to lower vibrations through misuse of will still have to come back again and relearn their path. [Darn! No guarantees then, even "up there."]

The vibration of DI exists far above emotion. Only intelligence exists where they are, there is no emotion. Only what we understand as joy. They assure me that joy, the highest vibration of the Universe, is what we as a species are working towards. We will all get there eventually though how long it takes is up to us.

DI guides us but won't "do it for us." When we are ready, we are "injected" with intelligence by them.

Q: Where are you from?

[In response] *I am shown a big, black, shiny, fly-like object and am "told" it is one of their flying ships. I see one of their beings at the controls as they traverse space. They are showing me brilliant sunlight. I am astral traveling!—leaving earth now—traveling in space from planet to planet as they do. The entities go out from their planet around the galaxy all the time, teaching, very busy, like Piccadilly Circus.* [I smile at their tongue-in-cheek analogy.] *Showing me a planet behind a sun where they are from.* [They don't give me a name.] *As guardians of the Universe, they also have a strong connection with another five planets. To help us through this dramatic transition to higher consciousness, some of them (DI) are now manifesting on earth as our version of aliens* [the gray men with huge, black, almond-shaped eyes].

DI welcomes all the spirits in the room to this group discussion. We can ask anything we want. Showing me a bar in my hands as if I am lifting weights. [Are they showing me my strength or suggesting I join the gym?]

"They want us to ask questions," I told Graham. He shrugged, for the present too stunned to speak. So in my mind, I ask.

Q: What is it like where you are from?

A: You would have no conception, nothing to relate to. Bright—no nature there. There are different physical forms but not that you would recognize. We are of matter but we do not experience pain. No genitals [not like humans at least]. *No sex. Big heads. All communication is tele-pathic. There is much activity. No leaders, more harmony than on earth. Everyone has own role. Many triangles and angular shapes where they are. Don't feel emotion as we know it. They are much freer. There is no sleep.*

Q: What is my exact role?

A: You are going to be a teacher, a prophet, teach other psychics to go out and nurture people. Raising consciousness. You have much work to do. [Great!] *Many psychics are needed. The learning has already begun. It is a choice between fear and love. You will be one of those teachers, light-bearers. You can only reach those with a higher consciousness, those who are willing to hear. The many that you will teach will spread the word.*

[Are you sure I volunteered for this job?]

Feel a shift of energy.

I am now seeing earth from above. Turbulence around crust, volca-noes erupting, earth dividing. Disasters, wind, rain. Looking down from planet in outer space. Much tragedy, death, screaming. Disasters come in bursts during turn of the century and over a period of time. [Those poor people! Why is it happening and what will happen afterwards?]

It is all for the good. A vortex of self-destruction needs to be dis-sipated, shaken up. There will be very big changes on earth. Don't be afraid of physical changes, earthquakes, etc. Go with them. [Easy for you to say!] *It is a preparation for a landing from a higher dimension, a New World. Despite the fact that we will go through much pain, it is all for our highest good. There is great love for all on earth and for our ultimate good.*

Over the next 15 years, the energy on the planet is speeding up, get-ting faster and faster. It will bring both fear and excitement. All the souls on the earth plane will divide into two levels of consciousness. At first, there will be individuals who will rise up and speak of a different way of being. These individuals will attract others who are curious, who are reminded of a truth they already know. Then these clusters of people will join one another and form large groups until eventually the think-ing on the earth plane will divide into two: those who are ready and willing to go with the higher consciousness and those who, out of fear of losing control, want to hang on to the old pedagogy.

But these stubborn people will not be able to refute the force of what is coming into being. Like a tidal wave, it will overwhelm them. They will leave or be taken from the planet to another dimension and continue their evolution at their own pace. This other planet is still in the same galaxy but evolution is slower. [Can I go and visit? I think some people I know will be there.]

Those who are willing to let go and grow will at first experience chaos on earth. Eventually they will rise to the surface and experience a more peaceful world existing on this higher and lighter plane of consciousness. [Must remember to buy myself a lifejacket!]

Q: What if I can't do this? Do I have a choice?

A: You always have a choice. However, if you do not follow this path, you will regress. We are all either in the process of growing or regressing. To grow will require courage. You need to believe in yourself. Your life this time, in this context, is not your own. You agreed to do this work, and it is time for it to begin.

[Let me see that contract!]

You chose to be a master number, a leader, a channel and to learn to be a teacher. You can refuse it but you really want to do it. [I do?] *It will be very exhausting. You must look after your physical body.*

*Don't forget humor, to laugh, to **be** humor.* [I'm trying!] *Humor is an essence in itself, a connection to a higher level, a raising of consciousness.*

My grandfather is patting my hand. There is a lot of work to do, he tells me. Physically all will be taken care of—operate just on psychic level. People will come to me. I will be prominent in this field of truth and enlightenment. Earth needs to be prepared for a new society as it raises its vibration. Only ten per cent of earth people have higher consciousness at this time. [That many, huh?] *Must draw them to me and nurture them. Each spirit has something different to offer. I have been chosen to do this path.* [Oy, vey!]

DI is influencing my vibration, lifting me up. Feeling a powerful force available to me [as if every spirit in the room was giving me all their love and support].

Look towards the sun. There will be a sign from the sun when it is about to happen. Don't worry about anything. Just do the work and you will be taken care of. Relax.

Tingling in left leg.

The energy suddenly cleared, and coming to, I blinked and glanced around the dimly lit room. Apart from Graham, it was empty and still.

"Are they gone?" Graham asked, putting down his pen and yawning.

"Yes, but I don't think it's over." I stretched out my arms and legs, amazed at myself that I could sit for so long in that position without cramping.

"Can't wait," Graham chuckled. "Are they gonna let us get some sleep first?"

"What time is it?"

"Late. Or early, depending on which day you're talking about."

4:03 a.m. loomed in red from the clock radio by Graham's side. They were right. There was no conception of time.

"How do you feel?" Graham asked.

I shrugged. How *did* I feel? "Stunned...like sleeping beauty. As if I've been asleep for a hundred years, but instead of a prince coming to bring me back to life with a kiss, this wonderful being shone his light on me and I woke up. Soul-kissed."

"That's neat."

"Of course, I am also terrified that I might be going stark raving bonkers."

Metaphysical Endnote 21

Free Will or Destiny?

As I observed the patterns and the seeming unpredictability of others' lives, one question always plagued me. Is there an immutable design for a person's life written in stone, or can we choose our fate? Is there such a thing as luck where some higher being toys with us like figures in a chess game, or do we by definition of our own personalities determine our future?

I came to the conclusion that there are both free will and destiny. And with a heightened awareness, there is no fate that cannot be overcome.

As I read palms, I study the fate line which arises either from the center of the palm near the wrist, or from the Mount of the Moon, the mound on the lower, outer side of the hand. The fate line coming up from the bottom center of the palm is indeed an indication that the person has an Agreement, contract, karma or destiny to fulfill. The fate line arising out of the Mount of the Moon signifies that the person can enjoy more free will and is, in effect, a freer spirit.

In some ways, while having a destiny is somewhat restrictive, it can be easier for some than having free will. Your life purpose and the characters in your movie are more pre-determined. What is yours will come to you. The free will that you *do* have comes into play when you decide to learn the lessons that are presented to you. Or not.

Just as the person with a destiny to fulfill has some free will, so, in a similar paradox, does the free-willed spirit have a script. But rather than having all the details of the destiny filled in, the free-will script is more of an outline. Free spirits choose how and when and with whom they will do the work. Some find this amount of freedom daunting while others enjoy the lifetime of all lifetimes. While their script still includes lessons, there are no karmic ties to the past, not for this lifetime at least.

Like everything in metaphysics, there is a duality or polarity. Often clients will have a destiny fate line *and* a line of free will, a branch that emanates from the Mount of the Moon and joins into the fate line higher in the palm. This means that, at some point in the life, usually later when the lessons have been learned and the work is done, the person can enjoy a period of free spiritedness. A reward for work well done. Yahoo!

But whether you are in free will or destiny mode, know that you can change your challenges by rising above them. To do this, you will have to become spiritually awake, changing the Agreements on the subconscious and soul level.

So read on!

WHITE BEAR

Where was that tapping coming from? I opened my eyes. For a moment, the unfamiliar room was disorienting. Where was I? Something big had happened, hadn't it? Oh, yes. Divine Intelligence had popped in for a chat. The muted sunlight filtering through white net curtains and the sound of waves crashing on a beach immediately brought me back. I'm in Oregon.

"Hello?" I responded groggily, now aware that someone was knocking at the door.

"Room service!" Graham's muffled voice came through the heavy door. As I leapt out of bed, I noticed it was already 10:10 a.m.

Graham, bless his cotton socks, was outside my door clutching a tray with two big steaming cups of coffee, a selection of muffins and fruit salad.

"Couldn't let you sleep the day away." He smiled as he stepped into the room. "And you need sustenance before you talk to those aliens again."

"Do you think there's more?"

"Oh, yes."

19 June 1985–11:10 a.m.–Kate's room

Feel very strong force around me, hovering, strange. My body is heavy, feet are tingling. The energy is a dark, powerful, native Indian. My friend, Amanda, is telling me to relax. Her arm is around me. My mouth is also tingling. Dr. Leonard is here, too. Someone (an Indian?) is telling me to leave my body which is getting really heavy. Feel weight in my chest. (Taking long, deep breaths.) I am outside my body now.

Feel pain and relief at the same time. (Breathing still very heavy.)

Oh! I realize that I am Indian. His (or my) name is "White Bear." Showing me a native woman and child, his family. They were taken from him by the White Man. He's still very angry about that and needs to forgive. He has feathers around his head indicating his chief status and the lines on his face show his wisdom. He was an Indian chief who died too young. Sitting cross-legged like I do. There is a lot of sorrow about beautiful land. It was all theirs and it was taken away. Their spirits are angry.

Showing me the mountains with a river running through the valley below. He tells me that five mountains represent the five senses (?). Look at the mountains and you will see. He is standing on the side of hill looking at the scene. [I realize he is showing me British Columbia just before the White Man came and polluted the pristine wilderness.] *Spirits are angry at the way the land has been abused. They want to get rid of people who are greedy and ignoring the land. I see destruction. There is a road-like crack, a fault-line, running through the valley, going all the way up through B.C., north to Kamloops. The land is dividing, shifting in opposite directions. But this comes later. The Big One.*

Animals from the north are moving down. When the land cracks, the animals will go crazy. So sad. Land was so beautiful. The White Man has come and destroyed.

Although White Man is more sophisticated in one way, not so in another. He is greedy and doesn't care about having a relationship with the land. There will be an end to the world as it is now. A lot of people will be killed. I hear crying and moaning, see fire, terrible scenes, smoldering smoke and devastation. A long time before man comes back.

He is pointing up to a full moon and telling me that darkness will come before this event as a sign. Also a change in the sun. Not quite an eclipse but something similar. Showing me the "listen" sign. You can warn them but they won't listen. Some will take heed and know the time is come, others won't believe.

Q: Can I prevent this, warn people, change the outcome?

A: You can't change what will happen. It will happen anyway. [Not sure whether he is right about that.] *Tell people if you want. White Bear is still very bitter towards White Man. He is happy about the earthquake. White Man is stupid and blind. Don't they know they can have both? The richness is in the soil. He is showing me his hands, very old, weather-beaten. But his lifeline is short.*

[I feel for him and want to heal his pain.] *He is stuck in his anger and bitterness. I suggest that he release it. He will feel better and be able to move on.*

Tingling in my right big toe where he is putting on a ring. It is a gift for me of great honor, showing me acceptance and thanks. Looking at me with love. I ask him to help me with the earthquake information. By doing so, I tell him, he will cleanse himself of his bitterness and be free. But I feel his frustration. He wants to go to the top of the mountain, beat his chest, then cry and cry so the gods can hear. He wants to be rid of pain and feel at peace. He felt helpless when the White Man came and didn't know what to do to protect the land. He loves the mountains, his home.

He is now sitting looking up to God with open arms and receiving love, embracing the Universe. He wants to be forgiven. Dove of peace flying around him now. I ask him again to help me with the earthquake but he has difficulty helping the White Man. It is as if I am teaching him love. He trusts me. I remind him that if he helps me, it will be a cleansing for him, forgiveness and a letting go. He screams as he expresses and releases his pain.

Q: Where is the earthquake going to be?

Showing me a line down Burrard Inlet. A big hand is coming up from underneath the city and shaking it. Water is separating and going up on each side, just to scare people. Not too much damage but enough to bring in awareness. Those who don't believe will stay and be destroyed....

For the next two hours, I was shown in great detail two "movies" of the earthquake to take place in Vancouver, one through the eyes of White Bear and another more factual account. Graham wrote everything down. At the end, White Bear didn't want to leave my body but just sit there and be in a physical body for a while. I gave him five minutes and then asked him to leave. I wanted my body back.

When it was over, Graham and I, both in shock, took the TR7 with the roof down for a scenic drive along the coast, letting the wind blow through our hair and our minds, trying to feel part of the normal world again.

Over dinner, as we sat on a patio looking out over a colorful array of boats lazing at their moorings in the early summer evening sun, I quipped, "This whole experience has been like the vision—an earth-shaking initiation into the psychic sisterhood!"

"Well, not the brotherhood. Sorry dear, but the earth didn't move for me." Graham chuckled.

"But the question is," I said more seriously, "what do I do with it?"

"Before you tell anybody anything, the first thing I would do is type up those notes and take them to a lawyer. Get them notarized."

"Why?"

"Oh, I dunno. Just a feeling. For your protection maybe. And then it's on record."

Metaphysical Endnote 22

Channeling

Some would say that we are all channels, receivers of sacred information from a higher source or Divine Intelligence. In my experience this is only partially true. We all have the potential to be channels, but I believe the quality and quantity of channeling is in direct correlation to the surrendering of the ego, to the vibrational frequency of the physical being and to the spiritual awareness of the channeler. To be a clear channel, we have to be willing to let go.

While some of us are indeed used as channels for the odd words of wisdom, we can also receive our own spiritual guidance. Many artists know that when they are in that state of creative bliss while composing, writing or painting they are channeling from a higher power, divine source, or at least their higher self. Creation is not coming from them, but through them.

If we are willing to suspend our egos for a while, we can all access intelligence of whatever we need to know. This intelligence often comes to us in our dreams when the ego is sleeping, but very few of us pay attention to that information.

During the '80s, spiritual channelers were popping up frequently to teach new age wisdom. Seth, who came through Jane Roberts, was popular again; Ramtha came through J.Z. Knight. Lazarus and Aurora were two other well-known entities that channeled through willing and evolved receivers. While the information those channelers voiced was, for us hungry spiritual seekers of the era, indeed enlightening, there were others claiming to be channels who made a big drama of entering a trance and then spouted verbiage from what, I suspected, was a disturbed subconscious mind. While some listeners gave them credence, I felt that the information was diluted by shades of a murky ego. So I left quietly by the back door.

I questioned why channelers needed to go into trance to receive this illuminating information. Don't they want to be present for it? Or on some level are they conscious of what is happening? Apparently, it depended on the person through whom the information was coming. While a few channelers told me they were aware of what was being communicated, some said they went "to the other side" or astral-traveled while their bodies were used as transmitters. But if a channeler's ego didn't voluntarily move out of the way, these wise old spirits would gently push that channeler's ego somewhere else so that the information could come through pure, unsullied and unlimited by ego thoughts.

Whatever you want to channel, whether it be occasional pearls of wisdom, your own guidance, mind-blowing art or Divine Intelligence's message to the earthlings, I believe we are all capable. There are, however, a few prerequisites.

❖ We have to be willing to suspend our own limited beliefs. This means temporarily completely shutting down the ego mind (the pea-brain level), so no dark or even remotely shady thoughts can cloud the channeling. If they are present, you may not channel the higher vibrations.

❖ Our energy has to be "clean" enough for the vibration that we are channeling. Cleanliness *is* next to Godliness. Flush out the lower vibrational energies in the emotional body such as resentment, fear, and anger. Also alcohol, junk food and drugs will definitely muddy the waters in the physical body and lower your vibration. Minimize or abstain.

❖ Just as the psychic uses intense focus to attune to spirit, it is equally challenging for the spirit to come down to our denser physical level. So the lighter your vibrations, the easier it is for spirit to commune with you. To be a channel for the highest and the best, we first need to be the highest and the best.

Although spirits show up regularly around me during my readings, and some of them want to come into my physical being—I can tell by the cold prickles on the back of my neck—I let them know it is not necessary for their spirits to enter my physical body to communicate. So I ask these visitors to telepathically show me what they need to express. And they do. My clients and I are often in tears, but many times they are tears of relief, solace and joy.

Like many other healers and psychics, I often channel in my readings. The information and the words that come to me are coming either from the querent's guides, my guides or the client's various levels of consciousness. I know that as I continue to work toward a higher consciousness and a higher frequency, the information that I channel will also be of a higher vibration. And when *your* spirit is willing to totally let go and surrender, the messages that come through *you* will also be of a higher vibration.

EARTHQUAKE!

Suffice it to say that on my return from Oregon I was a changed person, stunned, overwhelmed, excited and scared. What was I supposed to do with this information? Darn, I had forgotten to ask Divine Intelligence that question. It lay heavily on my spirit like a big bad meal. I wanted to share it, but with whom? Would my friends think I was crazy? Of course they would! I was still wondering whether I was unhinged myself. My self-doubt would hardly inspire confidence in others.

Well, first I would take Graham's advice and draft a letter to a Notary Public.

To Whom It May Concern:

My name is Kate Rosewood. I currently reside in Point Grey, Vancouver. I am a psychic.

On 17 June 1985, using the medium of automatic writing, I was given the message by Dr. Gordon Leonard (deceased) that on July 11 (no year), there would be an earthquake in Vancouver.

The message from the automatic writing was followed by two separate visions of where the earthquake would strike. Here is a summary of those visions.

Chinatown and Gastown are the main areas suffering structural damage. Something (or someone?) falling from the Sears Tower. Also a large building in that area might endure damage. The railway station and buildings at the junction of Hastings and Chinatown crumble. One of the yellow towers of the North Shore chemical plant, just below Lions Gate, explodes. Some land and houses on the North Shore slide closer to the water. But although there would be a lot of movement, there would not be many injuries sustained there. One part of the North Shore might break away in the Deep Cove area. West Vancouver, for some reason, is not really affected. Downtown, on Burrard between Georgia and Pender, buildings are stable, but I see glass exploding out of windows and people being cut and in shock. Glass everywhere. There is traffic chaos in that area, a bus colliding with a car and some black snake-like hoses (?) coming up through Georgia Street in front of the Royal Bank. I see a ship, possibly a freighter, being thrown against a seawall or onto the street, and a large crack running across Georgia at Jervis or Bute. There is a black line (?) running down Robson, water boiling over somewhere, a fire or explosion in one of the buildings on Robson, possibly the Sheraton. A woman is blown against a glass storefront, possibly from the black lines coming up through the street. While standing on Burrard in front of St. Paul's, I can hear a large explosion coming from somewhere else in the city. Or is it a volcanic explosion from even farther away? St. Paul's Hospital may have to be evacuated.

Lions Gate Bridge is yawing over, twisting, and may come apart in the middle. People are leaving their cars and running, panicking, although some are paralyzed and staying where they are. A pink building on English Bay will suffer damage. I see a body fall from a high window there. South West Marine Drive and parts of Richmond are flooded and something happens to the Oak St. Bridge although that is not clear. A piece of land around UBC area separates. The roof of the stadium will collapse or be unsafe. There is a lot of water displacement in Burrard Inlet and around the Coast, but I don't feel it is a massive tidal wave or tsunami.

Psychically, I sense that the earthquake will strike between 9:00 and 12:00 a.m. on July 11. Though I have no year, intuitively I feel it will be a Wednesday and a very, very hot summer's day with the temperature in the 100-degree range. The main shock will occur between 11:00 and 11:10 a.m. with at least one after-shock twenty-five minutes later.

In addition to these visions, two years ago, while living in the British Properties and looking out over the city, I received another image of a crack running through downtown Vancouver from east to west and a picture of the downtown core sinking into sand...

Then I called the Geological Institute in Sidney, Vancouver Island.

"Hello," I started nervously as I was put through to Dr. Hyndman*, one of the top geologists in B.C. "I am a psychic (this sounded very strange) and I have just experienced two detailed visions about an earthquake in Vancouver."

He didn't hang up, burst out laughing, or even sneer. "Yes?"

Encouraged, I continued. Choosing to edit out the Indian spirit who had "shown" me the vivid pictures, I relayed the whole vision to him while he listened intently. "I have some questions though," I concluded.

"Yes?"

"There wouldn't be a wind in an earthquake would there? Why do I see a woman blown against a window storefront on Robson Street?"

Without faltering, he responded, "The black snake-like things you saw bursting up through the streets would be gas mains."

"Oh."

I waited for a *Thank-you-very-much-don't-call-us-we'll-call-you.* But there was just a stunned silence on the other end. "Does it make any sense to you?" I asked finally.

"Well, actually, it's quite amazing."

"It is?"

"Mel Blaney*, Head of Emergency Services in Vancouver, and I wrote an article about what would happen hypothetically in an earthquake of 6.7 on the Richter scale. We based it on the technical and geological data we have."

"And?"

"It's eerily similar to your vision."

Aaagh!

"I'll send you a copy and you can see for yourself."

Now there are times as a psychic when you really want to be validated, to be told that what you saw actually did manifest in "real life," that you're not crazy. But this was not one of those times.

"Thank you," I murmured ungratefully.

Oh, God. What do I do now?

As if in response to my thought, he said, "You should get in contact with Mel Blaney. He's British, an ex-RAF pilot. You should probably tell him."

Oh, no! Not an ex-Air Force pilot. I had flown with many of them. As a breed, they were about as open to anything metaphysical as the

---

* Real names.

Pope. Yeah, he's going to *really* welcome a novice psychic with a huge vision of disaster.

I received the article in the mail a few days later. As I read it, my skin broke out in goose bumps. What Dr. Hyndman and Mel Blaney had written *was* my vision but in more horrific detail. Perhaps I had telepathically picked up on this exact information and turned it into a vision.

I consulted with Graham. What should I do?

"Well, if this is going to happen," he suggested sagely, "maybe you're not the only one to pick up on it. There must be other psychics out there."

Yes, that was it. Maybe if I was lucky, I could off-load this responsibility onto someone else. Calling all psychics! Calling all psychics!

Ten days later, after doing some speedy networking, I met with twelve professional and semi-professional psychics, Mel Blaney and Shelley Hanes, a young reporter from the Vancouver *Sun*. We gathered together in a friend's spacious but cozy living room. As Mr. Blaney introduced Shelley, he explained he had brought her hoping to get some media coverage around earthquake awareness.

I was wrong about Mel Blaney. He was a white-haired, handsome man casually but smartly dressed in a denim shirt and jeans. Instead of the cynicism I was expecting, he greeted me with a firm, warm handshake and thanked me effusively for including him in our meeting. Did I sense shades of relief in him, too? Maybe he felt like I did. Now he wouldn't be the only one to carry this burden.

Shelley Hanes, the reporter, didn't look older than 19. Tall and slim, she sat woodenly on her chair, her body stiff as if she was afraid even to twitch. Her eyes darted around the room as though she had wandered into the padded cell of a loony bin by mistake and was now surrounded by dangerous inmates. I supposed to the uninitiated it would be unnerving to be in the midst of such a motley collection of psychics. What *did* she think we were going to do in front of her? Start swiveling heads and spewing green ectoplasm?

I introduced myself to the group, explained why I had invited everyone, shared the details of what I had seen and then asked if anyone else had "received" any impressions or dates about an earthquake.

Out of the twelve psychics present that night, five had seen, felt or intuited visual information.

Vivian, a strong clairvoyant whom I had visited several times, stated emphatically, "It will happen in 1986." A year from now. While

Vivian's premonitions and mine meshed somewhat—she didn't envision anything happening to the Lions Gate Bridge—I hoped she was right about the date. At least we would know.

Deirdre, another older psychic, said she was walking her dog on the beach one day when she saw a flash of a huge wave coming towards her right down Burrard Inlet. Even her dog reacted to her vision, or his own, by growling and cowering in fear.

Mel Blaney, I noticed, furiously scribbled notes while the reporter's eyes just got bigger and more scared. Like a white-knuckler on a bumpy flight, if she hadn't been paralyzed by her own fear and frozen to her seat, she would have bolted.

The group discussed whether we should contact a radio station and do an interview providing specific details of our visions.

"I'm wondering if that's a wise way to go," I cautioned. "We don't want to scare everyone. If we plant the vision in people's minds, we might even create it. I don't want to be responsible for that." The group murmured agreement.

Mr. Blaney suggested that he initiate a program to make people more "quake aware" as in Los Angeles. "We definitely need to educate the population of Vancouver about how to be prepared and what to do in the event of such a disaster." Now that sounded like good common sense. "If you can believe this, many people are still unaware that we live in an earthquake zone."

Ahem! I had been one of those.

"We're thinking about putting more information in the front pages of BC Tel's phone book," he continued.

Good.

When we were done, Mr. Blaney thanked us all and invited us to contact him should we receive any more visions or other pertinent data. "I'll take all this information into account and be in touch with Kate."

Frank Vanyk, a psychic researcher, began talking about the future of the planet and how human beings would eventually, due to a much higher level of consciousness, be able to live without food, teleport our bodies and communicate telepathically. Vivian agreed but had slightly different interpretations of how the future planet would evolve. I just listened, while attempting to reconcile their visions with what I had seen in Oregon. Some of their prophecies matched mine and some didn't. Interpretation of psychic information can give rise to a lot of ambiguities. Who is to say who is right? The future would speak for itself.

Now they had moved on to talking about philosophy. "We're here to control our emotions," Vivian stated.

"Master them," I piped up. To me the word "control" implied repression, like caging a lion. Mastering was allowing the lion out but having trained it to use its raw power wisely.

"Control them," Vivian snapped back. As Monty Python said, I didn't come here for an argument. Psychics are renowned for their huge egos, and unsure of my own tentative place amongst these professionals, I deferred to her seniority.

Mr. Blaney stood up and thanked me. Shelley, seeing this as her opportunity to finally flee, quickly scooped up her bag and followed him, almost in his shoes, to the door.

The next day, I called Shelley to find out if she would be writing an article about our meeting.

Now safely back in her own environment and surrounded by her own kind, she stated firmly, "No. It isn't something the paper thought was appropriate at this time." *Quelle surprise!* But a big part of me experienced relief. Maybe they were right.

A week later, Mel Blaney called me at the house. "We've decided all we can do is make more people aware of what to do in the event of a large earthquake. We're putting four pages in the front section of the phone books, but our budget won't run to a Quake Aware program like in LA. However, what we *are* going to do is start a psychic hotline."

"What's that exactly?"

"If any psychic gets a premonition, vision or dream about anything, a bomb, earthquake, volcanic eruption, plane crash, they can register it on the psychic hotline. If more than one psychic independently registers a premonition of an event, then emergency services go on alert."

"Great idea. I'll let the other psychics know."

I thanked him, grateful to Mr. Blaney for his open-mindedness and the fact that he was taking action.

Well, I thought, mentally washing my hands of the whole affair, *I'm off the hook. I have done everything in my power to warn people.*

But had I?

A few days later, I presented my completed letter to the young lawyer.

...I have informed Dr. Rogers* and Dr. Hyndman of the Geophysical Society in Sidney on Vancouver Island, Mr. Mel Blaney at Vancouver City Hall and Shelley Hanes of the Sun. *I also called C-Fox Radio and spoke to Joanna requesting that they do an item on earthquakes in order*

to ensure that the population is aware of what to do in the event of this emergency. Her news editor turned down the idea.

I am well aware as a psychic that timing is often difficult for us to pinpoint, as we are not dealing with time but space. My intention in informing the aforementioned people was not to spread panic but to awaken people to the fact that a large earthquake is imminent and they have the information available. Preparation could save a lot of lives.

I arranged a meeting with the other psychics for Friday, 5 July 1985, to discover whether I had been the only one with a vision. Approximately twelve psychics attended. Mr. Blaney and Shelley Hanes from the Sun *were also present. Five other psychics had experienced the same or similar visions, and we felt the tremors would commence this year. The major quakes could begin in 1986. The tremors are a warning.*

I believe that a lot of people who are not even necessarily highly intuitive are also picking up on the vibrations. We discussed the possibility of organizing a psychic clearing house for all psychic predictions concerning major emergencies as is done in California. I volunteered to provide that link until Mel Blaney has spoken to the Provincial Government. He feels it would certainly be of great value.

I feel I have done all I can do. In the meantime, I am asking people to pray for our safety.

Kate Rosewood – 9 July 1985.

As the handsome young lawyer scribbled his signature across his notary impression at the bottom of my letter, he nervously glanced around his office on the tenth floor of the downtown building with its large glass windows and said, "I won't charge you."

Metaphysical Endnote 23

The Curse of Being a Psychic

No wonder I shied away from my destiny as a psychic. Much of the time, being known as a psychic is just not comfortable. I am not alone. Hiding in the psychic closet is also common amongst my extra-sensorially gifted colleagues and students. We are weary of the sixteenth-century ignorance that still pervades the present mass consciousness, the snide comments, the inane jokes and the old perception of being "cuckoo."

But is all this dismissiveness really disbelief or a deeply entrenched fear?

After all, it's not as if "Understanding the Psychic" is taught in schools. Because psychic communication has never been explained, many people are still understandably ignorant of how the psychic works. Even in this age of enlightenment and wonderful technology, including fiber optics, digital everything and cellular communication, not to mention good old electricity, why do the masses still refuse to believe in thought transference? "Seeing is believing" is still the mantra of most. *Yawn!* Let's move on, folks. Haven't we noticed that it works the other way around. Only when we believe can we see.

The disbelievers spout a litany of *really* corny jokes such as, "Oh, I don't have to tell *you!*" or, "But you would know *that.*" These are followed by gales of uproarious laughter. I wait for the hilarity to subside before I can proceed with an intelligent conversation. (My career as a flight attendant prepared me well. One just smiles beatifically and continually thinks up fresh and funny retorts, like the one to the older man on one flight who was trying to get the stewardess's attention by furiously clicking his fingers. The stewardess calmly approached his seat, leaned over and whispered, "I'm very sorry, sir, but we don't allow flamenco dancing on this aircraft.")

But I understand the disbeliever's confusion. (Just one reason for writing this book.)

My own development was a two-part process: first I was tuning in and seeing, then I had to understand *how* I was tuning in and seeing.

The most common misconceptions about psychics are:

❖ People think you know everything, especially winning lottery numbers. According to Gandhi, having wealth without work is one of the world's greatest sins. Being psychic is an awareness and is meant to be used for a higher purpose than the mere acquisition of wealth. (But hey, I still buy lottery tickets.)

❖ People think you are reading minds all the time. When I see their wary expressions, I reassure them with, "Don't worry. You have to pay me to work."

❖ People think you can predict anything, anywhere, anytime. If I was tuned in all the time, then I would be crazy. Generally, I only "switch on" for a reading.

❖ Some people think you remember every single little detail about their reading. I am channeling and I do not absorb into my conscious mind everything that passes from my lips. But I do my best.

❖ People think you know absolutely everything about everything. If I were that smart or that highly evolved, I wouldn't be here. (Perhaps having won the lottery, I would be relaxing on a beach in Barbados?)

❖ People think that to be a psychic is somehow unchristian. So why does the Bible write of prophets? And why did God give us the psychic gift? My spirituality honors all religions.

❖ Sometimes people call me "fortuneteller." Aaagh! I do not tell fortunes. But I do guide my clients towards their highest future potential, give them a deeper understanding of who they are and what they are creating with their thinking, reassure them when they are on the right track, suggest more positive alternatives when they are out of balance, encourage them not to give up on themselves, expose their latent talents and facilitate healing of their wounded spirits with messages from deceased friends and relatives. I also teach them that they have the ability to know all these truths by listening and trusting their own inner voice. But I do not tell fortunes!

My theory about the ignorance, and sometimes downright rudeness, of some people in relation to psychics is that they are afraid. We all retain a cellular memory of our past lives and on some level we remember the inquisitions, the genocides, the witch-hunts and persecutions of our past, when it wasn't safe to express our thoughts, to be different or, especially as women, to have power. So it is more comfortable to shun the psychic, to make inane jokes and to pretend that being psychic is not a part of who we all are at our highest potential.

But then that is just one advantage of being a psychic. I can see the truth.

OVERLOAD AND SHUTDOWN

My first instincts on meeting Mrs. Helman had proved correct. After six months, I was still enjoying my time in the mansion. And I enjoyed the children though felt some sadness for them. Their mother had died suddenly, their second (step)mother had also left and now they were living in a mausoleum of a house, the children at one end, their father and their newest stepmother at the other with an intercom as a means of connection. Though there was genuine affection between Mrs. Helman and her nine- and eleven-year-old stepchildren, quality outweighed quantity. Whenever the children had the chance to sit at the breakfast bar while I prepared meals, they would gush conversation as if they had been locked up in solitary confinement. I knew I would also have to leave them eventually and felt like the traitor that I was.

I continued to meet with Graham and receive more channelings. The information coming through was not as dramatic as in Oregon, and I began to doubt the validity of the odd ramblings of my mind. The thought that none of this was real was a constant. On another level, I knew it was very, very real and not just the over-imagining of an underworked brain.

Then one night, sitting alone in my apartment in the dark and staring out at the sparkling nightlights of the illuminated downtown Vancouver, another vision came to me, unwanted and unbidden.

This time I saw the city of New York, the high-rises of Manhattan engulfed in a yellow, fire-like light. At first, I thought it was a nuclear bomb, but because it was confined to the inner city and there was no nuclear fall-out, the image didn't make sense. Why was the destruction so contained in Manhattan? I was "shown" an Arab leader as the perpetrator of this atrocity.

Then I traveled (or was taken) in time to a period after the event. The United States had sunk into a great depression. The whole land mass was covered in black as though it had caved in on itself. I was "told" that it was karma for all that country's past arrogance and simplistic, skewed values. While I felt that this event wouldn't happen for many years to come, there were no exact dates and no details, maybe because this time I didn't ask and I didn't want to know. To have the responsibility for yet another disaster on my mind was the last thing I needed. Nor did I want to see more destruction and pain. If this is what being psychic meant, Divine Intelligence could keep it.

The next day I called Graham and told him I wanted to "cool it" for a while.

"That's just fine with me," he said, a smile in his voice. "It gets a bit overwhelming after a while, chuck, so God knows what it's like for you."

Like floating out in space without a lifeline, I thought. I felt strange, *too* connected and disconnected from others at the same time, as though I couldn't be near people without chunks of their energy attaching themselves to me. If I spent time in others' company, afterwards I had a great need to be alone for even longer periods until I had literally brushed off their energy and I could be just me again.

A lot of the time, I was also out of my body.

They say that on average every one of us astral travels approximately thirty times in a day. That's while we are in a conscious, waking state. The lights are on but nobody is home. I knew I was exceeding that number, more out than in, gone from home. The worst thing was I didn't *want* to be in the physical. My body felt heavy and dense and required so much work bathing, grooming and feeding. Being in the physical was to me a drag. I found myself able to vacate my body at will and be in spirit on the other side of the room. I just had to think of myself out of my body in another place and there I was, this wonderful, light being.

Mrs. H noticed my vacant stares, my lack of concentration, my inattention to details, and kindly but firmly informed me, "If you don't want to be here, I can easily find a replacement." She didn't have to remind me that I had a cushy job.

"I know. I'm sorry," I responded, genuinely apologetic.

For about ten seconds I considered confiding in her about my experiences, but wonderful as she was, she may not have allowed me within spitting distance of her stepchildren. So I chose to stay quiet. That same night, I had a nightmare. The images weren't as disturbing as the fears they aroused.

I was sitting in one of the comfy armchairs in my apartment living room. A large, black, amoeba-like energy oozed out of the cupboard in the wall and came over to the chair where I was sitting. It spun the chair around and around faster and faster until I felt I would be flung, spinning, to the outer reaches of the Universe, never to set foot on earth again.

I sat bolt upright in bed, wary of the darkness that surrounded me.

After I had calmed down and reassured myself it was just a dream, I decided that was it! All these visions, channelings, out-of-body experiences were too much for me. I needed help. The next day, I called FrankVanyk, the Psychic Researcher, and made an appointment.

As I sat in front of him in his small, technology-filled, normal-looking office, he closed his eyes and tuned in. "You are a very powerful psychic."

Yes...and...?

"You're a conscious medium."

I frowned.

"You don't need to go into trance to receive information. You just see things."

Now that explained a lot.

"Not too many like you out there." He smiled.

This is a good thing!

"But you're wide open at the moment, ungrounded."

Yep.

"You need to close off your energy. When you're wide open like that, just anybody or anything can get in. You might be prone to psychic attacks."

I relayed my nightmare to him.

"Yes, that was a psychic attack."

"I knew it didn't feel like an ordinary dream. Very disturbing. How do I close down?"

Frank guided me through a grounding exercise which closed off my psychic energy. As I left his office, I decided that now my chakras were closed, they could stay closed. If I was a physical body here on the earth plane, a human being with all its inherent physical requirements, then

I would have to live as one, behave as one. Despite Divine Intelligence's warning, I was determined to put this psychic business out of my head. *Sorry guys,* I told them. *Just can't do it.*

Mrs. H was happy to have the old me back.

Metaphysical Endnote 24

Grounding

You don't necessarily have to be psychic to go through periods where you feel disconnected from reality, as if you might float out into space, never to be seen again. Whenever any of us experiences complex emotions or spends too much time in our heads, keeping our feet on the ground can be a challenge. At these times, we are liable to become ungrounded because we are giving away too much of our energy to something or someone else. To center, we need to bring our thoughts and emotions back to the Self.

When psychics are ungrounded, however, it is downright scary because their energy becomes untamed, unfocused and unchanneled. Their eyes can take on a vacant or, even worse, a crazed look, and that is when psychics can be vulnerable to other chaotic energies.

So how do the ungrounded, both those aware of their psychic ability and those who are not, get back down to earth where they can function intelligently in the material world again?

Grounding, just like electricity, is about balancing all the energies. It is necessary to be present in the body as well as the mind. Meditation, gardening or just focusing on your kneecaps can do it for some people. But to make really sure your feet are firmly planted on terra firma, you can do the following exercise. (This process can also be used for healing, relaxing and manifesting.)

Sit upright in a chair with your feet firmly planted on the ground, hip width apart. Make sure your spine is straight in order to allow a clearer channel. Rest your hands, palms upright on your thighs.

Close your eyes and take three very deep breaths from the stomach area—your solar plexus and the seat of your intuition. Inhale through the nose, hold for three and exhale through the mouth. As you exhale, imagine a huge bowl directly in front of you. Imagine you are blowing all your tensions, fears and worries into that bowl and that your angels are taking them away while you just relax. (Don't worry. You can get them back afterwards.) Once you are relaxed, settle into a nice steady rhythm of breathing, and for a few minutes just focus on your breath, your spirit.

Now imagine that way, way up in the Universe is a huge sun of brilliant white light. This you recognize as Divine Intelligence, the source of your higher power. As you observe it and feel its brilliance, you see that a beam of white light is emanating from that sun and heading towards your aura and physical body. As you feel it enter your body through the crown chakra on the top of your head, you experience the light as a warm, soothing liquid gently permeating your skull, your brain and your facial muscles, relaxing and healing as it progresses. The light liquid then filters down, suffusing your neck and shoulders, all the way down your spine, melting away any tension there. At the same time, this healing light is traveling through your throat, heart and stomach, rebalancing each chakra as it goes. Eventually this whole liquid light travels through every cell in your body, taking with it any tension, stress or discomfort. Feel it as it travels all the way through your groin area, down your legs and into your feet.

The beam of light eventually leaves your body through the soles of your feet and continues to the core of the earth where there is another source of sun-like energy. Observe as this beam of light that has traveled from your body joins with this core energy. As it does, all your negative lower vibrations can be transmuted into a higher vibration of energy. In your mind, ask for whatever you feel you need at this time: forgiveness, clarity, strength, centeredness, faith, trust, willingness, surrender, wisdom, kindness and/or compassion. See how this core energy becomes even more radiant or changes color as it increases in vibration. Then observe as this more radiant beam of transmuted energy now travels back from this core at the center of the earth towards your body and enters your physical being again through the soles of your feet. This time, the light travels up through every muscle, bone and cell in your body, filling you with the intelligence you asked for. As it does, you feel the increase in vibration in your own body. The radiant light passes quickly through the trunk and out of your body at the top of your head. Observe as it reaches all the way up and joins again with the source in the Universe. If you choose to, you can now go into a meditation or creative visualization or just stay relaxed for a while. When you are ready, you can open your eyes and return to the room. You are now grounded.

And when you don't have time for this exercise, just bring all your thoughts back to you, your body in the present time, in your present environment. Now you are in the present, just focus on your kneecaps. There now, doesn't that feel good?

GRANDIE'S FUNERAL OR MINE?

*I*t was 1986, the year the Challenger exploded before our very eyes on televisions in living rooms, my first year as a bona fide landed immigrant in Canada, the year of my foray into working with street kids, and the year my grandmother died.

After leaving the Helmans', I moved with three friends into a large house in Kitsilano, just a few blocks from the beach. I continued to study metaphysics and started a business which I believed was needed and would help people. Maybe my motivation was to compensate Divine Intelligence for not following my psychic path: to assuage my cowardly guilt, I did the next best thing. It would be years before I would be able to look back on this time and realize that Divine Intelligence had meant it when they said that if I refused the psychic path, I would regress. Well, they were right. My life soon descended into chaos and stayed there for a lo–o–o–o–ng time.

I called my project the Focus Support Network, the idea being to connect people who needed people: fledgling entrepreneurs with business consultants and people who needed physical and nutritional guidance with trusted practitioners who could provide emotional counseling and spiritual guidance to lost souls.

On a rare phone call from England, when I had endeavored to explain the concept to Grandie, she commented wistfully, "I wish it was something a little more *tangible*, dear." But I smiled at her mild disapproval. Little did I know they would be her last words to me.

Ultimately, I envisioned the Focus Support Network situated in a huge, rambling property or converted warehouse where I would rent out rooms to accountants, yoga teachers, healers, and counselors. In this supportive environment would be a dance studio, art classes, a music lab and a place where teens could discover their creative selves, perhaps with a bistro in the center as the meeting place. Eventually, when it became a club, a place for people to belong, we would publish a newsletter for all members. Ten per cent of the profits would support those in crisis, those who wanted to grow but couldn't afford the necessary guidance at the time. Once they were on their feet, they would repay the Network and thereby fund some other person in need and facilitate another's healing.

That was the vision.

And then Pamela showed up.

She was a 30-something, dynamic, petite, high-energy, Montreal-Jewish single mother-of-two with a singing voice to send shivers down your spine. As a hypno-therapist she used her huge, laughing blue eyes to their full potential. An Englishman who stopped me one evening on the stairs of my health club had introduced her to me. He didn't know why, he said, but he had felt guided to put Pamela and me together. When I met the little fireball, I understood.

We had the same vision.

Well, at first, anyway. Then Pamela wanted to change the focus. Instead of giving ten per cent of the profits to the generally unsupported, she decided that the whole project should cater specifically to street kids.

"Street kids!" I responded, aghast. "Isn't that a little dangerous?"

As her huge eyes bored into mine, she said, "Kate, they're just children who need a good home."

Well, that was it. Something clicked inside me (I am convinced she hypnotized me), and the deal was sealed. Though I was scared of what we were taking on, I pushed my trepidations aside and my plan was revamped.

You might be thinking at this point that we would have to be crazy to take on a project of such magnitude without any experience in that area except our own affection-starved backgrounds. And maybe that was enough. But you wouldn't be wrong either. The thought, *are you quite mad?* popped into my mind at least once every day.

So back to the drawing board we went. Instead of a business, we opted to start a society. Instead of making money, we would have to raise it. We spread the word amongst our wealthy and not-so-wealthy acquaintances and friends, one of whom sponsored us to fly to San Francisco to tour the Delancey Street Foundation. Totally inspired by their success, we chose to model our own project on their system. On our return, we contacted numerous corporations, radio stations and government agencies to raise funds, and we consulted with non-profit organizations that were already working with street kids for advice. Pamela and I were going to save the world, well, at least the street kids of Vancouver.

Meanwhile, in my chosen role as a *non-psychic*, I attempted to put the whole psychic business behind me and focus on being like everyone else—normal.

It didn't work.

Though I was known as a palmist amongst friends and acquaintances and I was sought out regularly for readings, my talents were viewed (by me anyway) as a conversation piece or party trick more than a serious clairvoyant ability. One day, another Mastery "cultee," Rebecca, who was a dabbling Tarot card reader, asked me for a reading. She seemed to be in crisis so I agreed. Rebecca was my age with intense blue eyes and a keen intelligence. She was in total rebellion against her Jewish background, so much so that she lived a Gypsy life with her ten-year-old son. But when we sat in my cramped bedroom, cross-legged on the bed, I saw a huge veil of anger in both her palms, a layer of white misty energy that wouldn't allow me to see beyond or underneath it.

"You're really mad at someone, aren't you?" I grinned.

Rebecca didn't smile back.

"This anger is coming up now to be healed. Feels like your parents are the culprits or at least you feel that they are."

Rebecca rolled her eyes and snorted. "They are."

"This is interesting. It's as if your anger is taking up all your energy. There's no room for anything else."

"Wouldn't surprise me."

"Rebecca, you need to deal with that anger first. I can't see anything beyond that. When it's resolved, come back for another reading. Then and only then will I be able to see your future. Does that make any sense?"

"Yes, actually, it makes perfect sense."

I continued to tune into the energy emanating from her palms. Suddenly, what was in her parents' minds came to me, and I was able to communicate their side of the story to Rebecca. While they felt a lot of love for their daughter, being devout Jews they were stubbornly refusing to give up their expectations of how she should behave. And Rebecca, as the daughter, not only totally rebelled against those expectations but also refused to give up *her* demands of how her parents should allow her those choices. Each side wanted the other to see them for who they really were and be accepted.

"Maybe if you let go of your expectations and let them just be who they are and still do your thing, the relationship will be a lot easier between you."

Rebecca nodded, inspecting the lines on her hand.

"Their opinion of you is important to you; otherwise you wouldn't care. But you do. You need to have a good honest chat with your parents," I added. Even though her eyes reflected understanding, I had little faith that Rebecca would take my advice. But that was up to her.

The expectations impasse between parents and children would be a common dynamic that I would encounter in future readings, but the first time I saw it, something huge was revealed to me. Not only could I read the minds of my client who sat before me, I could also see into the beliefs of those people affecting my clients. It felt good to be able to pass on to Rebecca the different perspectives of those involved.

When I came downstairs after the reading, Keith, one of my room-mates, commented, "You know, Kate, I've noticed that whenever you do a reading, you have this glow about you afterwards. It's good for you."

I had to admit it, Keith had a point. Readings were something that flowed through me, like a meditation. Afterwards, I felt calm, as if something had been released *through* me. I wondered if it was like an artist after having channeled a painting. I was well aware that medi-tation would be healthy but I was too afraid to let my mind go. What images would I see? More disasters?

Keith's comments made me reconsider. Should I put a sign on my door that read *Psychic Readings Here*? Or should I just keep a low pro-file and provide them to friends and acquaintances, by request only. Although my palmistry sessions were still freebies—I didn't feel good enough to charge—I sensed that, even as a "non-psychic," my readings were becoming stronger, more accurate, the images and their interpre-tations becoming clearer to me.

And then Grandie died.

After twenty years of hearing Grandie state without complaint, "Oh, I'm ready for my little box now, dear," and crying myself to sleep at night from the age of ten through my early teens wondering how awful life would be without my beloved grandmother, I lost her when she finally succumbed at the age of 86 to a variety of ailments. She was born in 1900 and lived through two world wars, so I felt lucky to have had her, my kindred spirit, in my life for so long. We had talked a week earlier and, without our consciously knowing, had said our goodbyes.

My oldest brother called to give me the news. "I'll pay for you and Luke to fly back...first class," he offered.

"Well, thank you, Mark," I said, though thinking cynically that the real motivation for his generosity was not wanting to go alone to face my mother and our other siblings. Yep, we were all damaged. I was also afraid of facing my mother, the monster. I accepted his kind offer. Though for Grandie, I would have gone anyway.

When the funeral service was over, for the first time in years all five of us "children" were together. Once we were seated in a restaurant with our mother, the brooding matriarch, at the head of the table, the recriminations started. I don't even know what we were fighting about but everyone seemed to be really angry about something. Janet pointed her finger at me, Alex laid into Janet, Mark was shaking his head, trembling with rage and glaring at all of us. My mother, I noticed, just sat and watched and puffed a lot of cigarette smoke, with a very cold look on her face as if to say, *Did I really waste most of my life rearing these awful specimens of humanity?*

But later it got worse, much worse.

The following day, Luke and I decided to take a one-day train trip up north to see Janet's children and her ex-husband in Manchester. Around nine o'clock, we arrived back at Grandie's flat in South London, where we were all staying. The place was in darkness. Luke and I could do nothing except sit on the stairs and wait in the shadowy, cold hallway for my mother to return and let us in.

Twenty minutes later, as soon as she and Mark got out of the car, even from their yellow-tinged forms silhouetted against the fluorescent light of the street lamp, I could see the anger in their dark shapes as they teetered up the path. Oh, God! They were drunk. And for some reason, I already knew they were very angry with me, just me. I envisioned it all in a flash. For the last few hours, my mother and Mark had been chugging down g & t's while she filled my brother's head with what "a little whore, bitch and slut" I was and "Who the hell does she think she is?" My stomach clenched as if protecting my innards. There was going to be a scene, an ugly scene.

With Grandie only gone a few days, fresh fruit still ripe in the silver bowl on the antique sideboard in her living room, my mother, my oldest brother and my sister proceeded to verbally assault me. It was shred-Kate-night. They attacked who I was, who I wasn't, what I had done, what I hadn't done, how I spoke, who I dated, what I was doing (though they didn't actually know because they hadn't asked). My mother sneered, shouted, hissed and pointed. Mark paced and yelled. My sister accused, blamed and huffed. I sat impaled on the couch by their nasty rage, stunned into paralysis.

There was no point in trying to defend myself against their hysterical ranting. Why fight insanity with insanity? Why waste energy on untruths? I thought about leaving. But then it occurred to me why should *I* leave and roam the dark empty streets of London on a cold February night. I was already the cold outsider. And I wasn't the one committing the offence. And anyway, some masochistic, or courageous, part of me wanted to get to the truth. Maybe if I stayed, some secret would be revealed. Or maybe I could finally get to the root cause of this anger that exploded whenever my family came together.

So a part of me separated from myself and retreated to a place slightly above them. In times of crisis, it had always been my way of gaining perspective, getting a sense of the ridiculous, surviving. If I hadn't been related to these insane Monty Pythonesque characters, this scene might have even been funny. But I *was* related to them and I wasn't laughing. And even as I sat there under psychic attack, I realized it wasn't their words that hurt me because they weren't speaking the truth. What disturbed me more was that these people were mad and I carried the same genes. As they continued to rant, I viewed them like caged rats in a laboratory, with me, the observer, asking the question, *What is it that makes them behave like that?*

I searched the past for reasons they should hate me. But it wasn't hate. Their accusations, I knew, were masking a much deeper affront, as if I were a threat to them in some way. But why? Were they jealous of my closeness to Grandie? Or was I just a scapegoat for their grief?

At one point, my oldest brother came at me with his fist. "Just do it!" he screamed, the fist lingering threateningly two inches above my face.

"That's right," I challenged him. "Be a *real* man and hit your little sister."

The fist dropped and so did his shoulders, in shame.

"Anyway, do what?" I asked.

"What you're meant to be doing!" he yelled.

Was I missing the brain cell or was he? I just couldn't fathom what he was talking about.

"But I am," I told him, mystified. The Future Youth Society was just about to be officially born, we had a board of directors, a successful model to follow, funds looked as if they might be on the horizon. Okay, I was putting a lot of my own money into the project, which probably wasn't very smart, but I had faith it would all work out in the end.

"No, you're not," Mark snarled.

"You tell me then, what *it* is."

"No," he snapped. "You've got so much potential and you're not doing it. I'm not going to tell you because you know." He jabbed his tight knuckles at me, his brown eyes flashing rage. "You know."

Er, excuse me, I thought. *Not everyone wants to be a millionaire like you. Is that what you're talking about? And why should my choice of career cause you so much frustration anyway?*

My mother sat in her chair. The chaos and the hatred that she had no doubt set in motion amongst her offspring, now all aimed at me, was very satisfying to her. I saw the smug smirk on her face, her beady brown eyes glinting with satisfaction that someone else was tearing me down. Now that she had convinced Mark I was the enemy, she did everything but stand ringside and cheer him on. I had no idea why she hated me with such venom. I scanned my memory for offences committed. Sure, she irritated me sometimes. Her refusal to treat me as older than three could be a little exasperating. Her put-downs, insults and wounding comments weren't particularly conducive to my trusting her. I had defended myself when I could, but I had never been deliberately vindictive towards her. I couldn't think what I had ever done to my mother except be born. She had slapped me more than once and told me that she wished she'd never had me. Later, I had been the only one who had stuck by her side. Maybe just being a sucker was my crime?

Luke sat on the piano stool, his face distraught, as if on the verge of tears. Every now and then he would mutter a few words in my defence but he got screamed down. Janet sat beside me on the couch and vacillated between protecting me and jumping in with insults. It lasted for hours.

At one point, I looked up at Mark, pacing the room, stabbing his forefinger accusingly at me, a cigarette laden with ash between his fingers. He was almost foaming at the mouth. I thought, *My God, he's got the same insanity as my mother; it's something in the brain. It is genetic. Janet has signs of it. Maybe I've got it, too.*

The assault lasted into the early hours of the morning. When Luke and I finally retreated to our rooms, he frowned. "Why do they always attack you like that?"

"I have no idea," I replied, my self-esteem and aura in shreds, still trembling from the violence and the vehemence of their rage. I hadn't trusted my mother for a long time, well aware of her violent feelings towards me. And I feared her, hated her yet still cared about her. (Now that was insane!) But now I added my oldest brother to the list of untrusted and unhinged members of the family.

It would be months before my aura stopped reverberating from the trauma, and years before I would understand why.

Metaphysical Endnote 25

Possession? Or Good, Good Vibrations?

Did you have the courage to watch *The Exorcist*?

Not me. Being psychically vulnerable, I knew I might be suscep-tible to its influence, and I didn't want those images impaled on my consciousness. Whenever we are not strong, low-life energies only need a tiny chink in the aura to be able to enter. I also avoided it because the movie's premise reminded me of my mother.

I know there is such a thing as possession because my mother was possessed. In those hellish days at Bramhall, if I hadn't seen with my own eyes how other entities rushed into my mother's body, I might have disagreed. It *is* possible for disembodied spirits to enter the living body of another.

There are no victims, however. These nasty entities don't enter just any old body. There is an unconscious agreement between a) the physi-cal vehicle, the possessed, and b) the spirit, the possessor. But who on earth would make such an agreement?

The possessors are low-life spirits who weren't very nice people while living. Just because they have died doesn't mean they become any nicer or wiser, especially if they didn't believe in a higher power, heaven or an afterlife. Death is only a transformation if we allow it to be.

These unhappy spirits have often died suddenly, too young or under dubious circumstances. They resist going home to the light, and with their own consciousness they create their own hell. *According to your beliefs, be it unto you* doesn't just apply to the living.

Now discarnate, or without a body, these unhappy spirits want desperately to get into a physical body again to wreak revenge for their own lives and deaths, to feel physical sensations again, including sexu-ality, and/or to create havoc with the living.

Who are the possessed? My mother was one example. Our thoughts are perpetually moving in vibrational, upward, creative spirals or in downward, destructive spirals steering us into creative, love-based or destructive, fear-based futures. She opted for the downward spiral, fu-elling her mind with low vibrational fear-based emotions such as hate, anger and revenge. Like attracts like and she attracted these nasty spirits with her thoughts. Instead of attempting to understand what had happened to her and recognizing her own part in it, she believed she was the powerless victim. Her intention was to avenge her own pain, and revenge always comes back to haunt the revenger.

So my mother ended up in a very dark vibration of rage, and evil. She was also an ungrounded psychic and wide open energetically, a prime target for possession. The "I'm-depressed-angry-and-an-ungrounded-psychic" metaphysical sign on my mother's forehead was an invitation for all the spirit low-lifes seeking a body to inhabit. The entities that showed up in her from time to time were indeed evil. They only had one intent—to damage. The problem was we never knew when they would appear. But when they did, there were no limits to the emotional pain they would perpetrate. No blow was too low.

Did my mother have control over this possession? Consciously maybe not. But unconsciously, she allowed them in and seemed to welcome their presence as though she had summoned the devil's cavalry. When these evil spirits were in her and around her, she no longer felt alone in what she perceived to be a hostile world.

So how do we guard against invading psychic perpetrators and evil spirits? Most of us will never have to worry about being possessed. But for those who are prone to severe depression or who are psychically vulnerable, the greatest protection you can use is simply not to entertain fear-based negative thoughts. Stay away from dark energies, especially Ouija boards, séances and any occult books, movies or activities. Be *willing* to entertain light thoughts.

When you walk into a dark room and switch on a light, what happens to the dark? It's gone. Higher vibrations always have more power over lower vibrations. Light is a higher vibration than dark. So when you are feeling fearful, surround yourself in a laser-like white bubble of light and think happy thoughts. Ask your angels to fill your mind with thoughts of love, light and laughter. Soon, your aura will be so luminous that nothing but the highest and the best will come to you.

Amen to that.

AT LEAST I TRIED

*W*hen the landlord of my home in Kitsilano decided that he wanted his house back, much as I hated moving (though I still did it frequently) I wasn't averse to a new environment. But this time, I wanted my own space. The beach house had always been filled with people and action, much of the hustle and bustle of my own making. Since the episode at Grandie's funeral three months previously, my nerves were still jangling and I felt a strong need for solitude.

The society was now formed, complete with an active and committed board of directors, one of whom was looking for a farmhouse out in the country so the kids could get off the streets. In the meantime, my new apartment, a house on West 2nd, was a one-bedroom, funky, attic space complete with sloping ceilings and mullion windows. It was here that I made my first foray into professional psychic reading.

I'm not sure what words I actually used in that ad in *The Georgia Straight* but what showed up did not match my preconceived ideas of what a spiritual healer's practice should look or feel like. Apart from dubious sounding men making heavy breathing calls late at night, there were needy women unable to eat breakfast without consulting a psychic. Other people called, whispering, as if somehow that was more spiritual. Angry, energy-sucking people who refused to take responsibility for their lives complained about their lots and then vehemently denounced every one of my predictions as impossible. Some sounded as if they needed peeling off ceilings. I had enough insanity in my family; I didn't need it from my clientele.

Why was I attracting so much wacky energy? Consequently, I was very choosy about who I let into my apartment. *Like attracts like* kept reverberating around my head. So what did that say about me? That I was weird too? Or was I merely manifesting all my imagined fears about being a psychic? Probably.

Not that they were all weird. I remember one of several people whom I feel I was able to help.

One April day, Carol, her blonde curls framing a pretty, blue-eyed face, came bounding up the stairs for her appointment. In her early thirties, she appeared fresh and innocent. And she looked so *normal*!

I invited her to sit on the couch while I pulled up a chair to face her. As I took her hands in mine and peered into her palms, the nuances of her energy started to make themselves known to me. I explained the significance of each line in the palms and then commented, "It feels like you are stuck."

She smiled. "That's why I've come to see you."

Though I picked up that she was recently and happily married, there was a deep pain that I felt was causing her grief, and that, if not handled, would cause blocks in all areas of her life, particularly her marriage.

"Something happened when you were three," I started. "Something big...feels like a male energy...in the family...."

I didn't need to finish. She gasped, looked up at me and then burst into tears.

"M—m—y uncle...he...he...when I was three," she sobbed. Shocked, I just sat back in my chair. This lovely looking girl didn't resemble the street kids with their shattered auras who had suffered this kind of abuse. Those kids never spoke of the many crimes committed against them. That was too painful. But the wounded, hunted and haunted looks in their eyes betrayed a thousand horror stories.

"I've never told anyone," Carol finally uttered, still staring at her palms as if wondering which line gave away her awful secret.

"That's why you're stuck," I reminded her gently. "The energy is blocked. You need to tell someone and you need to process the pain around it. I recommend that you go to see a counselor or psychologist. The three-year-old in you is still traumatized, and you need someone to help you untie all the knots in your mind so that the adult in you can not only cope but also heal. If you don't heal, the pain will probably overwhelm your whole life and get in the way of a good marriage."

She nodded. "It already is."

"But you're ready now to deal with it. Subconsciously you know that, and that's why you came to see me."

"Yes, yes," she agreed. While evidently not relishing the thought of having to dig up this painful memory, she said, "You're right." We finished up the reading, and though she was shaken, there was something freer about her energy. As she left, she thanked me profusely. Was it my imagination or did her aura look more expansive now?

Though I felt a great sense of reward at having helped Carol on her path to healing, there were too few like her. If mostly attracting extremely neurotic people was what being a psychic meant, I didn't want to be a psychic.

So I closed down...again.

Though I still passionately pursued studies in psychology, dream interpretation and all areas of human potential through books and more seminars, a practitioner, I decided, I was not.

Dave had found the farmhouse that he said would suit the society's purposes perfectly. We still had to continue fundraising for a year while we started our first business—collecting and redistributing horse manure (not my idea!). For that purpose, I had even sold my beloved TR7 and replaced it with an ugly-but-solid, red, Ford one-ton pick-up truck. The farmhouse would be vacant soon, and Pamela and I would be moving there in June. The Future Youth Society was now a reality.

A week later Pamela called. "I need to talk to you," she breathed down the phone.

Uh-oh.

When she arrived, she parked herself in the window seat. Her huge eyes stared vacantly down at the residential street where the cherry trees in full pink blossom were awash in sunshine. When I noticed that her eyes were furiously blinking as if trying to shut out all her thoughts, my heart sank. She didn't need to talk. Pamela was in overload.

"You want out, don't you?" I said.

She just turned and stared at me and blinked some more. If her eyeballs hadn't been attached, they might have rolled way into the back of her head.

This wasn't really news, I told myself. It was hard not to notice the signs that she had been gradually withdrawing from the project. Her dynamic enthusiasm had been replaced by long introspective moods, her penchant for bursting into joyous song long silenced.

But I couldn't leave now, I thought. We had gone too far. And though Pamela had been the instigator of the idea, I wondered why I had become even more possessed by it. Even if she had, unconsciously or deliberately, hypnotized me into cooperation, maybe the abandoned, homeless child in me needed to be healed. Whatever it was, on some level I related to these angry, brilliant, intuitive, wounded, manipulative, self-hating children in old-young bodies.

Though, like Pamela, my intuition was weighing heavily on the side of running as far away as possible, I gulped as I said, "It's okay. I'll carry on, Pamela. I can't quit now."

As if I had removed a 50-pound weight from her back, her shoulders suddenly slumped. At least this way, I reasoned, I wouldn't have to be a psychic. Maybe by doing this work, I was still appeasing Divine Intelligence.

Pamela called me again a few days later. Not only was the laughter back in her voice—I envied her newfound lightness of being—but she was also bursting with news.

"I've found someone to help you," she crowed. I understood now that she needed to replace herself to appease her own guilt. "His name is Ed Bross."

"Who is he?"

"I heard him talking on the radio. He's an ex-con who turned himself around in jail and teaches self-esteem workshops to youth."

"An ex-con!" *Lovely!*

"He's perfect," she said, not even having met him and undaunted by my cynicism.

"Uh…Pamela, what did he do exactly to get *into* jail?"

"He robbed banks and, oh," she chirped as if adding onions to her shopping list, "he killed a few people."

Getting better all the time.

"But he's turned around now," she said, as if everything was all right in the world and it was a "luverly day in the neighborhood."

"Aha."

"Let's get together with him," she urged. The old fireball Pamela was back.

Well, I told myself, I *would* need someone who had experience on the street, especially with the boys.

Rock or hard place? Hard place or rock? Hmm?

Again, I am not sure whether Pamela put me under another hypnotic spell, this time with her smooth voice. Even as my intuition screamed at me that I was on a perilous path, some other force was sucking me inexorably further down into this unfamiliar, strange world.

"Sure," I said. "We could meet." *Why not? What exactly do I have to lose?*

Three weeks later, Ed joined the Future Youth Society and moved to the farm.

My first and biggest mistake was to vastly overestimate the extent of the healing work Ed had done on himself and could, therefore, do with the kids. I realized too late that having been institutionalized for most of his life, he was just another wounded, angry, street kid but in a 40-year-old body with rippling muscles and tattoos on his arms.

He also hated his mother with a passion. That wasn't good for any woman in his life, colleague, friend or mate.

So one December evening, after only six months at the farmhouse, as we sat in the shadowy kitchen, Ed Bross successfully manipulated the board of seven men and one woman into believing "She has bitten off more than she can chew and should leave." They believed this man who, even by other criminals' standards, was somebody not to be messed with. Though I was devastated and dumbfounded by their blind acceptance of his summation of all my work, there was vindication for me in that final meeting. I wasn't the only sucker on the board.

Hearing the news, the Englishman who initially introduced me to Pamela and started me on this precarious journey called me at the farm. Crushed by a sense of failure, I wasn't too talkative. "Well, at least you tried," he commiserated. "Most people just go home at night and watch TV."

Yes, at least I tried.

Metaphysical Endnote 26

From Denial to Freedom

Too many people in their 40s and 50s and even 60s are still allowing the voice of their repressors, usually parents or abusive mates, to keep them stuck in a powerless place and in the beliefs of the damaged child they once were. That is why many of my readings are for clients who still don't know what they want to be when they grow up. Their desires are still buried in the basement of their beings, covered in dust and old programming.

Despite their protestations and denials, I insist that they take up activities that inspire latent talents—drama classes, writing workshops, music lessons, ballet classes, psychic development, trapeze swinging or elephant training. They often return to thank me, radiating joy because they have given themselves permission to finally express their true essences. What is great about discovering your childhood in later life is that you can choose what friends to play with, buy your own toys and stay up as late as you want!

Though no life path is easy, some are definitely more challenging than others. Out of all that struggle and pain, a greater purpose emerges. Once those in denial have run out of all other options, most of the time they will accept the next act in their scripts and follow what their souls are urging them to do—to become the creative beings they truly are.

Childhood may set in motion hurts or challenges—abusive parents, poverty or physical disadvantages that we can spend the rest of our lives overcoming. Sadly, some of us just love to continue to wallow in misery rather than opt for happiness. We choose victimhood over responsibility and denial over freedom long after the actual cause of the pain is gone. However, it is possible to recognize our own truth sooner rather than later and not waste our energies on what was, after all, a pre-life Agreement. We can begin to live as dynamic beings sooner and enjoy our gifts.

Our highest potential is to overcome the hurts and challenges put in our way. By this I don't mean merely burying or walking away from all those nasty experiences of the past. The purpose of our lives is to take the real meaning of our scripts and appreciate what they teach about our Selves, our souls and our spirits, then move forward with that enlightenment. Even at 90, we can be free-spirited, trusting, playful, creative, delightful children, contributing light to the world and joy to the mass consciousness. We *can* emerge victorious so that when we come back in our next incarnation, we won't have to do a boring old re-run. Instead, we can act out a new, exciting, more highly evolved plot. The bigger the set-up, the harder it may be to overcome, but then in the end, the greater the gift.

Don't let it take a lifetime.

PSYCHIC OR CRAZY?

*B*y the time I met Diane in 1986, I was thirty-four and I still didn't know what I wanted to do when I grew up. The now defunct street kid project hung over me like a failed marriage (as I imagined it anyway), and I needed some direction for my life. I still resisted the psychic path. Yes, I was fascinated by metaphysics, yes, I could read palms with some accuracy and yes, I felt I was destined to do something big. But what? Was being a psychic really me? *Aaagh!* Someone please just tell me what to do!

In one of my mother's more lucid, kinder moments, she had told me, "You have the world at your feet." But sometimes that much freedom can be more daunting than having none.

In July, as I strolled through the Pacific National Exhibition's Psychic Fair in a cool, sterile exhibition hall blindingly illuminated by yellow lights and suspiciously empty of people, I searched the different faces for someone, the right one, to give me the guidance I needed now. Contrary to the popular misconception that all psychics are rotund, black-haired ladies with hooped earrings, these practitioners, I noticed, came in all ages, shapes and sizes.

A woman about my age was sitting alone at a large round table. She was slim, with fine, short, red hair, her pale face devoid of make-up. She was dressed more for a stroll in the park than a psychic fair. I wasn't even sure she was one of them, her table separate from the other psychics and bare of the usual metaphysical accoutrements. Then her clear blue eyes locked onto mine.

"Do you want a reading?" she inquired, some invisible force drawing me automatically towards her.

As I sat down, I noticed that her simple psychic kit—a deck of well-thumbed Tarot cards, an amethyst crystal, a glass of water and a stubby white flickering candle—looked lost on the vast table. Something about her transparent skin and tragic eyes told me she was fragile. Was that a prerequisite for being psychic, a painful past?

"I'm Diane," she said, exhaling smoke and sitting up in her chair.

"Kate."

"Shuffle the cards and split them into three piles," she directed, grinding her cigarette into the ashtray. "And think about your question." I could feel her third eye boring into my soul as I rearranged the gold and blue Tarot deck. *Just don't tell me I'm psychic*, I begged, silently.

"Now, from left to right, put them back into one pile."

I obeyed, then Diane pulled the shuffled deck towards her. With eyes closed, she placed a hand on the single pile as if drawing information out of the cards. Her breathing was heavy, her body slumping slightly as if she was going into a trance. Then her eyes flew open.

Before the cards were even laid out on the table, she announced, "The relationship with your mother has been very difficult, hasn't it?"

Hallelujah. The first psychic to pick up on Mommie Dearest.

"Though it doesn't look that way, the love *is* there. The conflict is the Agreement that you made before you came here."

I leaned forward. "But why?"

"The lesson is to get you in touch with your power. Your mother is also psychic."

More like psycho.

"And you are very, very clairvoyant."

Here we go again.

Diane turned over more cards in a pattern I didn't recognize. "There is a man at a distance thinking about you. You have a very strong bond with him."

"Yes," I breathed.

"He's coming to see you this year."

"I know." Three months ago I had a sense that, after eight years of a seemingly endless separation, the love of my life, Alejandro, and I would finally be reunited this fall. My heart did a little somersault...

"But you may not end up together in this lifetime."

...and then landed with a heavy thud.

"If you don't marry him, it will be somebody like him, and he will love you just for who you are and will totally support what you do."

As long as he looks exactly like him, speaks like him, laughs like him....

Diane expertly flipped over another card, a sultry image that I couldn't make out. "You are a natural teacher, teaching others how to develop psychically. I see you standing in front of large groups of people. There will be short journeys but I also see you traveling the world."

More travel?

"There is success and *lots* of money. You may own a Rolls Royce or Bentley and will be flying on your own jet."

I laughed out loud at this prediction, far-fetched even for my gullible mind. *Rolls Royces and Bentleys weren't even my style, but I could get used to a jet. And me, that wealthy? Recently, I seemed to repel money, not attract it.* I glanced over at the surrounding psychic tables gradually filling up with more seekers of truth. I wondered if their readings about love, careers and finances were as outrageous as mine. Diane chose to ignore my cynicism and continued, staring at the cards as if they were talking to her.

"It feels like everyone wants a chunk of you. You must learn to say no, take care of yourself."

Certainly feels that way.

"St. Germaine or St. Hilarion, one of the ascendants, is one of your masters. St.Germaine is of the 7th Ray. They are there to help but you have to ask. Also Ramtha is giving instruction."

Never heard of the first two and what on earth was the 7th Ray? But this was the second psychic to mention Ramtha, the entity who channeled through J. Z. Knight. At that time in the 1980s, out of the many who professed to be channelers of the highest wisdom, only the teachings of Ramtha inspired me. I would have to research Germaine and Hilarion though.

Diane flipped some more cards over and sighed. "You're a very old soul. In fact, you were a guide once on another plane."

Neat.

"And you should write more. There are personal messages for you in automatic writing. Set some time aside."

But...but...the last time I did automatic writing, it got me into a lot of trouble.

"I see much growth," Diane continued. "You will experience growing pains, twinges in your body, which is just you adapting to the new energy. Open up to this energy through grounding exercises. Let it flow

through your heart. Teachings are coming to you in your dreams. You
will be taught and must learn how to teleport."

I didn't want to interrupt her psychic flow and I was intending to
save my questions for the end of the reading, but Diane paused to take
a sip of water. "Teleport?" I inquired. "What do you mean by that exactly?"

"Transfer your body physically."

That's what I thought but....

"You are good at manifesting, turning energy into matter, but you
must learn to de-materialize and re-materialize in other places. When
the time comes, you will be given one of the seven keys. These are keys
to the seven portals on the earth's surface which lead to the center of
the earth. Only seven people know of the keys."

*Okay, now you're really losing me. She was definitely psychic but
was she also crazy?*

"During the transformation, people will be teleported there and
your job is to assist them." I envisioned myself suddenly beaming down
to a cave entrance, a combination of Mary Poppins and Captain Kirk,
shooing stunned masses through a hidden door. The stuff of Asimov.
Sensing my disbelief, Diane warned, "Keep an open mind. Everything
you need you already have. It will all fit into place."

I often prayed to my higher power that the planet wouldn't go into
self-destruct, but all the prophecies had leaned that way. On a mass-
consciousness level, I knew we still had time to choose, but not much.
Maybe it wouldn't be necessary for me to do the Mary Poppins thing.
Might be fun though.

"It is your time to start teaching, but you are afraid to step out for
fear of abusing your power.... You were killed in another lifetime for
standing up for your beliefs."

*Yes! I'd always felt that I'd been burned at the stake for being a
witch. And my fear of being successful, being known, famous! My terror
of fire. It all made sense.*

"But you won't be killed this time."

Oh, goodie!

Palms downward, her hands fanned over the cards as if soaking
up information from them, she said, "Doing some past-life regressions
would really help you connect with and overcome your fears from those
lifetimes. You are clearing out, cleaning, opening up channels so your
intellect is becoming more in line with your intuition. Lots of emotional
disruption."

Tell me something I don't *know.*

"It is time to acknowledge yourself." Diane smiled beatifically at me as if to a child terrified of the dark. "There's nothing to be afraid of. You feel the responsibility, but remember, you are the messenger, not the message."

I heaved a huge sigh of relief as she uttered those magic words. Then, "You are a very powerful lady."

Please don't say that.

"See everything as a gift and know that you are taken care of," she added, finally gathering up the cards. We were done.

Sitting back in her chair, and puffing as if the wind had been forced out of her, Diane lit up another cigarette. I dug through my purse for two crisp twenties. As I handed her the money, she peered into my eyes.

"Kate, we know each other from Atlantis."

Why do psychics often claim this connection with me, as if having lived in that intellectually advanced culture was like belonging to some exclusive psychic sisterhood?

"Maybe," I said, my head already too full of the wild and wacky to want to discuss Atlantis. I thanked Diane, took her card, promised to book a past-life regression with her and left, stunned.

Metaphysical Endnote 27

Are You Psychic? Or Just Insane?

The definition of psychic: *being able to see and feel things of a non-physical nature.*

The definition of insane: *afflicted with a mental illness severe enough to make one incapable of leading a normal life, showing such affliction as being highly reckless or foolish.*

To the rational person, psychic and insane may look the same. Tragically, parents have locked up their offspring because their child saw spirits and demonstrated other psychic abilities (see *The Eagle and the Rose* by Rosemary Altea). Like so many rational people out there, those parents chose ignorance over understanding, fear over love. Therefore, a large percentage of people in mental health institutions may well not be crazy but extremely psychic. On the other hand, there are people walking the streets who should definitely be under lock and key.

Some might decide when you tell them that you're psychic that you *are* crazy. But until you have been given a clinical diagnosis of insanity, that is just their opinion. For many psychics who have survived the craziness of their dysfunctional or even psychotic families, the threat of insanity is very real and comes with the territory. So if *you* feel insecure about the solidity of your mental health, read on.

I have two theories.

First theory: In order to express your psychic self, you have to be willing to push the envelope of rational thought, or what the masses call sanity. The very process of becoming psychic means opening up the mind to all kinds of phenomena that the "sane" person would deem impossible or just imagination or crazy. And many energies in the Universe are of a non-physical nature that only psychics, dogs and children can see. But how do you know when you should be checking into a psych ward? Not until you have at least finished reading this book.

Second theory: What if, in order to be insane, you first have to be psychic? Some very psychic people of a lower vibration descend on that downward spiral of thought to an even lower vibration of depression and/or chaos, like my mother, for example. In that place, being psychically open and depressed, they join forces with low-life spirits who invade their bodies and their minds. This is known as possession which, for scared onlookers, can seem a lot like insanity and would account for such symptoms as hearing voices, multiple personalities and schizophrenia. If a person *is* totally unhinged, exhibiting violent, paranoid or self-destructive behavior, I suspect that they are not alone in their bodies or...they are in psychic overload. (There are also the eerily calm or wildly frenetic energies from whom I have also maintained a distance.)

But if someone is merely talking of parallel universes, little green men, lights, energies, hearing a voice, traveling in outer space, conversations with Jesus every night, I wouldn't be unduly worried. It is the whole energy I listen to and not just someone's conversation. My diagnosis would be "psychic until proven insane," and not the other way around.

So if a psychic ability is a form of brilliance—because we are using all levels of the mind—and there is a fine line between brilliance and insanity, what separates a psychic from insanity?

Intention.

Consciously or unconsciously, we *intend* the outcomes we want to create with our energy. Our intentions, a combination of our wills and thoughts, are continually manifesting in our physical world. Any gift comes with a responsibility and the responsibility is how that gift is applied. Insanity, therefore, could be a psychic ability gone wrong. Misdirected brilliance. A psychic ability used destructively instead of creatively—turned inwards instead of outwards—can definitely send the person on that downward spiral into chaos, lower vibration and insanity.

But as I wondered about Diane's sanity all those years ago, many of my clients have wondered about mine. Though my readings haven't been as far-fetched as hers, not to me anyway, and despite the client's questioning of my gray matter, I *gently* pass on the message anyway. When a client wants to refute my predictions, I remind them of three points: they won't do anything they don't want to, I could be misinterpreting the energy and I am merely the messenger. All my readings are taped for the client so that they may listen at their leisure to the reading and its subtler nuances. I constantly receive calls later from clients who inform me somewhat sheepishly, "I listened to your tape again. And you know you told me...and I didn't believe you? Well, guess what I'm doing now?"

Thank you. It's so nice to know I'm not insane.

HEALER, HEAL THYSELF

"You shouldn't be helping others while you still need to help yourself." These wise words came from my younger brother, Luke. An unlikely messenger, he was the one who was adamantly refusing to deal with his traumatic past. "Just put it all behind you," was his simplistic solution.

But I needed to understand me, my past and I, even luxuriate in analyzing it to death. So while I just couldn't *fuggedaboudit*, he was right about me not being ready to hang out my Counselor shingle. I had visited a few clairvoyants whose obviously damaged psyches bled into their psychic perceptions. What they "saw" was polluted by their own tangled wounds. The readings hadn't felt good. How could I then be facilitating healing for others when I was still a lost soul myself?

One dark and foggy evening, just as I was about to get into my car and drive away, Consuela, a Mexican counselor—who also happened to be a neighbor—accosted me in the street. Like a deer caught in the headlights, I froze in dread. She'd got me. But I saw something surreal about her that night. Was it the street lamp bouncing off her thick mane of long, curly black hair, or had Consuela been promoted to angel and developed a white aura?

"Kate, you ne–e–e–ed to come and see me–e–e," she said, almost pinning me to my car. My vacant stares and permanently stunned expressions must have given away my confused state. So I didn't take offence at her underlying inference. I needed help.

"Okay," I said, finally surrendering to something that I had known for a long time. Wherever I went, there I was. There was no escaping me and my skewed thinking.

After several months of meeting once a week, Consuela extracted and disentangled some of the stories of my childhood. She explained the dynamics of an abusive family, holding my memories out in front of me to see from an adult's perspective instead of the child's. My grandfather had been an extremely verbally cruel man to my mother and so it had been passed on. My mother abused us, particularly me, because she had been abused, because I was female like her, and because she could. The bullied become the bullies. With an emotionally detached father, a domineering mother and three older siblings who reveled in torturous mind games, I had to be strong, Consuela said.

Cruelty was something I could never understand. I just couldn't fathom why anyone would want to waste time making another's life so miserable. Consequently, I could never summon enough venom to combat my siblings. This inadequacy, I believed, was a weakness. But Consuela reassured me that my unwillingness to play their game was, in fact, a strength.

When I started the counseling, I believed that all my anger was directed at my mother. But after some digging, it became apparent that my father was also the bad guy for not protecting me from her. That's why I lashed out at the men in my life, never believing that they really cared about me. And while I had believed that my mother had just suddenly gone crazy when I was 17, Consuela pointed out that there had always been an underlying psychological malaise. The divorce only brought her schizophrenia out of the closet.

There were a lot of "ah-ha" moments, but the biggest release was when, one day, Consuela uttered the magic words, "Joo don't have a crazee bone in your bodee."

"Really?" I wanted to cry.

Consuela nodded solemnly.

"Could you put that in writing, please?" She thought I was joking.

"No, re-e-e-elly." She wanted me to understand this. After all, the reason I wouldn't let men get close or allow myself to have children was that I believed somewhere inside of me there was a monster like my mother just waiting to emerge. I was afraid of doing unto others what had been done unto me. "Jyour mother was always crazee and jyou have to give yourself credit for surviveeng. She was very, very jealous of jyou."

Jealous? Of me? But what about all those demeaning, nasty slurs over the years? Then the light went on. Of course! It made sense.

"Thanks God you had your grandmothurr."

Yes, thank God for Grandie.

With counseling, there is a time for active probing and a time for passive reflection. In my mind, both are equally important in the healing process. So after ten months of weekly sessions with Consuela, I told her I wanted a break. She understood. My confidence had started to resurrect itself, not enough to put me on top of the world but enough to allow me to get on with my life. Something still wasn't right, though.

By 1989, I was living in Kitsilano in an apartment two blocks from a busy beach. While working in television as an executive producer's assistant, immersed in an environment of glamorous but neurotic workaholic creativity (I felt *right* at home), I was inspired to follow my other passion—writing. So when the networks cancelled the four television shows on which I was employed and my duties dwindled to twiddling thumbs, I decided to leave and start a company called The Write Stuff. From the speeches, resumés, reports, letters, and promotional materials that I composed on behalf of others, I made a living.

Still heeding my brother's words that the healer first needs to heal, my psychic persona became a shadow of its former self though I still attracted others interested in the spirit realm. I studied a Course in Miracles and attended Unity Church, which held a non-denominational spiritual philosophy that promoted a wake-up, you-can-do-it line of thinking. My kind of people. I continued to go for the odd psychic reading, and occasionally I would read other budding psychics' palms. When I was told by these happy, non-paying clients that I was "bang on" or "powerful," I merely shrugged.

While Consuela had helped me to see my mother and the family dynamics from a more detached perspective and to see all my mother's abuse as a projection of her own self-hatred onto me, I still felt like a rotten apple, rosy and pink on the outside, black at the core. But hey, at least I wasn't crazy. Psychic maybe, but not crazy.

Soon, though, the lights would go on and even this rotten feeling would fade. It happened one Sunday afternoon when I switched on PBS and saw a bearded man using a butterfly mobile to demonstrate family dynamics. Perched on the edge of my couch, transfixed, I watched and listened as John Bradshaw paced the stage, explaining why, within a family, the children unconsciously take on roles according to the dynamics that have been set in motion by the parents. These roles included: a responsible one, the sibling to give the family dignity (my oldest brother by becoming wealthy), a clown and/or peacemaker (me), a black sheep (Alex, though in my eyes we were all black sheep), a spiritual/religious one (that must be me again) and a lost child (now was that Alex, me or my sister?). It was almost eerie as I recognized each and every one of us in those roles. As Mr. Bradshaw explained, the role that we unconsciously adopt could often be predicted by our position in the line of offspring. (Some schools of thought believe that our birth order in the family has more impact on our personality than environment, genetics or the stars under which we are born!) Mr. Bradshaw claimed that 95% of families are dysfunctional and further elucidated the types and degrees of aberrant behaviors in these clans.

My brain was popping "ah-ha's" like a popcorn maker. Did this mean then that being dysfunctional was actually *normal*? According to Mr. Bradshaw, it did. *So you mean we're not different! I don't need to feel ashamed of my family's abnormalities any more!*

Just as I thought about shame, he talked about a family poisoned by alcoholism, defining the specific habits and behaviors of alcoholics.

That's when the epiphany happened.

Mr. Bradshaw was describing my mother! And, to a lesser degree, he was describing my brothers, their nastiness always prompted by drinking. Like a checklist, I was mentally ticking them off, and the pieces of a jigsaw puzzle that had been forever out of place all suddenly clicked into one big picture. Finally, finally, I understood.

Ohmigod! My mother wasn't just crazy. She was an alcoholic!

For some reason, this truth liberated me, maybe because it gave me a choice. Craziness was genetic, and although alcoholism was too, it was something I could choose or choose not to be. I had power over that. This was cause for celebration, but maybe not by cracking open the wine!

"Alcoholics are often brilliant, funny, charming, sensitive, wonderful people...when sober," he said.

Yup. Mother had two personalities. Strangers and people who didn't get too close thought she was "charming," "so sweet," "great company," "interesting."

"When they drink they become angry, abusive, self-destructive, ugly."

Yup!

"They blame everyone else for their problems."

Her constant refrains: It's all your fault! You only think of you. You selfish little bitch. Oh, it's all right for you.

"Their behaviors are mostly shame-based."

That would be all the "Don't-tell-anybody's."

"They do not take responsibility for themselves or the destructiveness that they create."

Like my mother claiming, I just don't understand why my children aren't talking to me.

"They often project it onto those nearest and dearest to them."

That would be me because I was nearest, not dearest.

"They attract co-dependents, people who will enable or support them in drinking but will also make them right about blaming someone or something else for their misery."

That would be me again with "sucker" across the forehead. How many times had I said "Never again" and like Simon & Garfunkel's song, "The Boxer," kept going back for more?

"They are extremely clever at manipulating situations and people around them."

I can still hear her: Don't worry about me; I'll just stick my head in the oven. And the leukemia story. Poor me. I'll be all right.

"They are often secretive about their drinking."

Bottles of sherry in the broom cupboard and then claiming she was drinking "just tonic water" at 9:00 in the morning while reeking of gin.

"Alcoholism runs in families. You will either become one or marry one."

Aaagh! Well, I wasn't married. But was I an alcoholic?

I didn't drink all day.

I wasn't a binge drinker.

I didn't change personality and get nasty like Mommie Dearest.

In fact, I could rarely make it past the third glass without curling up into a fetal ball and sleeping. Obviously, I would have to keep an eye on myself.

Hallelujah! Praise the Lord! Finally the light had gone on illuminating the fuzzy, nebulous dark corners of my mind. The blackness that sat at my core I now recognized as not mine. While *intellectually* I had understood this from Consuela, something now shifted in me *physically,* on a cellular level. In an instant the self-hatred that I had taken on as my own from my mother (with a little assistance from the others) dissipated. I felt as if a black lump had been moved from inside me where, although aware of its murky presence, I couldn't see it to somewhere in front of me where I could observe the thing for what it really was: just a "mis-thought."

I finally understood that it wasn't me who was all wrong. The whole dang family was wacky, each in our own way and through dynamics that we had unconsciously set up within it. Beyond that were the dynamics of the bigger system, our grandparents and their parents, the society in which we found ourselves, in which I found myself. I was just a product of the environment, the effect of that system, the end result of a bigger organism, like the earth in our galaxy.

And though Consuela had led me part of the way along the right path, alcoholism had never been mentioned. I had assumed alcoholics were people who were red-faced, down-and-out tramps normally found in gutters. Why hadn't it ever occurred to me that my oh-so-respectable mother, who drank copious amounts of cooking sherry and gin and tonic, would be classed as an alcoholic?

Our family, every family, I understood now, is/was a manifestation of a thought, a concept, one aspect of Mind that had been set in motion a long time ago. All the "stuff" of our clan wasn't a creation *by* our family, more a reaction *to* what had been and the evolution of our ancestors. We were just trying to survive their unresolved stuff which had been passed down to us, and to the Selves that we had now become. But we weren't trapped within it. We could bring these patterns to the light of consciousness and there, through conscious effort, overcome.

Because I was sensitive, I had unconsciously but psychically picked up on my family's truths. As if standing naked before me, they couldn't hide from my unwitting ability to see them for who they really were. And because I still loved my family, at some deeper level, they knew I would accept their ugly projections of themselves onto me. We often show our darkest sides to the people closest to us, or those who will take it. The danger for me, therefore, had been not to understand the bigger picture, to be ignorant of the underlying reality and to take their abuses so personally. Wasn't that why I was driven to develop psychically, so I could see the truth behind the facades? Hadn't I relied on and honed this ability out of a crucial survival instinct?

At Grandie's funeral, I must have triggered or mirrored something in them that was, for them, very painful. Their guilt? Or something else that I should not have known, but because of my psychic ability, had sensed? Whatever it was, I loved them anyway. *That* made them uncomfortable because the gulf between the roles they had assumed and who they really were underneath was too great, the Big Divide. They couldn't make the leap. So when Mark had screamed at me that night in Grandie's flat, "Just do it!", he was really screaming inside himself. He couldn't name it because he didn't know what "it" was.

Phew! I had been declared innocent.

Well, almost.

Knowledge *is* power—if you use it. I had a choice now. Instead of allowing them to dictate who I was, I could embrace this innocent verdict. Like a phoenix rising from the ashes, the Self that had been projected onto me for so long began to disintegrate that Sunday afternoon. I emerged with a far greater sense of who I *really* was. Maybe I wasn't so bad after all. My crime, it seems, had merely been to be psychic.

I thought about Luke's words. While I realized I didn't have to be perfect (Who was?) in order to help others, there were still more layers of mis-thoughts for me to peel away before I would be ready. But at least I wasn't lost now. There was a path to follow.

Thank you, John Bradshaw.

So if he, as a self-confessed recovering sexaholic, workaholic and alcoholic could turn his lemons into lemonade and help others, wouldn't I be able to do the same?

Metaphysical Endnote 28

The Psychic Child

The truth is that as children, we are all psychic to some degree. We have just come from the spirit world where we are used to seeing everything as light. Our minds are open to anything, especially spirit and the magic of the Universe. So we can still see our invisible friends, our deceased relatives or the darker energies that sometimes plague sad or sensitive children.

Psychically gifted children, however, are exceptionally sensitive and attuned to energy. This sensitivity can be a curse when they are children because they may be judged by parents and siblings as being weak or strange, especially if they speak of seeing other entities. But later on in life, because it *is* a gift, sensitive children will have their day.

Alternatively, this heightened sensitivity might have been instigated in a dysfunctional or even violent environment or just by one trauma where the child learns that the world is not a safe place. The antennae go up and stay up, and children learn that when threatened, they can retreat to that world between worlds.

For the parents and siblings of a psychic child or children, the words that come out of their mouths can be anything from cute to downright scary. Though I was a psychic child myself, my mother never gave me any credit for having ESP (Extra Sensory Perception). My relatives did, however, though not until much later. The reason for my mother's denial of my gift, I realize now, is that I unwittingly exposed some of her secrets, innocently announcing these things to the whole family, unaware that this information was supposed to be hidden knowledge. Her only defence had been to call my comments "ridiculous."

If your child/children are making up fanciful stories, fanciful in your mind at least, just go along with them. Encourage your child to elaborate, even if it scares the bejabbers out of you. Then if you feel you need to, talk to a child psychologist, psychic, or spirit medium, someone who will be able to guide you and your child constructively through the experience. If they are only stories, the less you resist them, the sooner this kind of attention-getting tactic will fade. What they might be asking for, unconsciously, are more hugs from you, more reassurance that you love them or more time with you just listening to them, *really* listening. If they are just stories, they will soon cease.

My message to parents of all children is please do not crush your offspring, especially sensitive, spirit-seeing children, with your negative criticisms, rolling your eyes or making them feel wrong about who they are or what they see and feel. When we deny them their truth, we are severing the connection to their very essence, and we are shutting down much more than their psychic self. We are teaching them not to trust themselves. The worst damage comes when the adults that these shut-down children grow into try to numb or even kill off that sensitivity with drugs and/or alcohol. The lesser damage, though still unhealthy, will be to send them into a lifelong state of confusion where they will never listen to their own intuition, their connection to their souls. Until they resurrect that part of themselves, they can never be whole or happy.

How many of us, rather than trust our inner voices, consistently look for validation in things, people and events outside ourselves? This is not where the truth lies. The truth was, is and always will be right inside us.

FINAL SURRENDER

*B*y the early '90s, I had been living in Kitsilano for two years. With its constant wail of sirens disturbing the otherwise happy beach-side community, it was akin to living in downtown Jerusalem on a quiet night. I decided it was time to retreat to the countryside and chose the budding ski resort of Whistler.

My friend Laura had warned me it would not be easy. Apparently Whistler had per capita the highest number of PhDs in the whole country. Competition was tough. Lawyers and doctors were taking their sabbaticals as "lifties." Until one was accepted into the community as a local after about five years, everyone had to pay their dues by doing an apprenticeship of three seasonal jobs. Then you were rewarded with a "real" job which, with a year-round population at the time of just 3,000, were few. But far from having a small town mentality, the people of Whistler were the most interesting, well-traveled and stimulating characters I had met in one spot in a long time.

With the opportunity to begin a new life in this mountain paradise without the onus of being known as a psychic, I did not admit to my spiritual side. My psychic life, I decided, was behind me now. I would become a "normal" person. Blending into Whistler was challenge enough.

My psychic pursuits, I thought, had now been surpassed by my desire and fascination with writing. I compiled a monthly column for the *Whistler Journal,* was commissioned to script a murder mystery for corporate dinners, almost became a columnist on the *Financial Post* and continued with my other writing projects while selling ski tickets for Whistler and working part-time in a deli. I had never worked so hard and made so little money, but I was much happier than I had been in years. I loved life in the mountains within the dynamic, fun, happy community. And realizing my dream—though twenty years later than scheduled—as part-time ski bum, with the consequent improvement in my skiing, was a bonus.

After three years in Whistler, and feeling that it was my home, I was inspired for the first time since leaving Vancouver to do a palm reading for a colleague. When we were done, I whispered, "Now, don't tell anyone I do this." But that first little foray back into my dormant psychic talent rekindled something in me. I started taking notice of people's auras again. If some unsuspecting person was giving off interesting vibes, I would offer to read them. It couldn't hurt, could it? And it wasn't for money, just out of interest. Flattered, they held out their palms willingly. It was a diversion, a fun thing to do. I had no idea of the sleeping giant it would awaken.

By this time I had come to terms with the dysfunction of my family and was feeling more serene, finally able to file it away under "Past." My sister had disowned us all in 1989, so except for Luke and my father, I had very little contact with the other members of my immediate clan. Even my relationship with Luke had become distant. I felt sad that our previous closeness had dissipated over the years though I did joke with him one day, "*I* wanted to have a turn at disowning the family but there's only you left to disown."

A perennial student of growth, I attended *The Pursuit of Excellence* in Vancouver. It *was* an excellent workshop designed to help thirty- and forty-somethings gain clarity and manifest their goals and life purposes. The two-day seminar helped me define that my greatest wish at that time was to manifest a creative writing retreat for myself. As soon as the workshop was over, as if *he* was psychic, an American friend asked if I would house-sit his soon-to-be-vacated-for-the-winter home on San Juan Island.

Thank you!

And then I met Karl.

The workshop organizers wanted to bring *The Pursuit* to Whistler. It was at this introductory evening that I met the distinguished gray-haired and -bearded German. Karl reminded me of a professor and though he was obviously quite intellectual, he also loved the outdoors.

There was an instant empathy between us. He told me that he was divorced and looking for something but he didn't know what. (Weren't we all?) We arranged numerous dates, most of which I, being non-committal and perhaps in coward mode, cancelled at the last moment. When I finally enlightened him that I wasn't ready for a relationship as I was leaving on a five-month sabbatical, Karl persuaded me to join him for at least one date. So I did. He was fifteen years older but his gentle charm and sense of humor surprised me. While I enjoyed his company, I couldn't commit any further. My waterfront retreat was awaiting.

When I arrived on San Juan, and before he left for his winter in the sun, my soon-to-be-absentee landlord introduced me to Virginia. "You'll like her," he said. "She's nutty but nice."

Thanks...?

He was right. Virginia and I were kindred spirits. She was also a psychic, though she hadn't practiced in years. She told me that by the age of fifteen she was a well-known and highly paid clairvoyant in Los Angeles. One day when she was doing a reading at yet another Hollywood party, she glanced up at all the people lounging around. Suddenly she became intensely aware of the avarice, back-stabbing, petty jealousies, affairs and other nasty, "icky" energies in the room. Overwhelmed and filled with disgust, she fled, leaving her client aghast at the table and running out of the house and away from her psychic abilities. She hadn't done a reading since.

Until I pestered her to do one for me.

"Yes, you're going back to Whistler," she confirmed. I had been toying with the idea of trying to stay on the island. "There's a significant relationship coming up for you there but it won't be permanent. It'll last about two years."

Darn! Why can't it be permanent?

"You know him already."

"I do?"

"He's a Gemini."

I shrugged. No one came to mind.

"It's happening soon," she continued. "And I hate to tell you this, but you *are* going to be a full-time psychic." We had already bemoaned the uncomfortableness of the psychic life, the demeaning jokes and other demands, misconceptions and disadvantages that went with the territory.

"Traitor!" I smiled. "What about my writing?"

"That feels like it's going to take a while."

Figures.

I had always wondered whether I could be alone with myself for extended periods of time and whether I could write from dawn till dusk. Maybe it was just a fantasy. But on San Juan I discovered that I could do both. I loved it. My soul had been craving the time just to be and think and write without being bombarded by the energies of the outside world.

In the weeks of solitude that followed Virginia's reading, I also gave a lot of thought to my relationships with men. I understood intellectually why it had been such a struggle for me. Whenever I had allowed someone to get too close, I had panicked and sabotaged the intimacy, behaving in a way that I knew the person would find objectionable and so leave. And they did. Basically I was a coward and that was my choice. But I could choose differently.

One day, sitting in the oh-so-comfortable leather armchair, looking out at the rain splattering on a calm black ocean, I asked my Self the big question: *Self, do you want a relationship or not?*

Self replied, *Well, if it is the right relationship, of course, I want that. I am only on my own because...well...I have chosen to be.*

Only a week after arriving back in Whistler, I dropped by Chez Joel's with a friend and there was Karl. I nearly made him choke on a mouthful of après-ski beer as I slapped him on the back and said "Hi!" Despite the fact he had forgotten my name, we chatted and he invited me to his place for a barbecue the following night. I accepted.

From the beginning, Karl seemed to be smitten. At first, I held him at bay, not sure that he fitted the picture of my ideal mate, but he was persistent and courted me with great romantic finesse. Gradually I realized with delight how much we had in common, both enjoying the outdoors as well as entertaining, art shows and wine tastings. He even cautiously accepted my psychic/spiritual side. And he had a very British sense of humor. "It's a miracle," I would tease him, "a German with a sense of humor!"

So we continued to date and have fun. Then something in me started to come alive.

It is written (somewhere?) that we fall in love when we are away from each other. In August, Karl left for his hometown of Berlin. He had an idea of starting a tour business bringing Germans to Canada, specifically to Whistler. To my mild surprise, in those six weeks I missed Karl very much. And so it was. I was in love with him.

Not long after his return, we moved in together. He started to call me wife. As Karl was a Gemini (oh, boy, was he a Gemini!) and I had already known him when I went to San Juan, I surmised that this was the significant relationship that Virginia had predicted.

Karl and I settled into our own version of domestic bliss, and his two married daughters welcomed me into the family, often commenting, "Dad is so much more vibrant now that you're in his life." On our days off he organized picnics, bike rides and dinner parties. We had a lot of fun. I even caught myself experiencing an unfamiliar feeling—happiness. I was finally alive and in a relationship where I could love and was loved in return. So I surrendered, and not just to romance.

Maybe it was the glow in my aura or the serenity I was emitting, but the locals began seeking me out to do palm readings. This time it felt right. I didn't advertise (I had learned my lesson!), nor did I need to. My reputation grew by word of mouth. Apart from the average doses of neuroses and insecurities, my clients this time were for the most part "normal" healthy sparks of humanity. I enjoyed my readings and was delighted when I received so much positive feedback. Of course, the greatest compliment of all was the rapid increase in business.

Around this time, during a meditation, I had a little "chat" with Divine Intelligence, thanking them for the new flow in my life. Then I got it. The serenity was happening because I was finally channeling my psychic energies into healing others. *Okay, Divine Intelligence, I surrender. I admit I am a psychic and this is my path.*

In retrospect, it was odd that it was in Whistler, an environment that was all about the physical and not considered spiritual by many, where my psychic career was born. But it was not odd to me. Just being at the top of a mountain on a crisp sunny day or looking out on a full moon and the pink-purplish light illuminating the snow-covered peaks filled me with an overwhelming awe for the Universe and all of its creation.

Though Karl was, according to his two daughters, a complete cynic when it came to anything metaphysical, one night he asked me to read him.

"Oh, this is great," I cooed as I described the beautiful white light surrounding him. "In the next two years, you're going to go through a transformation."

Karl frowned.

"You're opening up spiritually. Probably under my influence," I teased.

He beamed then and nodded.

When more and more people made appointments, Karl accepted

this other talent of mine with equanimity. He would even vacate the house on occasion so my clients could be assured of complete privacy. The charges for my readings increased as I intuitively felt the value of my readings expand and develop.

As time went on, Karl and I discussed moving out of Whistler. We wanted to buy our own home, but Whistler was growing too fast and becoming too busy. Then Karl's good friend offered him a contract for a land management project in Kelowna.

"We could go there for a year and then buy a place on the Sunshine Coast," he suggested.

So that was the plan.

Just after Christmas of 1996, I was standing in our living room. It was early evening and Karl was sitting on the couch watching the news. Suddenly a "wind" rushed by my ear. As if someone had breathed the words, I heard, *A male, older and close to you, is going to die.* In my mind's eye, I saw a vague image of a man slumping to the floor, dropping dead. I quickly flicked through my mental list of older men: Uncle Jack (though I was fond of him, we weren't that close), Uncle Alan (about the same). *Ohmigod! My father!*

"My father's going to die!" I told Karl, panicking.

Considering I was the first psychic he had lived with, Karl was amazingly accepting of my predictive outbursts. "Well, you better go to England then." He shrugged as if it was perfectly natural for me to announce imminent deaths.

I returned two weeks later, sad but having accepted that it was the last time I would see my father.

One Wednesday morning in early February as we were eating breakfast, I looked up to see Karl staring at me with a big grin on his face. With his head tilted to one side and supported in his right hand, he asked coyly, "Will you marry me?"

I stopped, toast halfway to my mouth.

I don't know why I was so shocked. It had always been understood that we would end up together. We had called each other wife and husband for a long time now. But somehow when he put the proposal into words, it took my breath away. Maybe my disbelief stemmed from not being able to understand why, whenever I looked at Karl, I couldn't see a future with him. Yet I knew we would never break up.

"Yes," I breathed, smiling back. "But let's wait until we move. That'll be a lovely way to start our new life." I briefly envisioned myself in a white, flowing wedding gown. But for some reason, it didn't feel real.

"Okay, liebling," he beamed and then came around the table and we kissed.

A week later, Karl was dead.

Metaphysical Endnote 29

Are We Date-Stamped?

Do we come to this planet for a specific length of time or do we choose how long we stay? That is the question. Of course, when Karl died, I gave this question a lot of consideration. Was he date-stamped or had he chosen his time and manner of death?

Through my readings, I have intuitively learned that, as in much of life, there is not just one answer. In fact, the options about death can be very specific to the person I am reading. For some of us, particularly those children who die young from an illness or accident, there is a pre-life Agreement. The script of this Agreement includes the child and those whom the child affects—the parents, siblings and friends. That whole drama is, I believe, an agreed-upon event that each and every one of the players can choose to learn from. Or not.

Many of us with those karmic fate lines also have very specific work to do here on the physical plane. As mentioned, it may be unfinished business from other lifetimes or a path that our soul was very adamant about taking before we came to the life. Try as these people might to get themselves killed or to "leave early," their angels will make sure that they don't get off so easily, that they stay and finish the work. When the karma is rebalanced and the lessons are learned, then and only then can the soul shed its mortal coil and return "home."

Then there are those who choose the time of their death by actively or passively committing suicide. The active deaths, the suicides, are, of course, traumatic for the person doing the deed and for those left behind. Again, this transformation through death may be part of some script that all the players co-wrote before coming to the life. The passive suicides are those people who don't care or have given up. They will pursue behaviors they know will sooner or later kill them, such as smoking, drinking heavily, dangerous driving or addictive drug-taking. The even subtler versions of suicide involve those who allow their immune systems to break down so they contract a fatal disease. It doesn't look like suicide, and consciously they may fight their illness, but I can feel on a subconscious level when someone has surrendered their will to live.

Some of us have free will. When we've had enough and want to leave the party, we can manifest our own means of departure.

In Karl's case, although he talked enthusiastically of a future and I was assured of his love, at the moment of his death I just *knew* that he had chosen this way out. He probably did so because on an unconscious level he knew his heart was unhealthy and dreaded having his active lifestyle restricted. And he didn't want to be a burden. All of these thoughts came to me at the time of his death. Of course, later there were also a million *What ifs?*

I feel that Karl not only chose to die on a high note but that he also engineered the manner of his death under circumstances that reassured me that if he was meant to live, he would have. There are no accidents.

CLEAR AND PRESENT DANGER!

*I*n retrospect, there were plenty of signs warning me of Karl's death, but when his oldest daughter, Agnes, and I returned home from the gym and saw the fire engine outside my home that night, they didn't come to mind. Nor did they come to consciousness when I followed the fireman inside, aware that he was clutching some small device that had nothing to do with fire fighting. Or when I saw Karl lying on our kitchen floor, a fireman bent over his white face and prostrate body, pumping his chest. Only later would all the signs rush back to haunt me.

The fireman wouldn't let me get close to Karl, so from the other side of the breakfast bar, I screamed, "Karl, get back in your body!"

The young fireman stared up at me with a mixture of pity, confusion, disbelief and puzzlement, then he resumed his work. For some odd reason, I looked at the clock then. It was exactly 9:00 p.m. *He's gone,* I thought.

Agnes and I were shooed out onto the patio and then upstairs while the firemen continued to work on him. She sobbed as she called her husband. I tried to comfort her while reminding myself to breathe. After what seemed like an eternity, unable to bear the waiting, I went back downstairs. But the sickening "thud" sound coming from the kitchen and the murmur of subdued voices told me that, as a last resort, they were using the paddles. Though I wanted to get away from that awful noise, I stayed rooted to the spot.

It had been over twenty minutes now. Even if they could bring him back, he would have brain damage. What was the point? Then I just stood and watched a few minutes later as the stretcher with Karl on it left the house. I was driven in another red van, trailing the ambulance, to the clinic where at ten o'clock they pronounced him officially dead.

I started trembling that night and didn't stop for three months. As anyone will know who has lost someone suddenly, it is difficult for the mind to wrap itself around the concept. To have someone fill your life with their vibrant energy one moment and then disappear into thin air the next is tough to comprehend. Even though that night at the clinic I had kissed Karl's oh-so-white and cold cheek goodbye, part of my mind still expected him to poke his head around the living room door, a big mischievous grin on his face, and say, "I was just kidding." Now instead of a fresh and vital present, my life with him was relegated to rehashed memories. But the mind has its own amazing self-defense mechanism, and thankfully grief comes in waves.

On some level, we do know what's coming even though we often ignore the warnings. When I re-examined the previous months for signs, there were plenty staring me right in the face. But I hadn't listened. I hadn't wanted to. There is no problem so big that it cannot be run away from, for a while at least.

I remembered the dream two nights before his death. Karl and I were standing on a sailboat that was tipping sideways, with Karl at the bow and me amidships, an impassable laser line of light between us and a voice that kept saying *Clear and Present Danger!* But when I awoke there was no accompanying feeling of urgency. Mystified but not disturbed, I felt no immediate peril for Karl or myself. On the contrary, our lives were falling into place. His new job was becoming a reality and consequently, he was happier and less stressed. My reputation as a bona fide spiritual healer was expanding. Life was good. As well as his marriage proposal, his comments to me over the last two weeks had been so sweet and romantic. "The last two years with you have been the happiest of my life," he said. "I'm going to pay you back a hundredfold for everything you've done for me," and "If I hadn't met you, I don't know what I would have done." They were all lovely things to say, I thought at the time. But he was always a romantic. Little did I know he was saying goodbye.

The warning of death of the "older man" was, of course, not intended for my father but for Karl. I had never even allowed my partner into that equation. Ironically, my father flew from the UK to support me through the ordeal of Karl's funeral. A few weeks after my partner's death, when I went to see the firemen who had attended that night, the one who had given him CPR told me that there had been a chimney fire. Afterwards Karl had gone into the kitchen and, as in my vision, just collapsed. He was probably dead by the time he hit the floor, the fireman said.

Often when Karl and I had gone biking, hiking or skiing, after twenty minutes he would stop and clutch his chest, trying to catch his breath, but I was also gasping with a stitch in my side. He would then recover before I did and take off full of vim and vigor. I thought he was the fitter one.

I also remembered the psychic reading of the previous fall. The gentle clairvoyant with the sparkling blue eyes had been adamant that I had a spirit guide around me whose name was Karl. "No." I laughed. "That's my partner."

"But I see you with someone younger," she argued.

As a psychic, you would think I would have twigged.

Then three days prior, he had spread his palm and asked me to give him a reading. When I peered into his hand, I burst into a fit of giggles. "No, I'll do it later," I said finally, not knowing what was so funny. But as a flight attendant, when aware of potential danger (which with two out of three airlines was frequent!), my reaction had always been to dissolve into laughter, a form of hysteria I decided. Had I sensed the danger in his palm, and yet again, avoided it?

Finally, the bright white light that I had seen in his reading at the beginning of our relationship was indeed a spiritual transformation—his death.

Unable to handle all the sweet memories of Whistler that stared me in the face wherever I went, especially the mountains, I ran away to San Juan Island. This time Virginia begged *me* to do a reading for her. I wasn't sure I could focus. Karl had only been gone three weeks, and the grief lay so thick in and around me. I felt raw, everything hurt. "I'll try," I promised.

We were both delighted when her reading came through clear and succinct. In fact, focusing on someone else's energy, I found, instantly offered a marvelous relief from my own excruciating pain. As if I'd taken three Tylenol, for a whole hour the pain was temporarily tranquilized. I was in Virginia's energy, a much more comfortable place to be than my own.

So when I returned to Whistler, I didn't turn clients away. I was grateful for the brief respites these readings offered. Curiously enough, maybe because of my anguish, my insights became deeper, broader and lighter. An expansion was taking place. Having experienced this loss, I decided, allowed me to better tune in to their spirits. Or was it because I was constantly thinking of Karl and wondering exactly where he was and what he was experiencing in spirit that I became more aligned with the higher vibration?

I willingly read for many people during those first months. It was my salvation. I thanked God for my faith, the knowing that Karl was around in spirit and that only a thin veil separates this world from the next. My compassion and understanding deepened. It occurred to me that every experience in my life had been about feeling *all* emotions, all sides of the multi-prismed crystal, so I could understand all, have compassion for all and thereby be a more competent healer.

And I was not alone. As well as an army of wonderful friends who supported me through this time, I often felt Karl around me. In the mornings, when I came down to make myself a cup of tea (no more cups of tea in bed for moi!), the kitchen light would flicker for a good ten minutes as if he was saying, "Morning, honey."

For the first three months, I wondered if Karl was in as much shock at being dead as I was at having lost him. Maybe I was trying to pacify my own mind or did I really "see" him one day standing in the living room by the offending fireplace asking me, "Am I dead?"

One evening, when I was feeling particularly lonely and trying to lose myself in a movie, the lamp in front of me suddenly dimmed slowly all by itself and then was gradually turned back up again. I nodded, acknowledging Karl's way of letting me know he was with me. "I want you here in the *flesh*," I cried out loud, the second stage of grief—my anger—already in full swing.

But Karl's death was just the beginning of what was, as the Queen of England would say, my *annus horribilus*.

Death, I discovered, can bring out the best or the worst in people. It was immediately apparent that his family either blamed me for his death, wanted to erase me from his life as if their parents had never divorced and I didn't exist, or wanted to use me as a dartboard for all their pain. While I could understand their anger at losing their father so young, I had too much of my own devastation to deal with. Sadly, and for my own preservation, I removed myself from their line of fire, but not before they had ripped out what was left of my heart. Only a few days after the funeral, while I was still an emotional mess, the daughters and their husbands insisted on stripping our home and my memories of his things. It was like he died all over again.

But...there is no problem so big that it cannot be run away from. So I went to Mexico.

On my return, the owners of the house decided to remove the killer fireplace and put another one in the outside wall. The only problem was that, after creating a huge hole in the side of the living room, the contractor forgot to come back. Despite irate calls to the landlord and the deaf contractor, for two months I lived in fear that the big black bear roaming regularly through the back garden would either join me or have me for dinner.

But there is no problem so big that it cannot be run away from.

This time I went back to England for six weeks to see my father and his wife. My compassionate boss understood when I told her I was quitting my high-stress managerial position but still wanted to work in the company on a part-time basis. The readings were starting to take up every spare minute of my time.

When I came back to Whistler in August, although the hole in the living room was filled in with a new fireplace, the house was still a horrible, dusty mess. I started the part-time job, and people were knocking down my door for psychic readings.

In September, while running down my steps before leaping onto my bike, my left ankle decided to go in the opposite direction from my left foot. I came home from the same clinic where Karl had lain, this time on crutches with a severe tear in my ankle. Now I couldn't run anywhere, not even in the car.

Two weeks before Christmas, Karl's ex-wife and his daughters attempted to thwart my meager inheritance by claiming that I was not Karl's partner, but his landlady. (What a nice landlady I was!) If she'd asked me, I would have just given her the darn money. I didn't care about that. But I did care that by dishonoring me, they were dishonoring Karl's memory and his choices. So I hired a lawyer, a rude one, I discovered. (Maybe there's no other kind?) Despite his lack of couth and professionalism, I won.

In February, on the anniversary of his death, not knowing what else to do, I gratefully accepted an invitation to go skiing with friends. This time I ripped my right knee, second-degree media collateral tear. I went back to the dreaded clinic and back on crutches.

While confined to the couch, staring at the shiny, new fireplace, I decided I was cursed. Intuitively I knew it had something to do with my name. When I was finally off the crutches, I visited a numerologist, one of the good psychics.

"You need to change your name," was her first comment.

"Funny you should say that"—though from one psychic to another, it wasn't funny at all—"I've been thinking about that. But I want to keep the 'K'."

She raised her hands in mock horror. "No! Get rid of the 'K'! It's that letter that's been causing all your struggle."

Oh, so that's it. One lousy letter in my name?

Three months later, Natasha was born and my life changed... again.

Metaphysical Endnote 30

What Happens After We Die

Depending on our consciousness at the time of death, there are differing scenarios as to what occurs after our spirits leave our bodies. The standard rite of passage is as follows.

Once the heart has stopped, the spirit separates from the physical body. Either before or at the time of death, our previously deceased family and friends, guardian angels and guides will appear to accompany us through our transformation. The bright white light that people speak of is either a function of the brain dying or, as I prefer to see it, the opening into a much higher spiritual vibration, that place of unconditional love that the soul calls "home."

Initially, there are joyous reunions with loved ones including spirits who chose not to reincarnate this time around. In spirit everything is Consciousness, Mind or Thought. Spirits do not recognize each other in a physical form but as light vibrations. The higher our consciousness, the higher our vibration, the brighter our light shines.

At this time, I believe, the spirit that was ours for this lifetime is also reunited with that part of our soul we left behind. Together with our spirit guides, we then review our last life and how we performed in our movie. Did we stick to our Agreement, fulfill the contracts, live up to our greatest potential, or did we put off our growth? While we are our own judges, our guides will, nevertheless, assist us in recognizing our weak points. What do we need to relearn? Where did we allow our fears to stop us?

Reunited with friends, family and lovers, we resume our life in the spirit world. Often we live out the playful, creative life in spirit that we did not allow ourselves on earth. (That's why we call it heaven!) And according to our level of vibration, the learning continues.

Eventually, when we are ready and if we so desire, we may choose to return to earth, the physical plane. Our function then is to pick up from where we left off in our soul's evolution, finish off the unfinished business, make good on past errors, and, if we are willing to do this learning without incurring any additional negative karma, we will rise to a higher vibration. Unfortunately, some spirits regress. Fortunately, though, the urge of the soul, while striving for balance, is always to evolve. So eventually, sooner or later, we all do rise up.

There are, however, variations on this transformation we call death. The following are just a few:

❖ When older people or those who have been ill for extended periods die, their souls are often weary. After death, their spirits enter a deep "sleep" where they stay until they have recuperated.

❖ Persons who die suddenly and totally resist their death, because they were too young, not prepared, guilty or attached to someone on the earth plane, may not want to leave. Karl's spirit, for instance, was "in and out." He was in just as much shock at being dead as the people he left. In the case of a sudden demise, it can take three months to a year in our time before a spirit can accept and adjust to the idea of his/her own death.

❖ If a person dies guilt-ridden or is traumatized before death, the spirit may stay attached to the earth plane as a ghost to recover from or rectify the situation or repay the debt.

❖ If a bereaved person is clinging to the deceased for longer than is healthy, this unhealthy attachment, sometimes due to guilt, can delay the deceased spirit's progress.

❖ If the deceased failed in the role of spouse, parent, uncle, friend, the spirit of that person may volunteer to return and make good by acting as protector to the living person he/she failed.

❖ If the deceased is of a very low vibration, does not believe in an afterlife, and/or has unfinished business on the physical plane, such as revenge, that spirit often sticks to the physical world, becoming a ghost or attempting to "possess" a physical body through which he/she can enact that revenge.

❖ Some suicides may need prayers to release their unhappy spirits from the physical world. Once back in spirit, some suicides are ecstatic to be out of the physical struggle and *do* move on while others can remain stuck in their own remorse-filled consciousness.

❖ A spirit can return to the physical vibration as an observer to learn vicariously through the living who are learning the same lessons that the deceased rejected while on earth.

❖ Sometimes the spirit almost immediately reincarnates and enters into another body and another movie because they either chose to or need to.

In one of the Buddhist traditions, friends and relatives hold a "burning" 49 days after the person's passing. They create a bonfire on which they place a piece of clothing or a possession belonging to the deceased. This ritual is to celebrate the life of the deceased spirit and to encourage those on the earth plane to let go of that person so that all the spirits, in this world and the next, can get on with living.

So don't believe what your Uncle Charlie says about not believing. When his angels show up and that beautiful bright light shines down upon him, where do you think he chooses to go? Home to heaven! Of course, there are those who *don't* believe in an afterlife and they don't change their minds after death. But eventually, even these spirits tire of being stuck in no-man's land and finally succumb to the white light.

For those left behind, grief is an intensely personal journey. The most nurturing thing we can do when someone we love passes is release them and go through the process of grief with compassion for ourselves. Allow the pain to be there. When it is time to move on, the cloud will lift. You will know it is time to live again.

And so will they!

SOUL MATES

*I*t was the last day of another visit and writing session with Virginia on San Juan Island. I was savoring a cup of coffee in the Front Street Café overlooking a cozy inlet and a harbor full of boats bobbing on the water. Half the tourists in the café, I assumed, were, like me, waiting for a large white ferry which was due to appear within the next half hour on the horizon of that blue but blustery ocean.

"Kate?"

I turned around.

"Helen!" I had always admired this strong-featured, forty-some-thing blonde, mainly for her commitment to her family, the community and, at the same time, the pursuit of her spiritual path. She had proven that one commitment didn't have to preclude the other. "What are *you* doing here?" I asked, not bothering to inform her of my name change.

"Writing," she responded as she took the seat on the other side of the wooden table.

"Me, too! What are you writing?"

"A book on soul mates."

"Oh."

Funny she should mention that word. Since Karl's death, I had half-expected Alejandro, my soul mate (as far as I was concerned), to magically appear as he had done twice before to rescue me from myself. Since I had met him all those years ago, he had never been out of my thoughts for long. It didn't help that every psychic I had visited consis-tently described him to me, predicting conflicting outcomes. But it had been ten years since our last meeting, seventeen years since our first fateful encounter. When I met Karl, I had told him about Alejandro. For a while at least, I had been able to put thoughts of my "soul mate" aside though never totally out of my mind, maybe because for me there was something left unfinished. So it didn't take much to spark the happy memories.

It was October 1978, the hellish year of my nervous exhaustion. Maria and I were supposed to be flying on a two-week holiday to Barbados. We were standby passengers on the first British Airways plane out of Heathrow on the first day of their lifted staff embargo. But most BA crew, it seemed, were also taking their winter holiday in the Caribbean. As Maria and I were at the bottom of the standby totem pole, we didn't stand a chance. Resigned to the hour's drive back from Heathrow to Maria's house in the gray October rain, she and I consoled ourselves with dinner at the local pub. Not quite rum punch under a palm tree!

Two days later, British Caledonian and Viasa Airways transported us the pretty way, via Caracas, to the Caribbean. Spending a five-hour night-stop in orange plastic chairs in a terminal painted in orange and purple zigzags wasn't very conducive to sleep. Despite the fact that we met a fascinating selection of international travelers that night, I was feeling cheated of the three days of our holiday that we had lost in getting there.

But the wait turned out to be worth it. Barbados was a perfect paradise. As if I had my own palm-waving slave, I lay on a white sandy beach under a coconut tree, the wafting leaves acting as both sun-protector and cooler. Without the threat of phone calls from Crewing—though they had been known to hunt down needed crewmembers in the jungles of South America and at funerals on the Outer Hebrides—I finally began to relax. My skin soon darkened to a deep brown and my hair became blonder in the baking humidity.

I was out of the black pit now but I still felt numb and isolated in my glass bottle. The soothing heat gradually began to melt the iciness in my bones and relax my sore muscles. Physically, at least, I was healing. And I fell in love with Barbados, almost as if I had come home.

So ten days later, when it was time for us to leave, I told Maria I wasn't ready to part with my beach chair, my palm tree, the white grainy sand, the blue, blue ocean or my daily pina colada. I needed another three days, my full holiday.

"Well, what shall I tell the airline?" she asked, already agreeing to do the dirty work.

"That I fell into a vat of rum punch and drowned?"

"No, how about the usual stories?" She smiled. "You got kidnapped by a giant sea urchin or a pirate abducted you off the Jolly Roger?"

Crewing had heard them all. It was difficult to be original any more. And though it was not in my nature to lie, I felt that my karmic relationship with Crewing deserved a little rebalancing, in my favor. So I stayed.

By Saturday, after two days of solitude, I was ready for some company. Standing at the beach bar, I was waiting patiently (one has no choice in Barbados!) for a cocktail to be prepared when a few girls from a British Airways crew invited me to join them for dinner.

As we teetered in our high heels along the pot-holed road from the Hilton to the open-air restaurant on the beach, I suggested that afterwards we could all go to a great club called the Garage. Under a full moon, only a few feet away from crashing waves and a silvery ocean twinkling like diamonds, we ate fresh flying fish and chips and exchanged outrageous flying stories. After dinner, the girls announced they were too tired to go anywhere else but the hotel. An expert on fatigue, I understood. So we returned to the Hilton and the Flambeau Club downstairs.

When I looked back on that night, I knew it was fate that we arrived three days late in Barbados, and so it was fate that guided me to stay the three extra days. Wasn't it also fate then that brought me to the Flambeau instead of the Garage, and fate when the waiter brought me a marguerita instead of a pina colada?

When I made my way to the bar to change the drink, the seething mêlée of other internationals waiting to be served was daunting. I was just about to give up and return to my seat when I heard the words, "I was just going to ask you to dance."

As I turned towards the soft American voice accented with a gentle Spanish lilt and saw the boyish grinning face, I felt my breath taken away. "And I was just going to change my drink," I responded on automatic, already spellbound and in love with this man. But it was more than love, more like recognition, as if I had known him before, not in this lifetime, but a long, long time ago. The joy of seeing him again filled me until I was brimming over. And when what seemed like a few seconds later, he presented me with a fresh cocktail, something mystical happened. The noise of the music, the sound of people talking, all stilled into silence as if I was caught in a time warp. Then the dark numbness in my whole body just melted, lifted and was gone. I heard a "ka-thunk" and, in an instant, as if a huge light on a movie set had been switched on, every cell in my being was filled with light. He could have been one of those southern healers who smacked me on the forehead and declared, "Yooo arrr heeeled." But instead he just smiled at me. I was alive again. Hallelujah! Praise the Lord!

So we danced, Alejandro and I. And I couldn't take the smile from my face.

But the dance of our relationship would be a lot more complex, romantic, exciting and painful than I ever could have imagined.

"What's the premise of your book?" I asked Helen.

She took a sip of the frothy cappuccino for which this café was famous. "Well," she leaned back in the wooden chair, "most people think that a) we have only one soul mate and b) when we meet that soul mate, we will come together like magnets," she smacked her hands together for emphasis, "and that we live happily ever after."

"We don't?" She had my attention.

In March of the following year, on my first trip with my new long-haul airline employer to Bangor, Maine, Alejandro and I had met again. When I called him at his office, I didn't even have to say my name, just, "Hi." He immediately knew who I was.

"I'm coming to see you," he said, causing me to stop breathing momentarily.

My new friends on the crew didn't understand how I could be so confident of my feelings for him after such a brief encounter followed by a six-month separation. But I knew. And when I saw him again, I struggled to contain the joy that I felt. Even though he stayed just one night, with a kiss on each cheek at the end of the evening, the happiness of seeing him filled me again. "I will be coming to London for two weeks in June," he told me. Though I was mystified by his contradictory cool and loving approach towards me, I couldn't wait.

"When soul mates meet, they don't automatically stay together."

Funny you should say that.

"The opposite can actually happen. They meet and, of course, at first it's all wonderful. But often the feelings can be so tremendously powerful that the people, because they're not used to such intensity, run away terrified, scared, overwhelmed."

That would explain my extreme happiness in his presence; I thought my heart would burst through my chest. At the same time, an overwhelming urge to flee would sometimes overtake me. But I thought that was just my own neurotic make-up. Intimacy never was my strong suit in those days. Maybe I didn't trust that anyone could be that happy, for long anyway.

When I arrived home from my Toronto trip in June, my flat mate, Maggie, had left notes all over the house. "Alejandro called." I was so ecstatic during those first four days with him, I couldn't even eat. And I was terrified, terrified that I would drown him in this tidal wave of love I was experiencing, terrified that I would scare him away forever and terrified that he might not feel the same way.

One night, just as we were about to get into a passionate embrace, the words just tumbled unbidden out of my mouth. "Are you married?" He sighed, retreated and replied, "Yes."

With that devastating news, I decided that after he left England, while he was married I could never see him again. A few days after he had gone, leaving me numb, I was just climbing into my car when a voice whispered in my ear, "You won't be together now, but later. Much later." Well, I could wait, I thought.

Helen may have suspected from my captivated expression that her information was hitting home. Pennies were dropping like a jackpot in Vegas.

"And when you think about it," she continued, "it makes perfect sense."

"What do you mean?"

"You and your soul mate may have experienced many lifetimes together but maybe not always in a romantic context. They might have been a brother, sister, friend, grandmother."

The image of Alejandro and me as children often preoccupied me as did another flash of us living on a tropical island. But maybe that was because we had met in Barbados...?

"In those roles, there's been murder, betrayal, adultery, sacrifice, loss, illness, abandonment, all kinds of challenges to a relationship. We go through so much. Meeting your soul mate again is like meeting someone you've been married to for thousands of years and all that entails. With them you have gone through every emotion. While the love is there, a huge amount of unconscious fear and distrust is also present, depending on how you left each other the last time."

Was that why Alejandro and I couldn't be together? The intense love was there, on my part anyway, but maybe there was some horrific past that unconsciously we recognized but didn't allow ourselves to acknowledge. If we got together, maybe our relationship would be destructive. I had witnessed it in others.

To echo my thoughts, Helen added, "Soul mate energy is tough because the lesson *is* the relationship. If you do decide to be together, you may have to go through hell before you come out the other side, having forgiven and understood the past so you can be happy in the present. It's a lot of entanglement, a lot of work. Not many people at this level of consciousness are able to handle it."

Er, that would include me.

"You are better off meeting up with a twin soul than a soul mate."

"How do you define twin soul?"

"Two souls who come together to share the life journey but who are not entangled in each other's emotions. You are there to share and support each other in your individual life's purpose. It's not nearly as intense. The learning isn't *about* the relationship, but about what you do with your life. The twin soul is there to love you while you carry out your purpose."

"But what about soul mates? How do they break through their fears so they can be together?"

"It's like anything else in life. When we decide that love is greater than fear."

Oh, the "F" word again.

Helen stood up. "I'm going to get a refill," she said. "How about you?"

"I'm fine, thanks." As I glanced out over the horizon and saw a white blob on the line where the ocean met the sky—the incoming ferry—I wondered if the angels had sent Helen as their messenger to offer me understanding and allow me to let go of the ghost of Alejandro. Because that's what he had become. And anyway, the question of whether I would be with him or not was now redundant.

Diane, the psychic, and I were right in 1987 when we had both predicted that this man from afar with whom I had a special bond would make an appearance later that year. That November, during a session in a flotation tank where I often received psychic visions, I "saw" Alejandro walking into a room, coming over to me and putting his arms around me. When I returned home that night, my brother rang to inform me that Alejandro, after eight years' absence with only a few phone conversations between us, had called looking for me. After my friend had peeled me off the ceiling, I spoke with Alejandro. He told me that he and his wife had separated.

A month later, he and I were in Whistler, watching a movie, enjoying each other's company, when I decided that I couldn't contain my feelings any longer. I had to tell him. And so I did. Maybe the timing wasn't right, or he was afraid to admit his feelings, but I didn't get the response

I had hoped for. I retreated into my little shell and he into his. As we said our farewells at the airport the next day, his last words to me were, "Keep in touch." A month later I tried to, but he had disappeared.

So I told myself that Alejandro was an illusion, a fantasy, and that so much happiness really isn't possible in the long term anyway. There had to have been some other purpose for our meeting that I didn't understand. If we had engineered a life together, maybe we would have become like so many other couples, taking one another for granted, snapping, irritated. Familiarity breeds contempt. Or as my brother Alex once quipped, familiarity just breeds.

My faith in the institution of marriage had always been fragile. While it worked for some people, it didn't seem to be my destiny. I got that message loud and clear when Karl was ripped out of my life a week after his proposal.

Was I still holding on to the faint hope that Alejandro and I would one day, by some miracle, be together? Probably, although it had faded over the years. I know it's why I hadn't allowed anyone else into my heart in my thirties. There wasn't room, he had filled it to overflowing.

Well, now it was later, much later, and I didn't even know where he was or whether he was married or single, dead or alive. By his absence it was apparent that he didn't feel the same way about me. Or was it too intense for him, too? One of these days, when I had the courage, I would have to find him and write him a letter. Then I could finally let it all go. *One of these days.*

Just as Helen returned to the table, I noticed that the ferry had arrived and a motley collection of tourists and locals were pouring out of its underbelly. "I have to go," I said standing up, gathering up my thoughts and my writing materials.

"Tell me, Kate," Helen inquired, "have you met your soul mate?"

"Yes…one of them."

Metaphysical Endnote 31

The Importance of Loving Self

In an old "Monty Python" sketch, John Cleese is sitting on the edge of his bed, totally absorbed in his own reflection in the bedroom mirror. When his wife walks into the room and sees him sitting there, she says, "Really, David, do you have to keep staring at yourself like that?" David replies, "No, darling, you don't understand. This time *it's the real thing!*"

Humor is truth. We *are* meant to be in love with ourselves, to recognize that we are a spark of the divine. What we love in others, soul mates or otherwise, is only what is already present within us. Loving Self is what we came here to do.

When reading the hand, I can determine not only by the markings, depth and shape of the heart line but also by the energy in the whole hand how much or how little the client accepts him- or herself. By rejecting ourselves, we are not only rejecting that divinity from which we come, we are also not able to accept the love that surrounds us, especially from soul mates. And isn't earth a training ground for the Gods/Goddesses that we are in the process of becoming? What kind of creators will we be if we insist on being knotted masses of insecurities?

Yet loving the Self seems to be our greatest challenge. Why is it so *hard?*

"Just be yourself," we are often told. But if you have been taught that "yourself" is not acceptable or you don't know who you are, who are you going to be? If you don't know you, then how can you love you?

Understanding is knowing and knowing is loving.

On this path to self-love we are thrown many challenges and tests: abandonment, abuse, rejection and betrayal. How can we survive all this with our self-esteem not merely intact, but thriving? We need to remember that this adventure we call life is just a movie and these characters and events are all merely tests to motivate us to go deeper, find our power, our strength, find out how really valuable, cherished and adorable we are. In that consciousness, we can then repel any idea that we are not of the highest and the best.

If you feel any doubt about your own worth at any time, no matter how ugly or rejected you feel, remember you are a manifestation of that beautiful brilliant white light in the sky. You *are* a spark of the divine, a piece of heaven. If anybody tells you differently, then remember they are merely projecting onto you what they have forgotten about themselves and where they came from.

The main reasons you might not love yourself:

❖ *You are holding guilt from this or another lifetime.* Dig deep until you discover the source of that guilt. You may need help. Then forgive yourself. Let it go. You *are* an innocent.

❖ *You are afraid.* So do something that scares you! Take a (calculated) risk. Facing fear is invigorating and will set you free.

❖ *You have been taught to hate yourself.* Change the tape and the story about "not being good enough." That was just one person's not-very-highly-evolved opinion of you.

To love our Selves, our authentic Selves, *is* the real thing. Without it, we can never attract, and keep, our soul mates. After all, loving our Selves unconditionally is one of the most important functions of our evolution.

LEAP OF FAITH

"You know, Kate, I mean Natasha, the first year is all about doing it." My sister-in-law, Sarah, was calling me from Calgary and talking about grief. "There is nothing you can do but go through it." She knew what she was talking about. A few years before she met my brother, her fiancé of five years had, after an unresolved quarrel, committed suicide. Sarah had survived it with her sanity intact and a lot of grace. So I listened to her advice.

She was right. In April of 1997, fourteen months after Karl's death, as if I was emerging out of a thick black cloud, the intense weight of grief lightened. Although I loved Whistler, my thriving psychic practice and a circle of wonderful friends, I felt a strong urge to move away. Everywhere I looked, everyone I saw, reminded me of my past with Karl. It was time to move forward.

I decided to buy a house. But where?

One day in the kitchen, that same voice that had warned me of Karl's death urged me to go to the Sunshine Coast, as Karl and I had once planned. As if to accentuate the point, I felt my guide giving me a strong metaphysical shove in that direction.

I wasn't giving too much thought to when, where and how I would make a living on this long strip of land accessible only by ferry, but an idea came to me when my realtor instantly found a brand new, four-bedroom house. It sounded perfect. When I saw it, I envisioned a mini healing center, the bedrooms filled with massage tables and other healing practitioners and a steady flow of psychic clientele coming to me for readings. But it would take a while to build up that business. In the meantime, until I got acquainted with the community and they with me, I would rent out one of the rooms. That's when I met Neville.

Not knowing a soul in my new hometown apart from my realtor and now Neville, my new tenant, I still kept one foot in the door of Whistler, clinging to my part-time job, part-time home and juggling appointments with Whistler clients. To spark a psychic business in Sechelt, despite my apprehensions about advertising and people recognizing my face, I took the plunge and put an advertisement in the local paper, complete with photo.

After a few weeks of bouncing between Whistler and Sechelt, I was supposed to be setting out for Whistler one Monday morning when I was overcome by dizziness. Too light-headed to drive, I plunked myself on the couch and stayed there, trying to regain my equilibrium. I knew why I was so unbalanced. The to-ing and fro-ing between two homes, a new business and a part-time job was too much. I needed to make a decision and commit to one place. Which one would it be? Sechelt or Whistler? If I stayed in Sechelt, with a population of only 27,000 on the Coast, would there be enough business for me to make a living?

"Let your clients come to you," my housemate suggested, sounding like Kevin Costner in *Field of Dreams*. "And they will." So with Neville's encouragement, I committed to Sechelt as my home. I hoped I would now become the full-time psychic that so many other clairvoyants had predicted. The same psychic who had told me Karl was my spirit guide had also told me that I would need to take a leap of faith. Was this it?

Elizabeth, one of my girlfriends and a client from Whistler, called later that week to tell me she had met and was madly in love with the man I had predicted for her earlier that year.

"That's great," I said. "I'm so happy for you." I was also happy to be validated. Elizabeth, an accountant by trade, had accused me of losing my marbles when I had described how she would get to know him. I had envisioned her sitting at a computer and writing. "But I never write," she had retorted. A few months after the reading, she had met him over the Internet and wrote to him three times a day for months before finally meeting in person.

Oh, to be in love again, I thought.

"What about you?" she asked, sensing my wistfulness. "Any interesting men in Sechelt?"

"Haven't really looked, but I do believe I'm ready now for another relationship. I refuse to date though."

"How are you going to meet him then?"

"I'm just going to wait until somebody is standing right in front of me telling me he loves me."

"Good luck," Elizabeth snorted. By the tone in her voice, I could tell she still believed some of my marbles were missing. She obviously didn't believe in the art of manifesting, drawing what you want to you by thought.

It was only a month later when this scene actually unfolded with Neville. Suddenly and happily, I found myself at the beginning of a new relationship. I wondered if the psychic who had indicated that Karl was my spirit guide was right. Perhaps his spirit had somehow engineered my buying this house so Neville and I could come together. My vision of the house as a healing center also manifested, although not quite in the way I had imagined. While the house and our relationship facilitated a healing for both our painful pasts, when Neville's three delightful children came to live with us, I suddenly found myself ensconced in a loving family. Nurturing them through their temporary separation from their mother was challenging, delightful and above all, great medicine.

I need not have worried about my psychic business blossoming. Very soon a steady flow of people was trooping to my door. Also in demand in Vancouver, Whistler and then Calgary, I traveled. The local school board contracted me to do classes, corporations and hotels hired me for their special events including team building and I even had my own live radio show. Friends started calling me "Frasier."

It's really amazing what can happen when we take a leap of faith.

Metaphysical Endnote 32

The Magic of Manifesting

You *can* do magic! Or what appears to be magic. The art of manifesting is, as all things are, based on the laws of physics. If you want to create your own future successfully, understanding and mastering the art of manifestation is paramount.

Whether you want to manifest a larger house, a wonderful relationship, increased prosperity, a harmonious outcome to a conflict or a slimmer svelter you, the Universe doesn't care. It just takes orders.

Imagine that you have put your order in with the Universe. Implant the image of what you want *clearly* in your mind. And hold it. What is in the future already exists out there in the ether as a potential in some form. Your order is just waiting for you to claim it. What is yours will come to you.

Thoughts are magnetic impulses. Therefore, every time you envision driving that brand new car, making dinner in your new kitchen, the compliments on your new figure, or all the zeroes on that cheque, you are increasing the density of the magnetism, drawing your dream ever closer to you.

In the world according to Natasha, there is an equation for manifestation, and in order for your dream to become a reality, no matter how big or small, each part of the formula needs to be engaged in with passion! My formula is:

Desire + Visualization + Faith + Deservability = Manifestation

- ❖ *Desire:* Desire is the motivation that propels you into willing your dream into physical form. It is a "I-just-have-to-have-it" feeling rather than a "well-that-would-be-nice-if...." Either you desire it or you don't. Which one is it?
- ❖ *Visualization:* Your thoughts are magnets. Visualize your dream in your mind's eye in great detail as if your dream has already manifested. Keep visualizing your dream at least twice a day until it shows up in physical form.
- ❖ *Faith:* You have 260 million cells in your body (give or take a few thou). Each and every one of those cells needs to believe that whatever reality you are visualizing is already yours.
- ❖ *Deservability:* You will only allow yourself to receive what you

believe you deserve. If your dream isn't manifesting, it probably means you don't believe that you really deserve it.

So desire it, visualize it, think big, believe it and know that you deserve to have whatever your little heart desires.

It works! You *really* can do magic with your mind.

DON'T SIT ON THE GRANDMOTHER!

*A*fter two days of steady psychic readings in Whistler, I was looking forward to relaxing with my friend, Georgia, at David's summer solstice party. The forecast had been for a balmy, starry night. Instead the heavens had opened up and the rain came down in a solid wall.

David had refused to cancel the party, so Georgia and I made our way around his house to the back garden where we saw long sheets of orange tarpaulin strung between thick-branched old elms. Mosquito-repelling candles flickered precariously on tables and tree stumps. Trying to ignore the rain, the guests stood around in clusters under the sagging nylon, clutching paper plates of barbecued meat and limp salad and plastic glasses of wine.

As Georgia and I moved from tarp to tarp, mingling, I saw him. "My God, there's Blondie!"

"Who's Blondie?" Georgia frowned, chomping on a chicken leg.

"Remember the fair-haired, rugby-playing, younger-than-you, go-ing-to-make-you-laugh guy that I saw for you?" Over two years earlier I had predicted that Georgia would meet this man, marry him, have two children, and live on Easy Street. (There really is an Easy Street in Whistler.)

"Yeah, yeah," she muttered, eyeing Blondie.

As if the gods were complying, David suddenly appeared with Blondie in tow. "Georgia and Natasha, meet Doug." Was it my imagination or did I see sparks fly as they shook hands?

For a June night it was surprisingly chilly and the wine was beginning to have a soporific effect. By the time the rain had finally dwindled to a drizzle, Georgia and Doug were chatting easily together. Though happy for my friend, I began to feel a little excluded from their repartee.

Suddenly tired, I told Georgia, "I'm going into the house for a while."

"I'll come with you," she said. "I need a refill."

Georgia excused herself from a crestfallen Doug, and we climbed the wooden stairs on the outside of the house into the main living area on the second floor. As soon as I entered through the sliding glass doors, I felt an overwhelming presence, as if I was walking into a thick, unfriendly fog. An antique, glass-fronted china cabinet filled with dainty teacups was sitting inside on the left.

"The furniture is the grandmother's," I announced, spinning around to face Georgia.

She eyed the cabinet. "How do you know that?"

"The grandmother is here." I sensed her unwelcoming energy everywhere.

"Oooh, I'm going to check this out with David," Georgia chuckled gleefully and disappeared outside again.

I wandered through a hallway-cum-dining room into the kitchen. Four young men, all in black baggy jeans and t-shirts, were lounging at the round kitchen table, drinking beer and talking. In the living room, I found a square, faded, yellow tartan armchair in front of an unlit fireplace and an old tweed couch along one wall. I opted for the couch, lay down, and closed my eyes. Heaven!

Then somebody was shaking my shoulder. "Natasha. Wake up."

"Hmmm?" I was in that half-awake place between this world and another.

Georgia was standing in front of me, waving her hands excitedly. I came into a half-sitting position as she exclaimed, "You're right! David told me it *is* his Grandmother's furniture, all of it. How do you do that, girl?"

"I just feel it," I murmured, lying down again.

"Wait till the girls hear this one!" Georgia giggled.

Hazily I saw that she was now standing in the middle of the room clutching a glass of wine. Through half-closed eyes, I watched as she backed up towards the ancient armchair. Then she parked her glutei on the wooden arm, and I knew what she was about to do.

Bolting upright, I raised a hand to stop her but she started to slide back into the chair. *"Don't sit on the grandmother!"* I yelled.

In an attempt to defy gravity, Georgia flung both arms outward.

Her eyes, wide and terrified, nearly popped out of her head, but she managed to lean forward and leap off the chair. Amazingly, she balanced her wine without spilling a drop.

"Didn't mean to scare you, but the grandmother is sitting in that chair," I said, chuckling.

Georgia sank gingerly onto the end of the couch. Her glass trembling in her hand, she stared at the empty chair.

"Can you really see her?" she asked.

"Yes," I said, lying back down.

"Cool." I envisioned my friend telling this story for weeks.

"That's her favorite chair," I informed Georgia. "And she's not very happy."

"How come? I didn't *actually* sit on her. Did I?"

We both laughed. "She doesn't like what's going on in this house."

"What do you mean?"

"The people in the kitchen, the drinking. She'd like to get rid of everyone. She's very protective of her furniture. And of David." I was becoming drowsy again. "She doesn't approve of the party," I murmured, the words barely audible as I snuggled down.

"This is *so* cool," Georgia exclaimed, standing up. "I *have* to tell David." She was gone. I slept.

Only minutes later Georgia was shaking me again. "Can't a girl get a nap around here?" I complained.

"David is dying to tell you something," Georgia urged. "Come outside."

The grandmother, I noticed, was still in the chair, feet firmly planted on the floor, a thunderous look on her tough face, and frustrated, knowing she was powerless to change anything. *Must be hard being a ghost.* "Sorry, Granny," I said as I left.

I followed Georgia outside. Most of the people had gone, the temperature had dropped, the rain was just an intermittent plopping on the tarpaulins. The garden was in darkness except for a crackling fire in the far corner where a small cluster of people were warming their hands. Someone was strumming a guitar. Doug's eyes lit up as Georgia reappeared. David made a space for me on the wooden bench in front of the fire while Georgia sidled up to her new friend and rekindled their conversation.

"Hi." David greeted me casually as though I was returning a set of keys to him and not reporting on a close encounter with his dead grandmother. (Not nearly as close as Georgia's, though.)

"Your Grandmother loves you a lot," I told him, warming my hands at the fire.

David smiled. "We were always very close."

"She doesn't like strangers in the house, though."

"My grandmother's father was an alcoholic," he explained, nursing a beer, "and back in those days it caused a terrible scandal. Her family lost everything. So the rest of the family made a vow that none of them would ever drink or allow their children to drink. She was married to my grandfather for fifty years, and if they went to a gathering where she even suspected there might be alcohol, she would let him go in and she would sit in the car all night."

"Didn't I tell you?" Georgia told Doug. "She's a very good psychic." I should officially appoint Georgia as my agent or at the very least, president of my fan club.

Blondie was eyeing Georgia wistfully. Would he ask her out?

"Georgia, you can stay if you want but I really need to go," I stated.

"I'll come too," she said, putting her glass down.

Darn. What about the new romance?

Blondie looked as if someone had stolen his lollipop. *Do something,* I silently urged.

"Can I catch a ride with you?" he asked Georgia. "I live just up the hill."

Yay.

The three of us made a dash through the rain for the front porch while we waited for the Whistler Taxi. I shivered while Georgia and Blondie talked like old friends. *Maybe my prediction will come true after all.* They sat in the back seat together while I hogged the heater in the front. Georgia was friendly as she called goodnight to Doug.

"So, Georgia," I inquired, attempting a casual tone, "did you like him?" *Do you think he could be the one, hmmm?*

"Nah," she shrugged. "Nice enough guy, just not my type."

But, but, Georgia, I pleaded with her silently, *maybe if you just gave him a chance.* Knowing my stubborn friend, I would not be able to persuade her otherwise.

So that was that.

As a psychic, one encounters certain occupational hazards, the oxymoronic psychic *un*predictability of never knowing when or where the spiritual information will come from.

And because of the vagaries of free will that we all possess, no matter how wonderful a future one predicts, clients will do what they want to do anyway. Hence psychics cannot be right *all* the time. Some people would just rather be safe and cozy in their comfort zones than risk dipping one big toe into the pool of joy. There is often a great gnashing of teeth as I watch the bait for a wonderful future dangle in front of a client and then have to observe powerlessly as they ignore their potential for happiness.

My advice to apprentice psychics? Get used to it. You can't win 'em all. But don't make yourself wrong about your predictions. You can lead your clients right to the trough of happiness, but you cannot force them to drink from it. Many of us, I swear, are born with a lemming instinct drawing us habitually towards unhappiness.

And while I saved the grandmother the abhorrent indignity of being sat upon by my slightly inebriated friend, I could not force that same friend to explore a path to happily-ever-after.

At the time of writing, Georgia is living in Los Angeles and is still single.

The Blessings

If I have given you the idea that the life of a psychic is all pain and struggle, that's not the whole story. Though there are challenges, there are also gifts.

While I initially rejected being a psychic because it didn't appeal to my ego's image of who I was, I probably couldn't stop doing the readings now even if I wanted to. For me tuning in on a regular basis is like breathing. There are rewards. And I don't mean financial. (Where is that Lear jet anyway?)

First, I am honored that people who barely know me, mostly on a recommendation from a friend, are prepared to allow me to see into their souls' deepest, darkest corners. Through my clients, the wisdom of the Universe is revealed to me along with all the love, magic and limitlessness out there. The strength I witness in my clients, their drive to survive and their lessons are also inspirational for me.

Second, when I am able to facilitate a healing in some way, then yes, there are plenty of blessings, whether it be through a renewed clarity, a deeper understanding, a message from a deceased loved one, a fractured past forgiven, a released guilt or a resolved conflict or whether it be that a latent gift is revealed, a predicted soul mate arrives, a serious illness is prevented, a warning is heeded, a beautiful resolution appears, or a happily-ever-after manifests.

I am especially rewarded, however, when clients, rather than just follow my advice, listen to and trust their own inner voices. Then they can follow what their souls are urging them to do: grow.

Although now I have a busy practice and work hard, my life is an unending adventure. One week I am flying in a helicopter to the top of a mountain to do readings in a tent and the next week I am honored with an invitation to participate in a weekend Native healing ceremony. It is not just the physical adventure that is thrilling, it's also the adventure of the mind. And that is infinite for all of us.

The greatest blessing, however, is the gift of awareness. When we step into our higher potential, the universe is, indeed, a magical place. My own earthly evolution is far from over and I'm a long way from Perfect (I'm still here, aren't I?), but at least I know which path to follow. I'm also in great company. When the load becomes too heavy, I have angels to help me carry my bags.

So do you.

MAKING PEACE WITH THE PARENT

28H. A girl to the left, a woman to the right, knees in my back, and I am looking forward to ten hours of floundering uncertainty. Will my mother be dead or alive when I land in Scotland?

"She's had a stroke," my younger brother Luke had told me just before my flight was due to leave from Vancouver on Saturday. He sounded homesick for Canada, a lonely little boy's voice coming down the line.

As Air Transat spirits me over the Atlantic surrounded by fluffy white clouds in a blanket of blue sky, I remember the question Alejandro once asked me. What are the highlights of your life? My response had surprised me. Are highlights only about the good times or are they *all* memories, good and bad, that stick in your mind like cooked spaghetti to a wall? On this day of June 10, 2001, I wonder if my mother is scanning the seventy-eight years of her life and taking inventory of her spaghetti.

The call had come on Tuesday. "There's no urgency," my oldest brother, Mark, had reassured me, now on his way back to Canada. But something told me there was.

It is now Sunday and my eighty-year-old father is accompanying me, his supportive arm around my shoulder, to his ex-wife's room on the fourth floor. Dumfries, home to Robbie Burns, and its hospital—which took in the Lockerbie Air disaster victims in 1989—is now home to my dying mother.

My brother Luke's eyes light up, relief oozing out of every pore, as we enter her room. He leaves almost instantly for a cigarette to escape the sight of my shrunken mother and the suffocating smell of death.

My father leans over his wife of thirty-one years, mother of his five children and a woman he hasn't seen in twenty-three summers and gently mutters something. I think it's "good-bye."

"Just in case I don't see her again," he tells me, his voice cracking. As he prepares to leave, there are tears in his eyes. We hug before the door closes behind him and I am alone. With her.

I pull up a chair to the pristine white bed. Her eyes are half-open, her breathing steady but labored, her emaciated form no longer a threat, not a physical one anyway. I am relieved by her vulnerability, that she is no longer the big, bullying woman who intimidated me for so long. Yet it is not so much her physicality that did the damage but her words. My fears are assuaged: she cannot lash out at me with that now dormant tongue. Still I cannot bring myself to touch her clawed hand lying white and still on an even whiter sheet. Those hands, like small, rough bricks, had stung me too many times when she had suddenly slugged me across my face for offences unknown.

As I wait anxiously for my brother to return, I stare at her helpless form. Why does a bright, intelligent, beautiful, generous woman who had been devoted to her children transform into a vengeful, vicious monster? Was it the devastation of a failed marriage and the ensuing alcoholism, or had that particular strain of insanity always coursed through her veins only ignited by the divorce? Then how had she been able to maintain so many loyal friendships with charming, educated people without ever revealing that savage force within her? Those friends will probably accuse us of being cold-hearted, ungrateful children, abandoning their mother. Should I tell them that trying to love her was akin to hugging a porcupine with serrated, rotating switchblades on the end of each poisoned quill?

"The heeerring is the last thing to go-o," Alistair, the nurse, tells me in his soft Scottish accent as we settle in for a night of watching and waiting. "She'll know you're heerre." This is meant to reassure but it doesn't. Had news of my impending arrival instigated her stroke? But then the doctor had allowed her a glass of wine with dinner on the Friday. And it was Friday when she had learned that my father, her ex-husband, would be traveling from Wales to pay her a visit. Maybe it was all three.

It is now Monday afternoon and she is still alive, her imminent death postponed, temporarily at least. Luke and I make a decision, after two days without sleep, to go to our mother's home to rest. On the half-hour ride there in Luke's rented car, the lush green hillsides are soothing after the clinical harshness of the hospital. "Thay'll bee no–o–o coos," a Scottish passenger had warned me. He was right. Due to the indiscriminate foot-and-mouth disease, the fields are eerily bare of cattle.

While I am enjoying the scenery, Luke, having been alone with our mother and his own thoughts for the last four days, is dying to talk. "Do you think she was sick or evil?" he blurts.

I ponder my answer. Being a spiritual healer, I know that evil is merely the lowest vibration of fear. "I'd like to believe she was sick."

"Nah. She was evil," he hisses between clenched teeth.

Yes. He's right. When my mother had tormented her prey, namely her children, with her terrible words, the hard glint of victory that glistened in her eyes was like the very devil gloating "Gottcha."

The home that my oldest brother Mark had provided for her was spacious, cozy and clean. Not having seen her for the last ten years, I was shocked to see old-people equipment around the house: a walker in the living room, a special emergency telephone device, a chair in her shower with grab handles. Had she really been that frail? When I had talked to her only last year, she had sounded so vital. In fact, she still had the strength to wound. While knowing that she wouldn't give me credit for anything, I had still entered the viper's nest and enquired about my psychic ability as a child. Of course, she had denied any recognition of this talent. "When you were three years old, you were *such* a bully" was all she could say. Her last words to me.

A string of phone calls prohibits sleep. One by one her friends confess that they won't be coming to visit Sylvia now. They say she is no longer the Sylvia they knew, and they want to remember her the way she was. We can relate.

Her neighbor and friend, Beth, pops over for tea. She informs me that my mother is a humanist.

A humanist? Then Beth explains that it means she doesn't believe in any afterlife. When the physical body is dead, that's it.

This is not comforting to me. I am well aware that our beliefs determine where our spirits go. If my mother's spirit stays stuck on the earth plane, she could haunt me in death as well as in life. *Aaagh!* I pray for guidance.

Later, Luke and I set about going through the practicalities of death, sorting through paperwork, cupboards and clothes, assigning mementos for friends and family. When my niece calls from France to tell me my older sister is not coming to her mother's deathbed, I am not surprised. It is just my long lost brother, Alex, we need to track down now.

"I have a feeling today's the day," I say the next morning as we pull into the hospital's sloping car park.

"God, I hope so." Luke notices my shock at his response. "Well, she can't be comfortable like that," he reasons, "and I don't want to have to leave you on your own."

No. I was dreading Luke's leaving. Just how long can a person live without a liver?

A terrible groaning noise is emanating from our mother's room. Is this the death rattle? Alistair, when called, assures me she is not in any pain. I do not believe him. After three hours of watching her agonized twitching and having to listen to that rhythmic, constipated grunting, I finally persuade Alistair to give her morphine. The painkiller and the rearrangement of her withered body soothe her. She breathes silently again and is out of the pain that she wasn't in. As he leaves the room, he tells us how much he and the other nurses love our mother. "She's so—o—o wonderrrful," he says. Luke and I just nod, used to the duality of her.

It's Wednesday and the nurses apparently have no idea how long my mother will hang on. "Och, it's vairry harrd to taill," they all say as if that is the one phrase they learn at nursing school. So we continue our vigil punctuated by frequent breaks away from the intensity of the tiny, disinfected but stinky cubicle.

As Luke and I stand over her, relaying loving messages from friends and relatives, her half-open eyes, now reduced to black pinpricks, swivel back and forth as if reading the timbre of our voices. Slowly, she turns her head towards me. Those bullet-hard eyes search my face as she strains through an agonized grunting noise to make herself under-stood. I step back involuntarily, not sure of what she is so desperate to communicate. Is she saying, *Thank you for coming. I love you, please forgive me,* or *What the hell are* you *doing here, you little bitch?* I opt for the former.

When I finally track down Alex on his cell, he is on his way to Heathrow. He responds with a long, weary sigh. "No, I'm not coming," he says. I hope he doesn't live to regret it. Nothing worse than guilt to mess up your life.

"Any message for her?" I ask, providing him with a last chance at redemption.

"Just say I'm sorry for being such a rotten son."

I falter briefly, struggling to keep the tears down. Why are we, the abused, apologizing for crimes committed against us? "None of us ever wanted to hurt *her,* Alex," I say. "Remember that."

He talks passionately then about coming to Canada, about us all getting together, about healing the rifts. I listen but I know it will never happen.

"Have a good flight," I say as I hang up, not knowing if I will ever hear from him again.

On the fourth day, Luke has to return to his business in Canada. As I wave him off at a sunny but deserted Dumfries station early Thursday morning, I also feel deserted. His relieved, boyish face smiling out of the train window is another strand of spaghetti on my wall. Now there is just me.

I cry on the way to the hospital, telling myself that I can do this. *I can do this.*

I get lost in Dumfries' one-way system, my first time driving on the left and in the UK for ten years and my first time in this town. Then I panic when I arrive at her room and the bed is made, empty of my mother. *My God, has she died?* Then I notice that the decor is different. I am on the wrong floor.

When I find her, my mother is sleeping peacefully.

So I settle into the big armchair and start to write more cards to friends in her address book. I feel though as if I am betraying her, wishing her already gone by sitting in the same room writing of her death while her spirit is still in her body.

"Focus on the good times," my aunt encourages me over the phone from London. Had there been good times? The nightmare of her had been so long and brutal, it was hard to remember whether there had ever been anything else except a belligerent, satanic force. I return to her room and stare into those glazed eyes, trying to excavate the good times. Nothing comes.

As I drive alone that night to my mother's empty house, spent from juggling emotions and fighting persistent jet lag, I attempt to blot out the offensive smell of her hospital room clinging to the innermost sanctum of my nostrils. As I am negotiating a roundabout, reminding my stunned mind to drive on the *left* side of the road, I meet with a sight that melts away time, like flicking the pages of a book backwards. The Gypsies!

I slow the small Mini Metro almost to a crawl so I can follow the sight for a wee while. Cars are coming the other way on the narrow road, giving me an excuse to stay behind and enjoy the sight. Bright blue canopied wagons sitting on large spindled wheels are pulled by thick-ankled horses clip-clopping along the road, their long matted manes swaying in time with their lumbering gait. A man dressed in drab, dark jeans and jacket with sleeves four inches too short for his hairy arms is strolling alongside his Gypsy train.

An array of memories floods back to me then of my childhood, long, long ago, in another world, a time when our family lived at the Mill in the wilds of Oxfordshire, the place where the five of us were born, a time when my mother was loving, when she was happy. I remember the mantra she recited to us before setting out down those long country roads to school, "Now don't talk to the Gypsies." I remember what the Gypsy had told me that day when we had come upon their wagon on the way home from school, "You've got the sight, you 'ave, dearie." Now that I had accepted my clairvoyant abilities, it all made total sense.

Now I reminisce, not just about the childhood memories that the Gypsies had evoked, but many other happy adventures we had shared as children: laughing with my mother as she danced in the kitchen, giggling when we made spaghetti, tossing the unruly strands at the wall to see if it was cooked, joyous family Christmases, lively conversations, friendship, laughter, lots of laughter.

Suddenly, I notice in my rear-view mirror a line of traffic building behind me. Slowly I pull alongside the Gypsy train and then finally in front of them until they are merely a tableau in my rear-view mirror. As I pass, I want to shout, "Thank you," to the man whose jacket sleeves are four inches too short and whose eyes are fixed on the gray tarmac. Thank you for reminding me of the happy times.

Alone in the house that night, while on the phone to Canada, I hear a key in the lock, the outside door clicks open and then the inner one. I put down the phone to go and see who is there. The hallway is empty and both doors are still shut.

Friday is a sunny day, the curtain is billowing gently through an open hospital window allowing fresh air to dilute the putrid smell. As I sit by my mother's bedside, her body appears to be shriveling before my very eyes. I wonder if she is hanging on for Alex's or even Janet's arrival. Mark had also told her he might come back but he won't, not now. I decide to tell her the truth so she can make her choice. I lean over her curled form, stroking her clammy forehead, and tell her softly that her other children are not coming. She twitches and grunts as if in response.

"You were a good mother," I say, grasping at the pleasant maternal memories, "and there *were* good times. There were some bad times, too." Her body stiffens, arching up off the bed, and she makes a noise as if desperately trying to say something. But she can only grunt, and her eyes remain closed. "Maybe you can forgive us for all the times we hurt you and we forgive you for all the times you hurt us." She now settles back into the bed, relaxed. "Just let it all go and go in peace," I add. "Wherever you're going, just go in peace."

There is a final sigh in response and she gently turns her head away from me as if to say, *Go now. It is done. And I want to die alone.* My last memory of my mother is her snuggling her head into the pillow as if for a peaceful night's sleep.

The next morning, I am prompted by my inner voice to light a candle for my mother. As I set it above the fireplace and the wick hisses into flame, I ask the angels to come and take her spirit so that she can be released from not just physical pain but also the mental anguish that she must have been in for so long. Somehow I know that when the candle burns out, my mother's spirit will leave her body.

That night, just as Beth and I finish dinner, the candle flame hisses and dies.

"What time is it?" I ask Beth.

But before she can answer, the phone rings. "Your mother has just passed," the nurse tells me.

My mother, I decided, was one of my upside-down angels. I sensed that she was also very psychic. The tragedy was that she didn't use her gift or her acute intelligence, not creatively anyway. So it ended up being turned inwards and becoming a destructive force instead.

But sometimes the dark side also has its purpose. Even the word "devil" reversed is "lived." And I know that if she hadn't terrorized me, I wouldn't have become someone who helps others unravel the mystery of who they are and discover their full potential. And yes, there were good times. Sometimes the worst times were the best because they taught me all of who I can be.

As I return to Canada, this time sprawled luxuriously across three airline seats, it occurs to me that this is what the journey is all about. A combination of moments. Some stick in our memory like spaghetti to a wall, for better, for worse, till death do us part. If we live fully in the moment, our future has unlimited potential. We can only do that if we make peace with our past.

Metaphysical Endnote 34

Forgiveness

Next to loving the self, forgiveness seems to be our most challenging issue. For all of us, it is the most important. We cannot be free to totally love ourselves if our light is muddied with guilt and resentment. Whether we feel bad about ourselves or anger towards another, pain is pain. Because pain is resistance, it prohibits the flow of our spiritual, mental, emotional and physical health.

If I believed in victimhood, for example, then I would also have to believe in powerlessness and the randomness of good or bad luck. I don't. Therefore, in my philosophy, there are no victims. Whatever happens to me, in some way on some level, I have earned as a karmic lesson, or I have allowed, invited and/or attracted.

Guilt is often the culprit. While we can appreciate that the function of guilt is to keep our consciences in a state of grace, many of us allow guilt to hold us hostage to the past. Guilt robs us of our present, inhibits our futures and makes sure that we are never truly happy because we think we don't deserve to be. Guilt instigates fear in us because at some time in some way we know our punishment is coming down the pipe. As if we carry an invisible "Dump Disasters Here" magnet on our foreheads, guilt keeps all the good away and attracts the bad. Guilt is just a thought. Guilt disturbs us because on a soul level we know that something is out of balance. Oh, how the soul hates to be out of balance! So how do we release guilt from our minds?

It's that "F" again. Forgive.

While it is a word that is easy to say, many of us know it is not so easy to do.

First, we need to forgive ourselves and anyone who ever hurt us, including hurts from past lifetimes (according to Deepak Chopra, you can achieve this forgiveness through deep meditation). Forgiveness *will* bring our minds back into balance. Forget about facelifts. Forgiveness can do wonders for our bodies, minds and spirits.

Forgiveness of the Self requires, above all, compassion and remembering that we are all sparks of the divine, here on the planet, for the first time in this particular role, to learn. The more compassion we have for our Selves, the more we will be able to embrace others. How can we expect to get everything right first time around? Our mistakes are our teachers, if we allow them to be. When we forgive, we relinquish the guilt which then erases the fear of punishment. We are then free to live as innocents, simply, in the present.

Here are a few suggestions for how to perceive forgiveness:

- ❖ Forgiveness is stating to the perpetrator, "I am not willing to carry the pain of what you did to me any more. I am now releasing you and my pain. You no longer have any power over me."
- ❖ Forgiveness is stating, "I understand what you were thinking/ feeling when you did this to me. I have compassion for you at that time and your fear-based thoughts. I now choose to perceive you and me as innocent sparks of the Divine in the process of learning our lessons."
- ❖ Forgiveness is being willing to state, "I completely let go and *totally* release this experience. I am now replacing my own fear-based thoughts with love for others and myself."

But there is more to forgiveness. It's also about understanding how and why you were bullied, betrayed or otherwise abused in the first place, then putting things back into balance for your own soul.

I suggest, therefore, that in the forgiveness process there are two steps we can take:

- ❖ First, go through *in your mind* what you would really like to do about that person, physically, spiritually, and emotionally. Allow yourself to feel the rage, indignation and hurt. It is healthy to let your emotions come to consciousness. Expressing your true feelings—in a healthy way—puts you back in your power. Once out of denial, you will feel empowered again.
- ❖ Second, say this out loud: *There are no victims. Therefore, I am not powerless. In fact, I have a great deal of power in this situation. I can choose to see my part in what took place. If I contributed to the creation of this problem, then equally I have the power to re-create a solution for rebalancing. All events, especially painful ones, are for my learning and my growth. Instead of perceiving this event as punishment and these people as my enemies, I can choose to see them as players in my movie.*
  Within this event is a gift, even though I am not aware of what the gift is yet. I can, therefore, thank my adversaries for being my greatest teachers. I can now let them go with compassion and/or love but especially with gratitude for playing their part in my growth. I am safe. All is well in my world, and everything in this moment is in Divine Right Order.

Keep repeating this until you reach a state of grace.

But what if the people we have hurt or who have hurt us have died?

There is still a path to closure. Write them a letter. Put it all down—how much they hurt you, how much you hate them, how much you love them. On a psychic level they will "hear" you because psychically is how we truly communicate. Bury or burn the letter while asking that the energy be transmuted into forgiveness and that glorious blessings be bestowed upon all those affected. Then have a good sob.

Whether the perpetrators are physically alive or living in the spirit world, expect a sign to let you know that they have heard you and understood. Now that you have done everything in your power to heal, you can go in peace. That just might be your gift. Amen.

WHAT NOW?

Since I started giving psychic readings 30 years ago, I have been delighted to see how much my clients have grown in their awareness. I used to feel as if I had to translate everything. But now I am rewarded by my clients' grasp of this higher spiritual dimension, evidenced by the way they understand and take responsibility in large part for their own lives. Now they see how they create their own circumstances with their energy and thinking. Most of them finally know what I am talking about. Oh, joy!

The learning is eternal, although it is not so much learning but remembering. We are already aware of who we are becoming, at some level. It is just a matter of bringing that awareness back to consciousness, of waking up.

Sixth sense, intuition, gut feeling, second sight, ESP or psychic ability, whichever of these terms you are most comfortable using, we are all born with the ability to sense. To become psychic, even if we are naturals, still means we have to work at it. I could also have been an elephant trainer, Olympic skier, Nobel Peace Prize-winner or cordon bleu chef if I had dedicated all my energy to those pursuits instead of studying metaphysics. But I didn't. Apparently, I chose to be a psychic and a writer (the writing still needs work but thank you for bearing with me!). I have no special powers except the ones I work on within myself. These are the same powers that exist within everyone.

Since my experience with Divine Intelligence all those years ago, I have not forgotten their vision of peace and joy for the planet. But as they also reminded me about choosing or not choosing my path, humanity also has to make a choice.

As you have witnessed in this book, when I turned my back on my ability to help others, my life descended into chaos. But as soon as I surrendered to my destiny—my Agreement—my life started to flow. The chaos that surrounded me calmed.

In the same way, on a mass consciousness level, we all have a choice about our collective future, whether to follow the highest path or regress. If we regress, there will be chaos and, on a grander scale, the planet will rid itself of the pest called humanity that has plundered Mother Earth. According to the prophecies of the Mayan and Hopi Indians, we only have until the year 2012 to get our act together.

It takes just one moment to decide.

All potentials already exist, including joy if we allow it to be there. History continues to demonstrate that it is the ego mind that constantly gets in the way of our highest good. So we need to surrender that part of our minds to a higher purpose and a more intelligent power, inviting it to guide us to that higher potential. We may not be in control of the world but we are in charge of what we allow to dwell in our minds, how we think, what we feel, what we project, and thereby what we contribute to the world's mass consciousness.

My function continues to evolve. I now coach more of my clients to listen to their own intuition rather than just consider my prognostications. As people become more in tune with themselves, they will require my psychic services less. I plan to make myself redundant as a psychic and focus more on facilitating intuitive awareness in all the areas that that can encompass. Corporate event planners now hire me to read and/or teach various groups including cardiologists, doctors, and insurance salespeople. Past Life Regressions, Psychic Development Workshops, Creating Your Own Future Seminars and Separating Peacefully are now a part of my teaching repertoire. It's not a dull life. So many interesting stories to tell—with the clients' permission, of course! But more wild and wacky tales in my next book.

Developing a psychic ability then is not merely about being able to tune in to your own or somebody else's future. Nor is it confined to the healing of the spirit. When you open up your mind, you are embracing a much greater, more powerful, more loving, more exciting Universe with all its endless possibilities for joy. I would love for you to share in that Universe with me. Just as Divine Intelligence said, "You always have a choice."

So what do you choose? To acknowledge your intuitiveness and/or psychic ability or not? To utilize all of your mind or just a part of it? To live only some of your potential or all of it? In misery or with elation? With limited or unlimited thinking? In struggle or with abundance?

Choose for yourself, and those who love you will be inspired by your happiness. You *can* create any past, present or future you want. And therein lies the magical power of you and your mind.

As Einstein said, "The best adventure is into the mysterious."
Thank you for sharing the journey...so far.

The End

RECOMMENDED READING

(Apart from my next book, of course!
See last page for more information.)

Author	Title	Publisher	Year
Richard Bach	*Illusions*	Laurel	1981
Joyce Wilson	*The Complete Book of Palmistry*	Bantam	1983
Rosemary Altea	*The Eagle and the Rose*	William & Morrow	1997
Sylvia Browne	*Conversations with the Other Side*	Hay House	2002
	The Other Side and Back	Penguin Putnam	1999
	Adventures of a Psychic	New American	1991
James Van Praagh	*Heaven on Earth*	Pocket Books	2002
	Reaching to Heaven	Signet	2000
	Talking to Heaven	Penguin	1997
John Edwards	*Crossing Over*	Jodere Group	2001
Mona Lisa Schulz	*Awakening Intuition*	Random	1999
Anne Marie Evers	*Affirmations: Your Passport to Prosperity/Money*	Affirmations Int.	2002

Author	Title	Publisher	Year
Shakti Gwain	*Creative Visualization*	Bantam	1997
Helen Shucman	*A Course in Miracles*	Foundation of Inner Peace	1975
Joseph Murphy	*The Power of the Subconscious*	Prentice Hall Trade	1963
Stuart Wilde	*Miracles*	White Dove Int.	1998
	The Quickening	White Dove Int.	1988
	The Force	White Dove Int.	1984
	(And other titles – anything by Stuart Wilde is worth reading.)		
James Allen	*As a Man Thinketh*	Putnam Pub. Group	1959
Ralph H. Blum	*The Book of Runes*	St. Martin's Press	1993

About the Author

After surviving life in a large, chaotic family in Oxfordshire, England, Natasha Rosewood, a reincarnation of a Gypsy, found her niche as a flight attendant and apprentice palmist and traveled extensively. She lived in Switzerland, Norway, Germany and Libya, studying the languages of those countries and picking up a few additional languages before immigrating to British Columbia, Canada. Since 1995, when she finally surrendered to her fate as a full-time psychic, Natasha has evolved from palm reader to psychic coach, facilitating spiritual healing and psychic development through corporate and private workshops, writing books and columns, and offering private and phone consultations to people around the world. Her mission is to make her work as a psychic coach redundant by training others to listen to and trust their own intuition.

TESTIMONIALS

Dear Natasha ...

"Thank you so much for the wonderful reading. You are so right on! I was very uplifted. Every time I watched John Edwards, I shed tears as I wanted to connect with my brother Don. And here he came through on your reading – first thing!" Jocelyn, Prince George.

"Thanks very much for all your help and good guidance. You were right on and a great help through my transitional times. Peace and Blessings!" Ken, Alberta.

"Thank you for your warm energy & support. Your compassion comes across in your voice and it makes such a difference." Love, Tanya, Quebec.

"My whole consciousness has expanded incredibly and so many new insights and information has flooded in to help me continue on my path and to expand because of all your counsel. God keep you well." Cecilia, Alaska.

"Thank you for your good medicine and thank you for your help on behalf of others and for always believing that all life is sacred." Cheryl, Vancouver.

"Thank you for being in my life, for your kindness, wisdom and loving help." Regina, Vancouver.

"My girlfriend Sandra absolutely thinks she has died and gone to heaven from seeing you. I told her you were the best psychic I had seen and now she believes me!" Colleen, Vancouver.

HOW TO ORDER BOOKS

ON-LINE: www.natashapsychic.com
www.amazon.com

BY MAIL: Complete order form on next page and send to:

Seven Keys Productions
Box 1426
Gibsons, B.C. Canada

E-MAIL: natasha_psychic@dccnet.com

SIGNED COPIES: Order from Seven Keys Productions and include the name and address of the person you wish the book to be signed for and sent to.

BOOKSTORES: Visit www.natashapsychic.com for a list of bookstores.

E-BOOKS: The following book titles will soon be available in e-book format on my website: www.natashapsychic.com.

Aaagh! I Think I'm Psychic (And You Can Be Too)
Aaagh! I See Spirits (And You Can Too)
Above The Clouds - Inspirations for Dynamic Spirituality
Into The Valley of Death - And Other Ghost Stories

These books can be purchased either as:

Complete books
or
Individual chapters

NEWSLETTER: Stay inspired by subscribing to Natasha's newsletter on www.natashapsychic.com. Keep informed about new writings, CDs, books-on-tape and the details of Natasha Rosewood's radio and TV shows, book tours, workshops, and talks.

ORDER FORM

Please send: **Aaagh! I Think I'm Psychic (And You Can Be Too)**

\# of copies: _____

Name_____

Address_____

Prov/State/County_____Postal/Zip_____

Country_____Tel_____

E-mail_____Web site_____

# of Copies	PRICE: Can $	Shipping & Handling	
1-5...............	28.00	$6.00 (per book)	includes GST
6-10.............	25.00	$6.00 (per book)	includes GST

Please go to www.natashapsychic.com for prices in other currencies.

<u>Methods of Payment</u>

Credit card over the Internet, by phone, or by mail. Cheque or money order by mail.

Credit Card: Visa/Mastercard #.....................................Expiry..............

Amount...Signed...

I enclose cheque/money order (NO CASH PLEASE) in the amount of.......................Can/US/Euro

Please make payable to: Natasha J. Rosewood
And mail to: Seven Keys Productions
                                         Box 1426, Gibsons
                                         B.C., Canada VON 1V0

Namaste
Thank You!

About Natasha Rosewood's
next book...

Coming soon ...

Aaagh! I See Spirits (And You Can Too)
"Do you see dead people?" a potential psychic client once asked Natasha.
"Oh, yes. All the time," she responded. **"And so can you ... if you are open."**
But seeing spirits is only a small element of Natasha Rosewood's life as a psychic development coach, spiritual healer and writer. Join Natasha in *Aaagh! I See Spirits (And You Can Too)* as she shares just some of the fun and fascinating true-life experiences from her personal and professional life as a psychic. In the tradition of her first book, *Aaagh! I Think I'm Psychic (And You Can Be Too),* Natasha's fast-paced, light-hearted storytelling entertains as it enlightens and empowers us all to explore our greatest mind potential. The 'Dear Natasha' responses that follow each out-of-this-world tale answer the questions that most of us would love to ask a psychic.

Above The Clouds: Inspirations for Dynamic Spirituality is a collection of Natasha's Dynamic Spirituality columns, as published in journals and newspapers around the world. This mini-book was inspired by the psychic guidance she has received over the years for her clients and their most frequent issues. The author provides spiritual tools that the reader can apply to these everyday challenges. Whether you want to get unstuck or make a new beginning or separate peacefully, Natasha's 10-tip programs could provide the inspiration you are looking for.

Into The Valley of Death (And Other Ghost Stories) is a collection of spooky tales based on the real-life experiences of this psychic and those close to her. The settings of these stories range from a youth hostel in France to a home in Death Valley, California, to the alien-invaded English countryside. Like the author, you will be wondering what is true and what is not ...

For availability and prices of books, e-books, e-chapters and books-on-tape, go to:

www.natashapsychic.com

ISBN 141202821-3

9 781412 028219